Romans

Salvation from A-Z

Romans
Salvation from A-Z

By

Dr. Bo Wagner

Word of His Mouth Publishers
Mooresboro, NC

All Scripture quotations are taken from the **King James Version** of the Bible.

ISBN: 978-1-941039-56-4
Printed in the United States of America
©2017 Dr. Bo Wagner
©2nd Edition 2022
©3rd Edition 2025

Word of His Mouth Publishers
Mooresboro, NC
www.wordofhismouth.com

Cover art by Chip Nuhrah.

Table of Contents

Chapter 1   An Introduction..7
Chapter 2   Bombs Away..21
Chapter 3   Complete Equality 35
Chapter 4   Don't Even Think About It............................51
Chapter 5   Examining Imputation 67
Chapter 6   Faith, Faith, and More Faith! 77
Chapter 7   Gifts Found Under the Justification Tree.......87
Chapter 8   How Can Two Men Be More Different........99
Chapter 9   If You Are Saved, Live Like It! 113
Chapter 10   Jeopardy from the One Closest to Us 129
Chapter 11   Kinship with Christ and Its Effects..............147
Chapter 12   Looking Ahead...169
Chapter 13   My Greatest Desire 183
Chapter 14   Neithers and Nots to Notice........................191
Chapter 15   Observations on Election 197
Chapter 16   Putting Christ in His Place...........................213
Chapter 17   Questions and Answers About Salvation.....223
Chapter 18   Remnants and Riches....................................235
Chapter 19   Severity and Goodness.................................243
Chapter 20   Transformed..253
Chapter 21   Us and We...261
Chapter 22   Vengeance...273
Chapter 23   Walking the Walk 279
Chapter 24   X-Rays of the Heart, Getting Below the
              Surface 293
Chapter 25   Your Relationship with Others 307
Chapter 26   Zenith of the Book 323
              Works Cited 337

Chapter One

A - An Introduction

Romans 1:1 *Paul, a servant of Jesus Christ, called to be an apostle, separated unto the gospel of God,* **2** *(Which he had promised afore by his prophets in the holy scriptures,)* **3** *Concerning his Son Jesus Christ our Lord, which was made of the seed of David according to the flesh;* **4** *And declared to be the Son of God with power, according to the spirit of holiness, by the resurrection from the dead:* **5** *By whom we have received grace and apostleship, for obedience to the faith among all nations, for his name:* **6** *Among whom are ye also the called of Jesus Christ:* **7** *To all that be in Rome, beloved of God, called to be saints: Grace to you and peace from God our Father, and the Lord Jesus Christ.* **8** *First, I thank my God through Jesus Christ for you all, that your faith is spoken of throughout the whole world.* **9** *For God is my witness, whom I serve with my spirit in the gospel of his Son, that without ceasing I make mention of you always in my prayers;* **10** *Making request, if by any means now at length I might have a prosperous journey by the will of God to come unto you.* **11** *For I long to see you, that I may impart unto you some spiritual gift, to the end ye may be established;* **12** *That is, that I may be comforted together with you by the mutual faith both of you and me.* **13** *Now I would not have you ignorant, brethren, that oftentimes I purposed to come unto you, (but was let hitherto,) that I might have some fruit among you also, even as among other Gentiles.* **14** *I am debtor both to the Greeks, and to the Barbarians; both to the wise, and to the* *unwise.* **15** *So, as much as in me is, I am ready to preach the gospel to you that are at Rome also.* **16** *For I am not ashamed of the gospel of Christ: for it is the power of God unto salvation to every one that believeth; to the Jew first, and also to the Greek.* **17** *For therein is the righteousness of God revealed from faith to faith: as it is written, The just shall live by faith.*

The year was A.D. 58 or 59, and the city was Rome, the great capital of the Roman Empire. Roughly a million people were living in close proximity to that great city, people who represented almost every nationality on earth.

If you had been there, you would have noticed an amazing road system. You would also have noticed that this was very much a party city. There were 159 holidays a year. Of these, ninety-three were devoted to games and performances at the government's expense. The oldest and largest was the Circus Maximus, which Paul would have passed right by after entering the Porta Capena on the Appian Way. That circus, at the time of Nero, held probably 200,000 people (Unger, 1090).

That is not all that you would have seen. You also would have a hard time missing the Forum, whose very ruins are still great today. There were parks; there were gardens; it was absolute luxury on every hand. Amidst it all, everywhere you looked, you would have seen temples or other structures dedicated to idols. Rome had a very polytheistic culture, sucking up every "new god" that came along.

The Romans believed that since there was no semblance of unity in the natural world, there could be no semblance of unity in the heavens. From that flawed premise, they leaped to the conclusion that there must, therefore, be a controlling god or spirit over every important object or class of objects, every person, and every process of nature. Doing the math on that, the one thing you know is that they believed that there were more gods than there were human beings ("Roman Empire," 2620).

And what did that odd and eclectic "theology" lead to? It led to the conclusion that anything that a person ever wanted to "do" to be saved, all he had to do was find the particular god that would allow him to be saved that way. It also led to the conclusion that if a person believed something, it must, therefore, be acceptable and right because if he looked long enough, he could find a god that agreed with him.

The entire jumble of polytheistic illogicality went on for a good while. But then, Greek philosophy began to work its magic. The Greek philosophers systematically undermined the Roman system of belief. They were so good at what they did that, ultimately, they made all of the Roman "gods" look foolish! ("Roman Empire," 2621)

But that left a vacuum. Now, there were millions of people across the empire whose false hope had been taken away but who had not been introduced to any real hope. There were a million people in Rome going about their lives in sorrow, knowing that when they were dead, they were just done and that while they lived, they had no real purpose.

But then, one day, something life-changing came to Rome. Maybe it was due to the travelers on the day of Pentecost, maybe it was due to the persecution in Jerusalem, but somehow, someway, Christianity arrived in Rome. People who had been living in hopelessness came to know Christ as their Savior, and a church was formed in the pagan city of Rome. A light began to shine in the darkness. And to that church, to that light in the darkness, God directed the Apostle Paul to write and send what has been called the Constitution of the Christian faith.

To believers in the midst of darkness, to people who were having to fight polytheism on one side and atheism on the other, Paul sent the amazing book of Romans. This book covers the subject of Salvation from A to Z.

The man, Paul

Romans 1:1 *Paul, a servant of Jesus Christ, called to be an apostle, separated unto the gospel of God,*

As the church in Rome opened the letter containing the book of Romans, the first thing they noticed was that it came from Paul. Churches everywhere knew Paul; he, who had been the chief persecutor of the church, was now its chief promoter.

Paul had lived a life, prior to salvation, that was unbelievably prominent—a Pharisee, trained by Gamaliel, a rising star in Judaism—that was Paul.

Paul gave all of that up to follow Christ. But even after giving all of that up, he only became more prominent. Now, all those in Judaism knew him better than they ever had because he was the defector from their ranks. And the church certainly knew him since he spent every day of his life preaching or soul-winning or writing or starting churches or going on missionary journeys.

But look at how he began his letter! *Paul, a servant of Jesus Christ...*

The word he used for servant was *doulos,* a bondslave. In the middle of the greatest city on earth with the greatest opportunity for personal advancement, he said, "Just think of me as a willing bondslave of Christ because that is what I am." His heart was ever the heart of the humble, and that is doubtless one of the reasons God used him so mightily.

After pointing out that he was a servant, he reminded them that he was also *called to be an apostle.* In the history of the church, there was never a higher position. That office, which ceased entirely in one generation after Christ, was a lofty office. But rather than use that as an occasion for pride, look at what Paul did: he noted that even his apostleship was to be credited to Christ. There was simply not very much Paul in Paul.

The third thing he noted of himself in his opening remarks was that he was *separated unto the gospel of God.* And the word he used for "separated" was a very pointed, intentional word. The word he used for separated was *aphoridzo.* That is the same word from which the Pharisees got their name; they were the *aphorismenoi,* the "separated ones."

When Paul, the former Pharisee, used that word, he was making an intentional point. The Pharisees were everywhere, running him down, mocking his beliefs, telling people, "Oh, you can't listen to Paul. He isn't even a Pharisee anymore; he is no longer a 'separated one.'"

When Paul used the word he used, it was his way of saying, "I am still a Pharisee… I am just separated unto something completely different now. I was separated unto the law; now I am separated unto the gospel of God."

Every Christian should be a Pharisee, but not the kind of Pharisee Jesus had to so often rebuke. We need to be the kind of "separated one" that Paul was: every day of our lives ought to be all about the gospel of God, all about the good news that Jesus came and died and was buried and rose again on the third day so that we could be saved.

The message of Paul

Romans 1:2 *(Which he had promised afore by his prophets in the holy scriptures,)*

The gospel that Paul spoke of in verse one has often been accused of being "an invention of Paul." Even in our day, many cults refer to it as such, proclaiming that Paul twisted and warped the words and teachings of Jesus and that only the gospels should be believed and followed.

In the very beginning of Romans, this treatise on salvation, Paul went right back to Scripture to remind everyone that the gospel was not a "Paul thing." The gospel had been promised all through the Old Testament.

Isaiah 7:14 and 9:16 told us He would come and that He would be born of a virgin. Psalm 22 and Isaiah 53 vividly told of the crucifixion hundreds of years before it happened and that it would be for our sins. The end of Isaiah 53 prophesied His resurrection, as did Psalm 16:10. You can find literally hundreds of Old Testament references to the coming gospel. In fact, the first one was way back in the Garden of Eden, Genesis 3:15. The Gospel was never a "Paul thing"—it was and is a Genesis to Revelation Jesus thing!

Romans 1:3 *Concerning his Son Jesus Christ our Lord, which was made of the seed of David according to the flesh;* **4** *And declared to be the Son of God with power, according to the spirit of holiness, by the resurrection from the dead:*

We are only three verses into the book, and Paul has mentioned Jesus now for the second time. There was no conflict at all between Jesus and Paul; Paul literally lived and died for Jesus, and here as elsewhere did not hesitate to call Him Lord.

Notice the description given of the humanity and deity of Christ. In verse three, we see He was *made* of the seed of David. That word *made* lets us know that He was not a normal person and did not come about by a normal process.

In verse four, we find that He was *declared to be the Son of God with power, according to the spirit of holiness, by the resurrection from the dead:*

The declaration of God the Father was and is that Jesus is His Son. And this was not a weak, timid declaration; it was declared *with power.* Furthermore, this powerful declaration was *according to the spirit of holiness.* This is not a reference to the Holy Spirit; it is a description of the spirit of the holy God on this subject. We can think of it something like this, "in accordance with what God has determined to be holy and right."

And how was this declaration of His Sonship made? By the resurrection. In other words, if you want to know who Jesus really is, check out the empty tomb! It is conclusive proof that He is who He said He was, the very Son of God.

Romans 1:5 *By whom we have received grace and apostleship, for obedience to the faith among all nations, for his name:*

Paul and others like him had received some very precious things from Jesus. They had received grace, which we, the saved, also have received, but they had also received apostleship—not for their own glory, not to make a profit and live in a mansion and drive a Bentley and wear a Rolex. Neither Paul nor Jesus would even recognize the charlatans parading about under the unearned name of "apostle" today. No, Paul and the other apostles received that apostleship so that they could "obey the faith among all nations for His name."

They were the ones chosen both to preach and practice the faith, the system of belief and behavior that Jesus built. They were the tip of the spear. They were the ones who were chosen

12

to sacrifice themselves to spread the message across the world to the very first generation to ever hear it in its entirety.

Romans 1:6 *Among whom are ye also the called of Jesus Christ: 7 To all that be in Rome, beloved of God, called to be saints: Grace to you and peace from God our Father, and the Lord Jesus Christ.*

Paul may have been called to be an apostle, but his first calling was to be saved. That calling, he refers to again in verse six, and he points out that his readers, and we the saved today, have that same effectual calling.

In verse seven, we find something that I regard as amazing. Do you remember what we learned about Rome and its citizens? This was a wicked, mixed-up, unbelieving, pleasure-seeking populace. But God looked at those sin-soaked souls, loved them, and offered them grace and peace.

This is more than just a general greeting to all of the lost and saved in Rome, though. Yes, the gospel was and is offered to all. But here, Paul addresses those who, through their belief, have become part of the family of God – saints. To these, Paul wishes grace, which tells us that he means far more than just saving grace.

This, by the way, is the second time that grace has been mentioned so far in this book. Do you want to know how important it is for salvation? It will be mentioned nineteen more times for a total of twenty-one. This is not a long book! But grace is so important to salvation that Paul will refer to it twenty-one times as he teaches on the subject of salvation.

The mentions of Paul

Romans 1:8 *First, I thank my God through Jesus Christ for you all, that your faith is spoken of throughout the whole world.*

Paul has thus far spoken of Jesus, the gospel, and himself. Now, he will, for the first time, directly mention the Roman believers themselves. When he does, notice that it is a positive mention. He began by telling them how grateful he was that their faith was spoken of throughout the whole world!

13

This was in the day before modern communication technology. It was roughly 1,800 years before the telegraph, 1,900 years before telephones, and 2,000 years before cell phones, texting, email, Facebook, and Twitter.

In a day when news had to be carried by hand and mouth as people walked from place to place, the entire world knew within just a few months or years about the faith of these new Christians in Rome. That is quite a testimony of how they lived!

Romans 1:9 *For God is my witness, whom I serve with my spirit in the gospel of his Son, that without ceasing I make mention of you always in my prayers;*

Paul had never met these dear people, yet he prayed for them constantly and called God, who he served as a gospel minister, as a witness to that fact. That speaks volumes both of them and of him. We should pray for Christians we have never met, but we should also live in such a way that people who have never met us will pray for us.

Romans 1:10 *Making request, if by any means now at length I might have a prosperous journey by the will of God to come unto you.*

It was the desire of Paul to meet these dear people. He longed for it; he specifically prayed for it; he asked God to allow it. He would eventually make it to Rome, but the letter he wrote would get there first by some years.

The mission of Paul

Romans 1:11 *For I long to see you, that I may impart unto you some spiritual gift, to the end ye may be established;*

Paul had already mentioned his great desire to travel to Rome and see the believers there. Now, he will tell them why. It was not so that he could *gain* but so that he could *give!* Paul wanted either to give them spiritual gifts or to use his spiritual gifts among them, or both, so that they could be established, made stronger and more effective in their faith.

It should ever be the desire of a preacher to give rather than to get. The Nicolaitan concept of shearing the sheep is wrong, and the Christ concept of laying down one's life for the sheep is right.

Every church should know how to take care of pastors and evangelists, but every pastor and evangelist should have as their focus giving of themselves for the precious people they are preaching to.

It was not just his mission to give, though, but also to grow together:

Romans 1:12 *That is, that I may be comforted together with you by the mutual faith both of you and me.*

The introductory phrase *that is* takes us back to the desire he expressed in verse eleven for their firmer establishment in the faith. Mutual faith working together produces mutual growth. The thought here that comforted Paul in his tribulations was that he and these Roman believers could draw nearer and nearer to Christ together. A preacher growing in faith is never as pleasant as a preacher and his people growing in faith together.

But Paul was not done. His mission was to give and to grow together, but it was also to gain fruit:

Romans 1:13 *Now I would not have you ignorant, brethren, that oftentimes I purposed to come unto you, (but was let hitherto,) that I might have some fruit among you also, even as among other Gentiles.*

In the life and ministry of Paul, we learn much of the will and workings of God. Paul had desired to go to Rome, but God had thus far not allowed him to do so. He had been *let hitherto,* meaning hindered up to that point. Everything about that desire was right and good, but God's plans and God's timing are, very often, not our own.

It was the desire of Paul to go to Rome so that he might *have some fruit* among them. In other words, he wanted both to win souls and to establish those who had been won. He desired to be productive and profitable to the Lord.

This should be the attitude of every Christian, without exception.

It was, lastly, the mission of Paul to gospelize every nationality:s

Romans 1:14 *I am debtor both to the Greeks, and to the Barbarians; both to the wise, and to the unwise.* **15** *So, as much as in me is, I am ready to preach the gospel to you that are at Rome also.*

Paul knew 2,000 years before many others seem to have learned, that the gospel is to be taken to everyone regardless of skin color or nationality or culture or education. Paul regarded himself as a debtor to all in this task, meaning that he regarded himself as under an obligation to them.

To the Greeks, he said, those cultured, skeptical underminers of pretty much everything! To the Barbarians, foreigners who were rough and coarse, vile and violent, hateful and dangerous! To the wise (educated Greeks), to the unwise (uneducated foreigners), to those in Rome! The Great Commission is not the Great Commission unless it is the General Commission, not a commission specific to only those who have the same skin color and culture as ourselves.

The mentality of Paul

Romans 1:16 *For I am not ashamed of the gospel of Christ: for it is the power of God unto salvation to every one that believeth; to the Jew first, and also to the Greek.*

In the last two verses of this section, we find the mentality of Paul; we find a picture window into his thinking. His mentality can be summed up in two words: absolute unashamedness.

Our current populace of mankind seems to be embarrassed, very embarrassed, in fact, over the gospel.

They are embarrassed by what they see as its "over simplicity..."

They are embarrassed because they regard it as "too bloody..."

They are embarrassed because they regard it as "too old-fashioned..."

But those who know God will never, ever be ashamed of the gospel of Christ. Paul said *it is the power of God unto salvation.* Apart from the substitutionary death, the burial, and

16

the bodily resurrection of Christ, there is no salvation. It is what Jesus did on Calvary, and only that, that satisfies the righteous demands of the Father:

1 John 2:2 *And he is the propitiation* [meaning the satisfactory sacrifice] *for our sins: and not for ours only, but also for the sins of the whole world.*

No gospel of Christ, no salvation.

Paul, in verse sixteen, noted that this salvation came first to the Jew. Yet John 1:11 tells us:

John 1:11 *He came unto his own, and his own received him not.*

What, then, was to be done with this precious gospel? Paul knew: take it to the Greeks, another way of designating the Gentiles. And he did. And it is that decision, directed by God, that has allowed us to be the recipients of salvation.

Romans 1:17 *For therein is the righteousness of God revealed from faith to faith: as it is written, The just shall live by faith.*

This verse is a watershed verse of Scripture. It teaches a doctrine that separates truth from error and lost from saved.

Paul said that therein, in the gospel, in the "good news" that Jesus died for our sins and rose again, the righteousness of God is revealed.

It almost seems counterintuitive. If we are talking about righteousness, it seems like that would be revealed by judgment, not by salvation. But what revealed the righteousness of God was judgment, not on us, but on His own Son who alone could bear it!

God fully punished our sin when Jesus went to Calvary. He showed His righteousness by lowering the hammer of judgment on His Son.

But as powerful as the phrase *"therein is the righteousness of God revealed"* is, the next phrase only adds to the power. It is revealed *from faith to faith.*

In other words, salvation begins with faith, it ends with faith, and there is nothing in between those two points. God gives us faith to place in Him, we place that faith in Him, and there is nothing of human works in the process. Right at the beginning of this treatise on salvation, Paul is saying, "Not of works! Not of works! Not of works! Not of works!" It is from faith to faith; it is by faith alone.

Closing out this section, Paul uttered a quote from Scripture and the absolutely immortal phrase: *as it is written, The just shall live by faith.*

That phrase appears in almost the same wording three times in Scripture, right here in Romans 1:17 and also in these places:

Habakkuk 2:4 *Behold, his soul which is lifted up is not upright in him: but the just shall live by his faith.*

Hebrews 10:38 *Now the just shall live by faith: but if any man draw back, my soul shall have no pleasure in him.*

This phrase can be applied to what happens after a person gets saved, but in context, especially in Romans 1:17, it really applies to salvation itself. The "just," which is a shortened form for "the justified, the saved," shall live, shall be made alive, by their faith. In other words, it is not works that save a person; it is faith and faith alone.

In the early 1500s, there was a devout young man in Germany named Martin Luther. He had been raised Roman Catholic, doing penance, taking the sacraments, performing work after work in the hopes of being saved.

But none of it brought Martin Luther any peace. He lived a very clean, pure life, but he was miserable and unsure of eternity.

For years he was a good monk in the Augustinian Monastery. He kept all of the rituals and forms of the church. But somehow, he still knew that something was wrong. The thought that gripped Martin Luther, the thought that eventually struck terror into his soul was "If there is a pure and holy God in heaven, how can I ever be clean in His sight?"

Since none of his works were working, in the year 1510 he decided to try something else. That something else was a pilgrimage to Rome.

That did not go so well. When he got there, to "Ground Zero" of the Catholic faith, he found a cesspool of sin! He found priests too drunk to stand up straight. He found priests bragging that they were righteous because they only slept with women. He found people worshiping idols that they called "relics." His biographer Roland Bainton says that Martin Luther concluded that "If there were a Hell, Rome was built upon it."

In 1515, something happened that changed everything. A man named Johann Staupitz appointed Luther to teach the Bible.

When he started studying his Bible, this man who had gone to Rome and not found what he needed went to Romans and found exactly what he needed! What he found was Romans 1:17:

Romans 1:17 *For therein is the righteousness of God revealed from faith to faith: as it is written, The just shall live by faith.*

The lights finally came on. Luther realized that he had been trying to live by works but was still dead. If he wanted to be made alive, it would have to be by faith.

Here is what he said in his own words:

"I greatly longed to understand Paul's Epistle to the Romans and nothing stood in the way but that one expression 'the justice (the righteousness) of God' because I took it to mean that justice whereby God is just and deals justly in punishing the unjust. My situation was that, although an impeccable monk, I stood before God as a sinner troubled in conscience and I had no confidence that my merit would assuage him. Therefore, I did not love a just and angry God, but rather hated and murmured against him. Yet I clung to the dear Paul and had a great yearning to know what he meant.

"Night and day, I pondered until I saw the connection between the justice (the righteousness) of God and the statement that 'the just shall live by his faith.' Then I grasped that the justice of God is that righteousness by which through grace and sincere mercy God justifies us through faith. Thereupon I felt myself to be reborn and to have gone through open doors into Paradise. The whole of Scripture took on a new meaning. Whereas before 'the justice of God' had filled me with hate, now it became inexpressibly sweet in greater love. This passage of Paul became to me a gate to heaven." (Bainton, 49-50)

Martin Luther got it! Salvation is not by works; it is by faith! Jesus paid it all, all to Him I owe. Sin had left a crimson stain; He washed it white as snow!

Why was Paul so unashamed of the gospel? Why was he so bold as to write an entire book about salvation? Because Paul tried the Martin Luther route. He lived as pure or more so than Luther had lived, and he was just as miserable as Luther. When you read about Paul before salvation, all you see is hatred and anger and misery. After he got saved, he could say:

Romans 1:16 *For I am not ashamed of the gospel of Christ: for it is the power of God unto salvation to every one that believeth; to the Jew first, and also to the Greek.* **17** *For therein is the righteousness of God revealed from faith to faith: as it is written, The just shall live by faith.*

The gospel works, and it <u>alone</u> works.

Chapter Two
B - Bombs Away

Romans 1:18 *For the wrath of God is revealed from heaven against all ungodliness and unrighteousness of men, who hold the truth in unrighteousness;* **19** *Because that which may be known of God is manifest in them; for God hath shewed it unto them.* **20** *For the invisible things of him from the creation of the world are clearly seen, being understood by the things that are made, even his eternal power and Godhead; so that they are without excuse:* **21** *Because that, when they knew God, they glorified him not as God, neither were thankful; but became vain in their imaginations, and their foolish heart was darkened.* **22** *Professing themselves to be wise, they became fools,* **23** *And changed the glory of the uncorruptible God into an image made like to corruptible man, and to birds, and fourfooted beasts, and creeping things.* **24** *Wherefore God also gave them up to uncleanness through the lusts of their own hearts, to dishonour their own bodies between themselves:* **25** *Who changed the truth of God into a lie, and worshipped and served the creature more than the Creator, who is blessed for ever. Amen.* **26** *For this cause God gave them up unto vile affections: for even their women did change the natural use into that which is against nature:* **27** *And likewise also the men, leaving the natural use of the woman, burned in their lust one toward another; men with men working that which is unseemly, and receiving in themselves that recompence of their error which was meet.* **28** *And even as they did not like to retain God in their knowledge,*

God gave them over to a reprobate mind, to do those things which are not convenient; **29** *Being filled with all unrighteousness, fornication, wickedness, covetousness, maliciousness; full of envy, murder, debate, deceit, malignity; whisperers,* **30** *Backbiters, haters of God, despiteful, proud, boasters, inventors of evil things, disobedient to parents,* **31** *Without understanding, covenantbreakers, without natural affection, implacable, unmerciful:* **32** *Who knowing the judgment of God, that they which commit such things are worthy of death, not only do the same, but have pleasure in them that do them.*

On December 7, 1941, a peaceful day was abruptly shattered as Japanese bombs fell on Pearl Harbor. A couple of years later, the Japanese were shocked beyond measure by the only two atomic bombs ever dropped during war, on Hiroshima and Nagasaki.

During the Gulf War, we were able to watch live coverage of bombs blowing bridges out from under people.

Nothing is so abrupt and awakening as a bomb. And no bombs ever dropped carry the same spiritual impact as the bombs that Paul is about to drop in our text. Verses one through seventeen ended on such a positive note: "The just shall live by faith." But truthfully, before people can get saved, they must realize themselves as lost! And no passage of Scripture brings home more forcibly the lost condition of mankind than Romans 1:18-32.

Throughout this text, we will over and over again go back and forth between three spiritual bombs: The revelation of wrath, the responsibility for wickedness, and the reward for wrongdoing.

The revelation of wrath

Romans 1:18a *For the wrath of God is revealed from heaven against all ungodliness and unrighteousness of men...*

Right after the comforting statement of verse seventeen, *the just shall live by faith,* the comfort is needfully shattered by the truth that the hot, burning, abiding wrath of God is revealed,

22

made known, against all ungodliness [*asebeia*, lack of reverence toward God] and unrighteousness.

Ladies and gentlemen of the jury, the only verdict we can arrive at is that God is angry at sin! He is not an all-tolerant, all-accepting, anything-goes kind of God. He does not excuse sin, nor does He allow excuses for it.

That very thought should frighten man senseless. Picture yourself in a pit of rattlesnakes that someone has been poking at with a long stick until they are furious and ready to strike. Such a thought should not be nearly as frightening as the wrath of an angry God, our Creator, whose holiness and purity have been offended.

The responsibility for wickedness

Romans 1:18b *...who hold the truth in unrighteousness;*
The word here for *hold* [*katecho*] means to hold down, to suppress. It is as if a messenger boy were running to the courtroom to deliver life-or-death information, and you tackle him so that he cannot bring that life-saving news. That is the picture! Men know the truth yet suppress it. Therefore, they are responsible. It is not as if man is ignorant of his sin. Mankind does actually know the truth; they just do everything in their power to suppress that truth.

Romans 1:19 *Because that which may be known of God is manifest in them; for God hath shewed it unto them.*
Notice the phrase *That which may be known of God.* At least now, in the flesh, there are things we cannot know or understand about God. But that which we can know is not hidden; He has shown us everything about Himself that, for right now, we need to know. Therefore, we are responsible.

Romans 1:20 *For the invisible things of him from the creation of the world are clearly seen, being understood by the things that are made, even his eternal power and Godhead; so that they are without excuse:*
Man says, "I cannot see Him!" But God says that from the very moment of creation, by looking at the creation which is visible, you can clearly see and easily understand the eternal

power and Godhead, meaning respectively His unending might and His divine nature.

No wonder the truth of the Genesis creation is so hated by modern man! If creation testifies to the existence and power of God, and it does, then man is without excuse, as Paul plainly states in this verse.

In more godly times, the most brilliant minds ever were able to look at creation and see the obvious. The founders of modern science, Sir Isaac Newton, Francis Bacon, Johannes Kepler, Galileo Galilei, Robert Boyle, Blaise Pascal, Michael Faraday, Louis Pasteur, and a host of others were creationists. These men who gave the world the laws of physics and motion and electromagnetism and calculus and optics and so many other things that every scientist in our day still uses were men who did what Romans 1:20 says. They looked at creation and clearly saw that creation was a testimony to the fact that there was and is an omnipotent God to whom we are responsible (Morris, 14).

Because all men everywhere have creation clearly demonstrating that there is a God, they are responsible. Every heathen in the deepest jungle can clearly see that there is a God. And whenever man responds to that witness of creation and genuinely seeks after the God who made that creation, God will respond by sending them more and more and more light that will, if they keep seeking, lead them all the way to Christ. 2 Peter 3:9 tells us that God is not willing that any should perish! God is just as interested in the Aborigine in the bush as He is in the white child in the suburbs.

But here is the most convicting part: because every heathen everywhere is still responsible for accepting Christ, it is our responsibility to get them the gospel! Christians regularly ask, "Well, Preacher, what about the heathen in the jungle that never hears the name of Jesus? Will God send him to hell?"

The answer is "No." God will not send him to hell; we will. God has given His people enough resources to get the gospel to every single person on the planet. If we use those resources for other things, if we fail to support the missionaries

24

needed to get the gospel to those heathens, God has not sent them to hell; we have.

Romans 1:21 *Because that, when they knew God, they glorified him not as God, neither were thankful; but became vain in their imaginations, and their foolish heart was darkened.*

Paul had some people in mind in his day and in days prior to his days. He was thinking of people who knew God from the witness of creation. But rather than glorify and thank Him, they made a choice to become vain in their imaginations, meaning worthless and empty in their thinking. As a result, their "foolish heart was darkened."

Notice that it was not their mind darkened but their heart! Some of the most brilliant minds on our planet today are just like the people of Paul's day. Their intelligence is unquestioned, but their hearts are dark and unreceptive. They can clearly see the magnificence of what God created; in fact, they know even better than we do how magnificent it is. But that knowledge in their head never is allowed to make it into their heart because if it ever did, their heart would bow before the Creator of the creation that they are studying.

Romans 1:22 *Professing themselves to be wise, they became fools,* **23** *And changed the glory of the uncorruptible God into an image made like to corruptible man, and to birds, and fourfooted beasts, and creeping things.*

Professing themselves to be wise means that they put themselves forward as being the wise ones in all of this. But by so doing, by seeing the truth yet refusing to acknowledge it and then claiming to be wise anyway, *they become fools.*

And what happens after they become fools? They change *the glory of the uncorruptible God into an image made like to corruptible man, and to birds, and fourfooted beasts, and creeping things.*

In other words, they lower God to an image with which they can be comfortable. Mankind used to do this with actual images, now he does it by teaching about God but by making God out to be the exact opposite of how He really is.

The Bible says that God is holy and that we are, therefore, to be holy. They make Him unconcerned in the least about holiness.

The Bible says that God is angry with sin; they make God out to be approving of sin. They even go so far as to claim that God made everyone how they are, and therefore, even the things that God said He abhorred are now perfectly fine with Him.

But none of those efforts change the fact that mankind is both sinful and responsible for his sin.

The revelation of wrath

Romans 1:24 *Wherefore God also gave them up to uncleanness through the lusts of their own hearts, to dishonour their own bodies between themselves:*

A man, by his very nature, moves toward sin and sinfulness just as hard as he can. God, in His mercy, sends conviction to restrain us. But there comes a point at which something horrifying happens.

God made it very clear in many places throughout the Bible that there is a deadline that we can cross while still alive that will keep us from ever being saved.

Genesis 6:3 *And the LORD said, My spirit shall not always strive with man...*

Isaiah 55:6 *Seek ye the LORD while he may be found, call ye upon him while he is near:*

We find that truth forcefully reiterated in Romans 1:24. God speaks of these sinners who have had all the light they need to get saved yet have chosen to debase God and bring Him down to a level that they can be comfortable with, and He says *wherefore,* because of that choice they made, He *gave them up...*

When God gives up on us, that is the worst form of His wrath!

And what did He give them up to? Uncleanness, spiritual and moral dirtiness through the lusts, the uncontrolled desires of their own hearts.

26

God does not make people do things that are wrong, nor does He make people pre-programmed to do what He says is wrong.

Man is born, thanks to Adam, with a sin nature. But God has given us all the information we need to get saved and then live right and overcome that sin nature. But when people choose not to do so, and when they then go so far as to debase God and bring Him down to their level, He will at some point give them up to uncleanness.

This will result in them *dishonouring their own bodies between themselves.*

Paul is about to very specifically point to homosexuality. And the description he gives of it here is fitting. It is a practice that dishonors [*atimadzo*, treats with contempt] the bodies of those who engage in it.

God made the man specifically for the woman, and the woman specifically for the man. When man and woman come together, everything works exactly as God intended it, and the body is not dishonored in any way. But when a man and a man or a woman and a woman come together, the body is dishonored. It is dirtied and damaged and sullied. There are physical and emotional and spiritual costs that will end up being manifested in the body.

The responsibility for wickedness

Romans 1:25 *Who changed the truth of God into a lie, and worshipped and served the creature more than the Creator, who is blessed for ever. Amen.*

The first phrase of this verse has the modern world, especially America, written all over it. Man takes the truth about God, His real character, His likes and dislikes, His expectations, and changes all of it into a lie.

Every time an adulterer says, "God wants me to be happy, and He has blessed me with this new person," he or she is changing the truth of God into a lie.

Every time a homosexual says, "God made me this way, and I am a gay Christian," he or she is changing the truth of God into a lie.

Every time someone says, "I am saved, and the church is not important to God or me. We do our own thing together," he or she is changing the truth of God into a lie.

Every time someone says, "Jesus wasn't hung up on sin; He came to combat social injustice," he or she is changing the truth of God into a lie.

Every time someone says, "All of the passages about an awful place called hell have been mistranslated and misunderstood," he or she is changing the truth of God into a lie.

Every time someone says, "People are all worshiping the same God, just by different names," he or she is changing the truth of God into a lie.

Every time a "Jesus documentary" tells you that Jesus was married to Mary Magdalene, had kids, escaped to a foreign country, and lived to a ripe old age, it is changing the truth of God into a lie.

Why do they do this? The last half of the verse tells us why. They want to worship and serve the creature, themselves, rather than the Creator, God. It is the exact same sin as the original sin of Satan. It is created beings deciding that they want to be God instead of letting God be God. Because of this, because it is a willing choice, they are responsible.

The revelation of wrath

Romans 1:26 *For this cause God gave them up unto vile affections: for even their women did change the natural use into that which is against nature:* **27** *And likewise also the men, leaving the natural use of the woman, burned in their lust one toward another; men with men working that which is unseemly...*

This is the second time that God says He *gave them up*, this time to what He calls *vile* [*atimia*, disgusting, from the same root as dishonored] affections. Please let it be clearly understood that not all "affection" is a good thing in the eyes of God. Some of it is vile, disgusting, wrong in His sight. The world says, "All affection is good." God disagrees.

It does not take long for Him to specify exactly what He is speaking about. He very clearly specified gay and lesbian behavior as that which He deems vile.

He spoke of the women first. He said that they have a *natural* use, and that is to be for man. But they, God says, have chosen to do the opposite, and He then says that what they are doing is *against nature*. Anyone with a brain, an ability to identify anatomical parts, and a shred of honesty can clearly see that men and women were designed by God for each other. A woman with a woman is unnatural. That is not my words or my evaluation; it is what God said Himself. It is what the Bible clearly says right here in front of our eyes.

He then spoke of men. He spoke of men leaving [*aphiemi*, abandoning] the *natural use* of the woman and *burning in their lust one toward another; men with men working that which is unseemly.* Please notice, first of all, that this is not about love; it is about "lust." And even that lust is not a natural thing; it is not the way that God designed it; it is *unseemly,* from the word *askaymosunay.* That word means "shameful and disgraceful."

Commentator Albert Barnes said, "Perhaps there is no sin which so deeply shows the depravity of man as this; none which would so much induce one to hang his head and blush to think himself a man." (Barnes, 42)

It could not be more clear that God despises this behavior. It could not be more clear that people are not born homosexuals. It could not be more clear that God designed a man for a woman and a woman for a man, and anything else flies in His face. It could not be more clear that this is an embarrassing, degrading, vile, shameful behavior.

Two entire cities were destroyed for this sin in Genesis 19. God forbade it throughout the law in places like Leviticus 18:22, 19:13, and many more. In Deuteronomy 23:18, He commanded that any money made from that practice could not even be accepted as tithe. Romans 1:26-27 is so graphic and clear as to be unmistakable. In 1 Corinthians 6:9-11 God said that people who engage in that behavior among others "will not inherit the kingdom of God." In Revelation 22:15, He used the term "dogs" the same way He did in the Old Testament as a metaphor for that behavior, and once again, He stated that they could not enter into heaven.

There is no desire by this author to be mean or hurtful. Rather, in love, it is my desire to communicate an unpopular truth so plainly as to give people the light they need to seek Christ and the escape He can give anyone from any behavior that will damage and ultimately doom them.

There is something that people say constantly that is an outright error. When people say, "All sins are the same to God," they are wrong. Any one sin is enough to send a person to hell, yes, but all sins are not the same to God. He does not speak of all sins in the same way and language; the sacrifices for some sins were much greater than for others, and the punishment and consequences for some sins were much greater than others.

The sin spoken of here in Romans 1, homosexuality, is right up at the top of the list. Go through your Bible, see what God said about it, and see how He dealt with it. You will not be able to escape the conclusion that it is among the worst of the worst of all sins in His sight.

And the fact that God *gives men up* to it is a revelation of His wrath against them.

The reward for wrongdoing

Romans 1:27b ...*and receiving in themselves that recompence of their error which was meet.*

The wrath of God, spoken of at the beginning of verse twenty-seven, does not end the story. It also includes what you see at the end of verse twenty-seven, the natural physical consequences of it when He says *and receiving in themselves that recompence of their error which was meet.* That phrase means that there are harmful consequences to the body that this behavior brings. That is not by accident; any deviation from God's design causes problems. And no matter what modern

30

medicine tries, no matter how hard doctors and scientists work, this behavior will always have some type of a natural, physical damage to the body associated with it, both in the ancient and even still now in the modern world.

The Gaston Gazette of June 1, 2001, was honest enough to report that the first five cases of AIDS were found among homosexual men in San Francisco. It used to be called GRIDS, "Gay Related Immune Deficiency Syndrome," until political pressure changed the name to something more acceptable. The Gazette was also honest enough to report that the vast number of AIDS cases continue to be found among homosexual men and Crack users.

Do innocent people often contract it? Yes. Sin has a terrible way of even impacting those who have not been involved with it. But if you are simply honest enough to look at the numbers and the other long-term damages associated with this behavior, you will have to conclude that there is a natural cost to this sin, and it is a very high cost.

The responsibility for wickedness

Romans 1:28 *And even as they did not like to retain God in their knowledge...*

Why is man responsible for his wickedness? Is it that they did not have knowledge of God? No, it is that they *did not like to retain God in their knowledge! Like* is from the word *dokimadzo,* and it means to approve of. They know God; they just do not like what they know about Him, they do not approve of Him and His expectations for them.

Why? Here is the answer:

John 3:19 *And this is the condemnation, that light is come into the world, and men loved darkness rather than light, because their deeds were evil.* **20** *For every one that doeth evil hateth the light, neither cometh to the light, lest his deeds should be reproved.*

It is a conscious choice. Men like their sin, and they do not want God or anyone else shining a light on it and pointing

31

out that it is wrong. Man is, therefore, responsible and utterly without excuse.

The revelation of wrath

Romans 1:28 *And even as they did not like to retain God in their knowledge, God gave them over to a reprobate mind, to do those things which are not convenient;*

This is the third time that God mentions giving people up. This time, He *gave them over to a reprobate mind.* Reprobate means "worthless, rejected, undiscerning," and there is a bit of wordplay found within it. It is from *adokimos,* which has the same root as *like, dokimadzo,* found at the beginning of the verse. In so many words, God said, "Your mind refuses to approve of me, so I will give you up to a mindset that I do not approve of."

There comes a point at which, especially with this sin, God turns off the light in a person's mind. Once that has happened, they are doomed while they live. You and I are not God; we do not know when that point will come, so we still have a responsibility to witness and try to win them. But there does come a point at which they cannot be won because God says, "I'm done!" and turns off the light and gives them over to an undiscerning mind. At that point, you could literally hang them over hell on a spider web, and they still would not turn from their sin.

God said that He ...*gave them over to a reprobate mind, to do those things which are not convenient.*

That word "convenient" means "proper and right." Our human minds desire wickedness. One of the greatest and most profound ways God ever reveals His wrath is by removing the restraints from our minds and allowing our minds to become reprobate, worthless, undiscerning. God "leaving us to our own devices" is very serious business.

The reward for wrongdoing

Romans 1:29 *Being filled with all unrighteousness, fornication, wickedness, covetousness, maliciousness; full of envy, murder, debate, deceit, malignity; whisperers,* **30** *Backbiters, haters of God, despiteful, proud, boasters, inventors of evil things, disobedient to parents,* **31** *Without understanding, covenantbreakers, without natural affection, implacable, unmerciful:*

You can tell what a person thinks of a vessel by what they allow it to be filled with. When a person has nice crystal glasses, they will never allow a child to put worms for the science project in them. The child will have to use a plastic cup for that.

In verses twenty-eight through thirty-one, God "rewards" man's wrongdoing by allowing him to be filled to the brim with a long list of very bad things:

Unrighteousness: the general term for wickedness and injustice

Fornication: every type of sexual wrongdoing

Wickedness: depravity, that which is low or base

Covetousness: greed, avarice, the desire for what belongs to others

Maliciousness: ill will toward others

Envy: jealousy over the blessings of others

Murder: taking innocent human life

Debate: contention, strife, argument

Deceit: fooling people in a harmful way

Malignity: subtlety, malice

Whisperers: talebearers, slanderers, people who stir up trouble

Backbiters: people who openly speak evil of those who are good

Haters of God: this one is self-explanatory

Despiteful: disregarding the needs of others

Proud: haughty, arrogant

Boasters: bragging

Inventors of evil things: as if the evil all around us already is not enough, they have to dream up more and more

Disobedient to parents: self-explanatory

Without understanding: foolish
Covenant-breakers: those who do not keep their word
Without natural affection: not having the affection they should have and having affections that they should not have
Implacable: one who will not make peace
Unmerciful: self-explanatory

Twenty-three very vile things to be filled with, twenty-three awful rewards for wrongdoing.

The responsibility for wickedness

Romans 1:32 *Who knowing the judgment of God, that they which commit such things are worthy of death, not only do the same, but have pleasure in them that do them.*

People say, "It is God who made me this way; it is His fault!" That sentiment is wholly incorrect. Even while doing these things, they know the judgment of God, *that they which commit such things are worthy of death.* Yet not only do they do them; they rejoice when others do as well, they *have pleasure* [*suneudokeo* to be pleased together with] *in them that do them*

Mankind is, therefore, once again, utterly responsible for his sin.

Now, do you see why I call this section "Bombs away?"

But it has to be said, and it has to be heard. Mankind is in a quagmire of sin, and they will never get out of it until they know the truth.

Chapter Three
C - Complete Equality:
God Despises Hypocrites of Any Nationality

Romans 2:1 *Therefore thou art inexcusable, O man, whosoever thou art that judgest: for wherein thou judgest another, thou condemnest thyself; for thou that judgest doest the same things.* **2** *But we are sure that the judgment of God is according to truth against them which commit such things.* **3** *And thinkest thou this, O man, that judgest them which do such things, and doest the same, that thou shalt escape the judgment of God?* **4** *Or despisest thou the riches of his goodness and forbearance and longsuffering; not knowing that the goodness of God leadeth thee to repentance?* **5** *But after thy hardness and impenitent heart treasurest up unto thyself wrath against the day of wrath and revelation of the righteous judgment of God;* **6** *Who will render to every man according to his deeds:* **7** *To them who by patient continuance in well doing seek for glory and honour and immortality, eternal life:* **8** *But unto them that are contentious, and do not obey the truth, but obey unrighteousness, indignation and wrath,* **9** *Tribulation and anguish, upon every soul of man that doeth evil, of the Jew first, and also of the Gentile;* **10** *But glory, honour, and peace, to every man that worketh good, to the Jew first, and also to the Gentile:* **11** *For there is no respect of persons with God.* **12** *For as many as have sinned without law shall also perish without law: and as many as have sinned in the law shall be judged by the law;* **13** *(For not the hearers of the law are just before God,* *but the doers of the law shall be justified. **14** For when the Gentiles, which have not the law, do by nature the things contained in the law, these, having not the law, are a law unto themselves: **15** Which shew the work of the law written in their hearts, their conscience also bearing witness, and their thoughts the mean while accusing or else excusing one another;) **16** In the day when God shall judge the secrets of men by Jesus Christ according to my gospel. **17** Behold, thou art called a Jew, and restest in the law, and makest thy boast of God, **18** And knowest his will, and approvest the things that are more excellent, being instructed out of the law; **19** And art confident that thou thyself art a guide of the blind, a light of them which are in darkness, **20** An instructor of the foolish, a teacher of babes, which hast the form of knowledge and of the truth in the law. **21** Thou therefore which teachest another, teachest thou not thyself? thou that preachest a man should not steal, dost thou steal? **22** Thou that sayest a man should not commit adultery, dost thou commit adultery? thou that abhorrest idols, dost thou commit sacrilege? **23** Thou that makest thy boast of the law, through breaking the law dishonourest thou God? **24** For the name of God is blasphemed among the Gentiles through you, as it is written. **25** For circumcision verily profiteth, if thou keep the law: but if thou be a breaker of the law, thy circumcision is made uncircumcision. **26** Therefore if the uncircumcision keep the righteousness of the law, shall not his uncircumcision be counted for circumcision? **27** And shall not uncircumcision which is by nature, if it fulfil the law, judge thee, who by the letter and circumcision dost transgress the law? **28** For he is not a Jew, which is one outwardly; neither is that circumcision, which is outward in the flesh: **29** But he is a Jew, which is one inwardly; and circumcision is that of the heart, in the spirit, and not in the letter; whose praise is not of men, but of God.*

He made free use of Christian vocabulary. He talked about the blessing of the Almighty and the Christian confessions, which would become the pillars of the new government. He assumed the earnestness of a man weighed down by historic responsibility. He handed out pious stories to the press, especially to the church papers. He showed his tattered Bible and declared that he drew the strength for his great work from it as scores of pious people welcomed him as a man sent from God.

Who was the spiritual giant? Who was this man who clearly possessed such a deep walk with God?

His name was Adolph Hitler, a man who knew how to put on an outward show without ever having to be bothered with any inward reality. (Today in the Word, June 3, 1989.)

We have a name for a person like that: hypocrite. A play actor. A person who pretends to be pious but inwardly is lost and wicked. Interestingly, that is not a new phenomenon; it has been going on for a very long time. In fact, it was going on in Paul's day. There were people who claimed to be saved and righteous and on their way to heaven when, in reality, they were lost and wicked and on their way to hell. Chapter two deals with that problem.

As we begin chapter two of the book of Romans, let me give you the words of Dr. James Qurollo that will summarize the template of the next couple of chapters.

"In Romans 2, Paul's first main divisions of Romans continues. It deals with man's lack of righteousness and with his consequent need for God's righteousness which is available to him only by faith. There are four subdivisions. In 1:18-32 the pagan Gentile is shown to lack righteousness, in 2:1-16 the moralizer is shown to lack righteousness; and in 2:17-3:8 the Jewish is shown to lack righteousness. In summary, all the world is shown to lack righteousness and stand universally condemned before God (3:9-20)" (Qurollo, 29)

A finger pointing

After such a cutting portion of Scripture as Romans 1:18-32, the natural tendency is to fancy that it is directed at others and not at ourselves. The desire of mankind in regard to this passage is to proclaim themselves innocent regardless of whether they actually are or not.

Romans 2:1 *Therefore thou art inexcusable, O man, whosoever thou art that judgest: for wherein thou judgest another, thou condemnest thyself; for thou that judgest doest the same things.*

In chapter one, verse twenty, we found the pronouncement that mankind was *without excuse* when it comes to the responsibility to know and serve God. We now find another area in which mankind is *inexcusable.*

Paul took great umbrage with the idea that people who were committing the kinds of wickedness spoken of in chapter one could turn an accusing finger at others who were engaged in that same wickedness.

When commands against judgment are given in Scripture, watch for the "why." Over and over, you are going to see commandments against judging given because of hypocrisy, not because there is anything wrong with pointing out the difference between right and wrong:

Matthew 7:1 *Judge not, that ye be not judged.* **2** *For with what judgment ye judge, ye shall be judged: and with what measure ye mete, it shall be measured to you again.* **3** *And why beholdest thou the mote that is in thy brother's eye, but considerest not the beam that is in thine own eye?* **4** *Or how wilt thou say to thy brother, Let me pull out the mote out of thine eye; and, behold, a beam is in thine own eye?* **5** *Thou hypocrite, first cast out the beam out of thine own eye; and then shalt thou see clearly to cast out the mote out of thy brother's eye.*

Paul was dealing with hypocrites in Romans 2 just like Jesus was in Matthew 7. God does not despise judging; Jesus Himself said in **John 7:24** *Judge not according to the appearance, but <u>judge righteous judgment</u>.*

God does not despise proper judging of what is right and wrong; He despises hypocrisy.

Some years ago, there was a "reverend" who became world-famous as a civil rights leader. He often pontificated about the need for purity and faithfulness. That is until he, the "Reverend" Jesse Jackson, was exposed for having cheated on his wife with his secretary and produced an illegitimate child.

Romans 2:2 *But we are sure that the judgment of God is according to truth against them which commit such things.*

Every one of the things mentioned in Romans 1:18-32 are wicked and judged so by God, not according to finger-pointing but according to *truth*. It is true to say that some things are wicked, even if mankind likes those things and makes sitcoms about them. It is true to say that some things are pure and right, even if mankind hates them and makes fun of them on late-night talk shows.

God's judgments are always based on truth. Man, on the other hand, wicked, liberal, God-hating man, always judges according to his own hypocritical finger-pointing.

A foolish philosophy

A philosophy is, in a basic sense, a way of thinking. And these hypocrites had a foolish way of thinking:

Romans 2:3 *And thinkest thou this, O man, that judgest them which do such things, and doest the same, that thou shalt escape the judgment of God?*

There are two things put forth in this verse that hypocrites think they will escape judgment for: their *deeds* and their *hypocrisy*. The clear implication of this verse, though, is that they will escape neither. We do not have to worry ourselves with things like that; God sees, God knows, and God will deal with it.

Romans 2:4 *Or despisest thou the riches of his goodness and forbearance and longsuffering; not knowing that the goodness of God leadeth thee to repentance?*

Why would a wicked man think he could get by with wickedness and hypocrisy? Because they mistake the goodness and forbearance and longsuffering of God for weakness, or maybe even for acceptance and approval. Paul put it this way, they *despise the riches of his goodness and forbearance and longsuffering. Despise* is from *kataphroneo,* meaning *to disdain, to think very little of.*

But pay very close attention to that last phrase: *the goodness of God leadeth thee to repentance.*

39

To think that we will get by with evil, any of us, to imagine that God will not act, that is a foolish philosophy! God still demands repentance. His goodness, His patience, is all designed to compel man to turn from sin to Him. But there will come a day when His patience runs out, and all that is left is His judgment.

A full payment

The goodness of God leads us to repent, but many will not follow that leading. They choose to go another way.

Romans 2:5 *But after thy hardness and impenitent heart treasurest up unto thyself wrath against the day of wrath and revelation of the righteous judgment of God;*

The concept of a hard heart is usually familiar to Christians, but this verse also calls it an impenitent heart. That descriptive means *a heart that refuses to change*. It is not that people *cannot* receive Christ and change; it is that they *will not*.

This verse tells us that they are treasuring up some things. They doubtless think that they are gathering the good things of life, but what they are really doing is treasuring up, heaping up like the proverbial dragon's treasure, wrath to themselves. There will be a day of reckoning, a day of wrath, a day of revealing the righteous judgment of God.

Romans 2:6 *Who will render to every man according to his deeds:*

We will meet up with our deeds again. Either at the Great White Throne for the lost or the Judgment Seat of Christ for the saved, we will answer for the deeds done in our bodies.

Yes, we, the saved, have it better than the lost. We do not have to go to hell. As far as our salvation is concerned, we are set. But we will still look the Lord in the eyes and answer for what we have done or not done since we got saved. We are going to either gain reward or suffer the loss of reward based on our deeds.

Romans 2:7 *To them who by patient continuance in well doing seek for glory and honour and immortality, eternal life:*

This verse gives the marks and rewards of one who has placed his or her faith in Christ, not a pattern by which one could somehow earn eternal life.

The marks of one who has placed his faith in Christ are that they will have patient continuance in well-doing, and by that patient continuance in well-doing, they will seek for glory, honor, and immortality. In other words, a real Christian will keep on living for the Lord and will have his sight set on things above.

Will he be perfect? No. But will he "continue?" Yes. One who is truly saved keeps going on for God. He may stumble, he may fall, but he gets back up and keeps going on for God.

Again, that is not how you get saved; it is how you prove that you *are* saved!

And what is the main reward of salvation? Eternal life! It is very hard to beat that.

Romans 2:8 *But unto them that are contentious, and do not obey the truth, but obey unrighteousness, indignation and wrath,* **9** *Tribulation and anguish, upon every soul of man that doeth evil, of the Jew first, and also of the Gentile;*

The last verse gave the marks and rewards of one who has placed his or her faith in Christ. These verses give the marks and rewards of one who has not placed his or her faith in Christ.

The marks of the sinner are that they are contentious and will not obey the truth. Instead, they obey unrighteousness. Please note that they will obey either way. Everyone obeys; the only question is what they obey.

Their reward for obeying unrighteousness is indignation (*thumos*, God's boiling anger), wrath (His punishing anger), tribulation (pressing, trouble, squeezing), and anguish (narrowness, being caught in a tight predicament).

But now please notice two incredibly significant words, words that show us the hinge that this entire passage swings on:

Upon every... (v. 9)

Look at the entire verse again.

Romans 2:9 *Tribulation and anguish, upon every soul of man that doeth evil, of the Jew first, and also of the Gentile;*

41

The Jewish people occupy a prized position: first in the heart of God, the very apple of His eye. But that lofty perch comes with a price: first in priority, therefore first in judgment.

Christ came first to the Jews, and they were the first to reject Him:

John 1:11 *He came unto his own, and his own received him not.*

The Jews believed that they could get by with sin because they were the seed of Abraham, but that God was going to harshly judge the Gentiles for those exact same sins because they were not the seed of Abraham.

God does not care who your father or grandfather were. There is complete equality with God; He despises hypocrites of any nationality.

Romans 2:10 *But glory, honour, and peace, to every man that worketh good, to the Jew first, and also to the Gentile:*

Yes, God equally despises hypocrites, no matter the nationality. But that is only the bad side of things; there is a good side as well: He also equally blesses those who are saved and live like it, of any nationality, with glory, honor, and peace. This is also "to the Jew first," but it is also equal in proportion. They will be at the front of the line for judgment, they will be at the front of the line for blessing, but everyone in the line will receive an equal blessing if their deeds have been equal.

Believe me, that is not something the Jews wanted to hear. But it was about to get even worse as far as they were concerned.

Romans 2:11 *For there is no respect of persons with God.*

This was like a nuclear blast. It shows that it was never about race; it was and is always about righteousness.

We Caucasian Gentiles are just like the Jews. We have it in our minds that God likes us best because we are white. Good luck with that. God does not care about your skin; He only cares about your sin.

You can be a Jew on your way to hell or a Gentile on your way to hell. You can be black on your way to hell, and you can be white on your way to hell. You can be any of those things and be on your way to heaven. Christianity is the most non-race-driven thing in the world because Christ the founder was utterly non-race-driven. He died for all.

A faithful performance

It is not our assertions that show what we are; it is our actions that show what we are. Here is how Paul begins to develop that thought.

Romans 2:12 *For as many as have sinned without law shall also perish without law: and as many as have sinned in the law shall be judged by the law;*

It is not necessary to have the law in order to have sinned, and it is the Jew's law, God's law, that Paul had in mind when he pointed this out. Men sinned before there ever was a Jewish code of law and perished (went to hell) before that law was ever penned. This means that sin is not a matter of disobeying a governmental authority; it is a matter of disobeying God.

If you have the law, you will be judged by the law. But whether you have the law or not, sin is still sin, and God will deal with it. There are plenty of things that the law allows but that God says are a sin. When that is the case, you need to understand that God is going to judge you based on His laws, not on ours.

Romans 2:13 *(For not the hearers of the law are just before God, but the doers of the law shall be justified.*

You can see from that parenthesis mark that verse thirteen begins a parenthesis of thought in this passage. He is going to use this parenthesis to deal with a Jewish mentality that was and is dead wrong. When he began to speak of the law in verse twelve, he knew that they thought, and many still think, that they were justified simply because they were God's chosen nation and because they received and heard the law. Paul himself used to feel that exact same way until he met Christ on the Damascus Road.

Paul was determined that his people not make the mistake that he made. He wanted them to know that simply hearing is not enough. A person would have to be a doer of the law for it to be enough.

But he had one more shoe to drop. One would have to do the entire law, all of it, perfectly, and that was utterly impossible. Without trying to run too far ahead, look at that fact from the very next chapter:

Romans 3:10 *As it is written, There is none righteous, no, not one:*

Romans 3:20 *Therefore by the deeds of the law there shall no flesh be justified in his sight: for by the law is the knowledge of sin.*

All of the law-abiding Jews, 1,500 years of them, tens of millions of them, and not one had ever yet been justified by the deeds of the law. It was and is utterly impossible to do so!

Romans 2:14 *For when the Gentiles, which have not the law, do by nature the things contained in the law, these, having not the law, are a law unto themselves:* **15** *Which shew the work of the law written in their hearts, their conscience also bearing witness, and their thoughts the mean while accusing or else excusing one another;)*

The Jews always believed themselves better than the Gentiles. But Paul the Jew made clear in these verses that the Gentiles, even without having had the benefit of the Mosaic law, still usually managed to keep the things contained in the law. Maybe not all of the ceremonial parts, but certainly many of the moral parts. God has put the concept of right and wrong down into the heart of man, Jew or Gentile. People know in their hearts when they or someone else is doing right or wrong.

This is another reason why people are without excuse. They have to fight against what God has put in their heart to try and justify the wicked ways that they are living.

This ends the parenthesis that began in verse thirteen.

Romans 2:16 *In the day when God shall judge the secrets of men by Jesus Christ according to my gospel.*

In order to understand verse sixteen, we need to take out the parenthesis and read it right after verse twelve:

Romans 2:12 *For as many as have sinned without law shall also perish without law: and as many as have sinned in the law shall be judged by the law;* **16** *In the day when God shall judge the secrets of men by Jesus Christ according to my gospel.*

Once again, Paul demonstrates that there is complete equality in God's sight. The first phrase of verse twelve describes Gentiles, the last phrase of verse twelve describes Jews, and the things that are waiting for any who have sinned are perishing and judgment.

Judgment day is coming. The world laughs at that thought; they relegate it to caricatures of some long-bearded, wild-eyed man on the street holding up a sign. But there will come a day when all of the laughter stops, and the harsh reality of judgment sets in.

And notice, please, who verse sixteen says will be doing the judging: sweet, sweet Jesus will be doing the judging. The Jesus that is supposedly tolerant of everything and everyone will be doing the judging.

But there is one more shocker in that verse. Please notice what Jesus will be using as a measuring stick: Paul's gospel! And since the context is law and judgment, the sin that necessitated the gospel will be part of the proceedings. The world loves to pretend that Jesus had nothing to do with anything but the first four books of the New Testament. In fact, they love to say that Jesus is actually opposed to the rest of the New Testament, especially what Paul wrote. But there will come a day when Jesus Christ will open the Bible and judge men out of it, and one of the places He will open to is the Pauline Epistles!

Jesus will read Romans 1:18-32 and judge homosexuals out of it.

Jesus will read 1 Thessalonians 4:3 and judge fornicators out of it.

Jesus will read Galatians 5 and judge adulterers and practitioners of witchcraft and idolaters and drunks out of it.

Jesus will point out that had Paul's gospel been followed, people would have repented of those and other sins and been saved and justified.

45

And it will not be those who have asserted that they are right who will be justified; it will be those whose actions were right, it will be those who truly got born again, and all who truly got born again will have lives that proved it.

A frightening pride

Romans 2:17 *Behold, thou art called a Jew, and restest in the law, and makest thy boast of God,* **18** *And knowest his will, and approvest the things that are more excellent, being instructed out of the law;* **19** *And art confident that thou thyself art a guide of the blind, a light of them which are in darkness,* **20** *An instructor of the foolish, a teacher of babes, which hast the form of knowledge and of the truth in the law.*

There are two rather significant words in this section of verses: *boast* in verse seventeen and *confident* in verse nineteen. They serve to show the frightening pride that the Jews especially held, pride that was keeping them from humbling themselves to accept Christ.

They had "title pride;" they were proud to be called Jews.

They "rested in the law," meaning that they were proud that they were the ones that the law was given to.

They "made their boast in God," meaning that they really believed that they had an inside track to God that no one else had.

They believed that they knew His will and that others did not.

They "approved the things that are excellent, being instructed out of the law." That means that they had very high standards and behavior and were very highly proud of their very high standards and behavior.

They were confident that they were *a guide of the blind, a light of them which are in darkness, an instructor of the foolish, a teacher of babes,*

In other words, they knew what they knew, and they knew that you did not know what they knew, and they knew that you were really nothing more than babes and fools compared to them.

46

Then, we find that they had *the form of knowledge and of the truth in* the law. Place a strong emphasis on that word form [*morphosis*] when you read it because that is all they had. The law/their religion was a veneer to them; they had no substance; they had no real walk with God.

But what they did have was lots and lots of pride, which all by itself has sent more people to hell than all other sins combined ever have.

A forceful point

This whole passage has been about hypocrisy, but now Paul is really going to bear down on it.

Romans 2:21 *Thou therefore which teachest another, teachest thou not thyself? thou that preachest a man should not steal, dost thou steal? 22 Thou that sayest a man should not commit adultery, dost thou commit adultery? thou that abhorrest idols, dost thou commit sacrilege? 23 Thou that makest thy boast of the law, through breaking the law dishonourest thou God?*

Paul asked five questions, and the obvious answer to every single question was the exact opposite of what it should have been. They taught others, but when Jesus showed up to teach them, they would not be taught, nor did they ever truly teach themselves what they were teaching others. They preached to others not to steal, then they institutionalized stealing right there in the temple, and the whole corrupt show was led by High Priests Annas and Caiaphas! They railed against adultery, then when Jesus said, "He who is without sin among you, let him first cast a stone," they had to slink away because they knew they were adulterers themselves! They said that they abhorred idols, then committed their own form of idolatry, revering the gold given to the Temple more than the Temple itself. They boasted in the law, then every time they found a law that they did not like, they came up with a custom or a teaching to get around it.

They were utter, complete hypocrites. And what was the result of that hypocrisy? The result was what you see in verse twenty-four:

Romans 2:24 *For the name of God is blasphemed among the Gentiles through you, as it is written.*

Quoting Isaiah 52:5 and Ezekiel 36:20-23, Paul pointed out that the Gentiles were looking at the hypocritical behavior of the Jews as listed above and blasphemed the God they believed must have been accepting of such.

But wait! Are we any better? Is modern so-called Christianity any better?

Deacons on Sunday who drink on Friday and Saturday.

Church members who curse at work then clock out and walk out to their cars with the church bumper sticker on the back.

Preachers who are unethical with money then brag about their big giving.

Ladies who sing in the choir then dress during the week in utterly immodest ways.

People who say amen and hallelujah and praise the Lord in the sanctuary and then post things that are sexual and sensual and suggestive on their Twitter or Facebook before they even leave the church parking lot.

If you say one thing and live another, people will see, and they will know, and they will go to hell because of you, and their blood will be on your hands.

A focused purity

Romans 2:25 *For circumcision verily profiteth, if thou keep the law: but if thou be a breaker of the law, thy circumcision is made uncircumcision.*

Paul has not changed subjects. He is still dealing with the law and those who were claiming to keep it. Circumcision was a foundational part of the law; it was the first part of the covenant given to Abraham; it was a symbol of having our sin removed from us. And if they had gone on to actually keep the law, it would have been a profitable thing, which is a thought he will more fully develop in the next chapter.

The Jews thought that since they were circumcised as babies, they got a pass on all other disobedience. But Paul

48

pointed out that your actions as adults are more important than a ritual performed on you as a child.

It does not matter what ritual, pick one. Whatever you pick, your actions as adults are more important than a ritual performed on you as a child. And the most important action you can take is to receive Christ as your Savior and then live for Him.

Romans 2:26 *Therefore if the uncircumcision keep the righteousness of the law, shall not his uncircumcision be counted for circumcision?*

This verse goes back again to the Jew's belief that they were better than the Gentiles [the uncircumcision], any Gentiles. Let me tell you what they really, truly believed: they truly believed that a Jew, just because he had been circumcised as a child, could be a murderer, adulterer, homosexual, drunk, thief, and yet be better than a Gentile who did not live like that, just because that Gentile had never been circumcised as a baby.

Do you see both the foolishness and hypocrisy? There were Gentiles that, after Calvary, accepted Christ, got forgiveness of their sins, and were on their way to heaven, and yet, they would have lost, wicked Jews look at them and say, "You are worthless! You are going to hell because you weren't circumcised!"

But Paul had a heavy hammer to drop on that; as far as God was concerned when looking at the Gentiles, if they kept the righteousness of the law, God not only gave them a pass on their uncircumcision, He actually regarded their right behavior as if it was circumcision, placing them on equal footing with Jews in that matter.

As shocking as that was, he was going to go even farther in verse twenty-seven.

Romans 2:27 *And shall not uncircumcision which is by nature, if it fulfil the law, judge thee, who by the letter and circumcision dost transgress the law?*

Paul said that those uncircumcised Gentiles who did right would actually be judges of circumcised Jews who did wrong. Their uncircumcision was *by nature*, it was the way God created them and everyone else, and He was not going to hold that against any of them in the context of who was more pleasing in His sight, choosing instead to focus on behavior. That very thought, the idea that Gentiles would ever in any context be the judge of Jews, condemning them as guilty, would make them boiling mad!

But Paul was right. No ritual performed on you as a baby is as important as the way you behave as an adult. Circumcision never makes up for hypocrisy.

But Paul was not yet done. He saved the best for last, in fact. He would use verses twenty-eight and twenty-nine to tell people how to be a "real" Jew:

Romans 2:28 *For he is not a Jew, which is one outwardly; neither is that circumcision, which is outward in the flesh:* **29** *But he is a Jew, which is one inwardly; and circumcision is that of the heart, in the spirit, and not in the letter; whose praise is not of men, but of God.*

In summary, national promises aside, you do not become God's chosen people *spiritually* because you had a *physical* operation performed on your reproductive instrument; you become God's chosen people *spiritually* because you had a *spiritual* operation performed on your heart. You do not get saved by keeping the law, not even to the very letter. That may bring you the praise of men, especially other religious men, but the praise of God only comes when the heart gets circumcised, when you get saved and have the old sinful you forever cut away.

Chapter Four
D - Don't Even Think About It!

Romans 3:1 *What advantage then hath the Jew? or what profit is there of circumcision?* **2** *Much every way: chiefly, because that unto them were committed the oracles of God.* **3** *For what if some did not believe? shall their unbelief make the faith of God without effect?* **4** *God forbid: yea, let God be true, but every man a liar; as it is written, That thou mightest be justified in thy sayings, and mightest overcome when thou art judged.* **5** *But if our unrighteousness commend the righteousness of God, what shall we say? Is God unrighteous who taketh vengeance? (I speak as a man)* **6** *God forbid: for then how shall God judge the world?* **7** *For if the truth of God hath more abounded through my lie unto his glory; why yet am I also judged as a sinner?* **8** *And not rather, (as we be slanderously reported, and as some affirm that we say,) Let us do evil, that good may come? whose damnation is just.* **9** *What then? are we better than they? No, in no wise: for we have before proved both Jews and Gentiles, that they are all under sin;* **10** *As it is written, There is none righteous, no, not one:* **11** *There is none that understandeth, there is none that seeketh after God.* **12** *They are all gone out of the way, they are together become unprofitable; there is none that doeth good, no, not one.* **13** *Their throat is an open sepulchre; with their tongues they have used deceit; the poison of asps is under their lips:* **14** *Whose mouth is full of cursing and bitterness:* **15** *Their feet are swift to shed blood:* **16** *Destruction and misery are in their ways:* **17** *And the way of*

51

peace have they not known: **18** *There is no fear of God before their eyes.* **19** *Now we know that what things soever the law saith, it saith to them who are under the law: that every mouth may be stopped, and all the world may become guilty before God.* **20** *Therefore by the deeds of the law there shall no flesh be justified in his sight: for by the law is the knowledge of sin.* **21** *But now the righteousness of God without the law is manifested, being witnessed by the law and the prophets;* **22** *Even the righteousness of God which is by faith of Jesus Christ unto all and upon all them that believe: for there is no difference:* **23** *For all have sinned, and come short of the glory of God;* **24** *Being justified freely by his grace through the redemption that is in Christ Jesus:* **25** *Whom God hath set forth to be a propitiation through faith in his blood, to declare his righteousness for the remission of sins that are past, through the forbearance of God;* **26** *To declare, I say, at this time his righteousness: that he might be just, and the justifier of him which believeth in Jesus.* **27** *Where is boasting then? It is excluded. By what law? of works? Nay: but by the law of faith.* **28** *Therefore we conclude that a man is justified by faith without the deeds of the law.* **29** *Is he the God of the Jews only? is he not also of the Gentiles? Yes, of the Gentiles also:* **30** *Seeing it is one God, which shall justify the circumcision by faith, and uncircumcision through faith.* **31** *Do we then make void the law through faith? God forbid: yea, we establish the law.*

The relationship between parents and children is a very unique thing, and as such, it produces some unique terminology. For instance, parents will often tell their children, "Don't even think about it."

Don't even think about smacking your sister! Don't even think about shoving that Cheerio up your nose! Don't even think about peeing in that bathtub! Don't even think about it!

Why in the world would we say such an unusual thing? How are we supposed to know what they are actually thinking? And why not just be content to tell them not to do a particular thing?

The reason we tell them, "Don't even think about it," is because we know that thoughts will produce actions.

Paul knew that as well. That is why Paul used Romans 3 to tell believers in Rome in so many words, "Don't even think about it!" There are some things they would think that he knew they did not need to be thinking. Let us delve into chapter three and find out what those things were.

Don't even think the problem with man is God or His Word

Jump ahead to verse four with me and notice a phrase that Paul used:

Romans 3:4a *God forbid...*

That phrase sets the tone of this chapter; we will see it multiple times.

Romans 3:1 *What advantage then hath the Jew? or what profit is there of circumcision?*

There is really no biblical debate about the fact that God called a specific, chosen people. All through the Old Testament, we find that He chose the Jews to be the nation by which He would send His Son.

When Paul said *what advantage then hath the Jew*, and *what profit is there of circumcision*, he was in no way indicating that God did not call the Jews to a very special position. And the question that he asked in verse one he would then answer in verse two:

Romans 3:2 *Much every way: chiefly, because that unto them were committed the oracles of God.*

The real advantage of the Jews was not in the circumstance of circumcision but in the fact that God sent the Scriptures to them (the oracles of God), specifically the Old Testament Scriptures. They received the light of the written Word of God much more fully and well before the Gentile world. Make no mistake, that is a huge advantage!

Romans 3:3 *For what if some did not believe? shall their unbelief make the faith of God without effect?*

In saying what he said in verse two, Paul knew that a rhetorical question would arise. He knew that the Jews would ask, "Why is this such an advantage compared to circumcision? After all, some people who received that Scripture did not believe!"

And certainly, many did not. Korah, Dathan, Abiram, Ahab, the list could go on forever. Seeing that, they would reason that there must be some problem with this doctrine of scriptural faith in God superseding circumcision. They would think that what Paul and others before him and with were teaching "had no effect." In short, they would be pointing out what they believed to be problems with God's Word and God Himself.

Romans 3:4 *God forbid: yea, let God be true, but every man a liar; as it is written, That thou mightest be justified in thy sayings, and mightest overcome when thou art judged.*

That phrase *God forbid* is obviously a very strong statement. It is the harshest term of condemnation in the Bible. Qurollo puts it this way, "It is an expression of utter abhorrence at the very idea of something." (Qurollo, 49). The very idea that God could somehow be at fault for the disbelief of others really upset Paul. Anyone who knew the Old Testament Scriptures knew better as well. Paul made the statement *let God be true but every man a liar*, and he then referred to Psalm 51:4 for this doctrine:

Psalm 51:4 *Against thee, thee only, have I sinned, and done this evil in thy sight: that thou mightest be justified when thou speakest, and be clear when thou judgest.*

Whenever God speaks, He is justified in whatever He has said because He speaks the truth in everything that He says. Therefore, any man who contradicts God or His Word in any way is the liar, not God.

The last phrase of verse four, *That thou mightest be justified in thy sayings, and mightest overcome when thou art judged*, requires us to understand who the pronouns refer to if we are going to understand it properly. This, then, is how you should understand it:

That thou [God] *mightest be justified in thy sayings, and mightest overcome when thou* [God] *art judged.* In other words, since God will always be the truth-teller and man always the liar in any conflict between the two, God will always ultimately be vindicated against any and all criticism.

The problem of man has never been any fault in the Word of God; it has been his fault in failing to follow the Word of God.

Don't even think that God is not right to judge us

As we did in the first section of verses, please jump ahead in this section of verses. Look quickly at verse six:

Romans 3:6 *God forbid...*

For the second time, Paul used the phrase *God forbid.* In other words, as we have been saying, "Don't even think about it!"

Romans 3:5 *But if our unrighteousness commend the righteousness of God, what shall we say? Is God unrighteous who taketh vengeance? (I speak as a man)*

Is God unrighteous who taketh vengeance? What a question! You could substitute literally anything for those last two words, *taketh vengeance,* and it would still be just as absurd. God is not unrighteous in anything!

The reasoning of the people to whom Paul was writing, the reasoning that he knew they would use in looking at this, basically says, "But my badness makes God's goodness look really good! So why should God judge me?"

It is almost inconceivable just how ridiculous such an argument is, and yet, Paul knew that people would make that very argument.

When Paul said in the parenthesis at the end of the verse, *I speak as a man,* it means, "I am speaking as I know a man would speak. I am using the reasoning that I know that you are going to use." And knowing that reasoning was coming, it is no wonder the next verse begins like this:

Romans 3:6 *God forbid: for then how shall God judge the world?*

Paul knew that his readers understood the Scripture well enough to know that God is one day going to judge the world. But if they had no problem with that idea, then how could they possibly also hold the idea that God could somehow be unrighteous? When God judges, it is always perfectly righteous, for He Himself is always perfectly righteous.

This belief is being discarded by our modern world. Mankind is now becoming so sin-soaked and indulgent that he has to reason away the coming judgment of God in order to go about his day-to-day activities. Every perversion, every sin, every outright blasphemy must somehow now be seen as acceptable, and God Himself must be the one who is unreasonable. God has now been reduced to a God of tolerance and acceptance rather than the Biblical God of holiness and judgment.

But He will judge the world, of this there is no real doubt, and He will be righteous in every one of his judgments.

Romans 3:7 *For if the truth of God hath more abounded through my lie unto his glory; why yet am I also judged as a sinner?* **8** *And not rather, (as we be slanderously reported, and as some affirm that we say,) Let us do evil, that good may come? whose damnation is just.*

Paul's argument in verse seven is a rephrasing of his argument in verse five. If bad things that we do (such as Paul's hypothetical lying) bring glory to God, why would God ever judge him for lying, even though it is clearly a sin?

In verse eight, Paul begins to expose an attack that was being leveled against him and the rest of the apostles. Paul and the apostles taught grace and salvation by grace through faith in Jesus Christ alone. This is the very doctrine that made Jesus run afoul of the Jewish leaders, and Paul and the apostles would fare no better.

In regards to this, Paul and the apostles were being slandered with a very grievous lie. Those who believed in salvation by works of the law were slanderously claiming that Paul and the apostles were encouraging people to sin!

Those who know the book of Romans will know that in Romans 6:1, Paul dealt with that very firmly. But even here, the very first time he mentioned it, he dealt with it in the brutal manner that it needed to be dealt with. He proclaimed that the people saying such things were under damnation and that their damnation was just! People who are perverting the doctrines of Scripture and of the Lord Jesus Christ, people who are lying about God's men who teach the pure doctrines of Scripture and of the Lord Jesus Christ, are absolutely under the condemnation of God, and their condemnation is indeed just.

What was Paul's basic admonition? If you think that God is not right to judge us, don't even think about it!

Don't even think that "we" are better than "they."

In verses nine through eighteen, eleven times you are going to find the negative terms no, not, and none.

Romans 3:9 *What then? are we better than they? No, in no wise: for we have before proved both Jews and Gentiles, that they are all under sin;*

There are differing views as to the identities of the *we* and the *they* in this verse. The latter half of the verse, to me, settles that issue: "*we*" refers to the Jews, and "*they*" refers to the Gentiles. In that context, the argument he is making goes back to the truth of verse four, that the Jews [the circumcision] had a huge advantage in that God sent the Scriptures to them. And yet, they were still no better, no more worthy of salvation than the Gentiles.

No matter who the "we/they" are, no one in their own righteousness is better than anyone else. Why?

To begin with, verse nine tells us that we are all under sin. Paul reminded them that he had *before proved* that, meaning he had established that clearly in the first two chapters of this epistle. And this is universal! *All,* anyone of any race, any religion, any creed, any belief is under sin. When it comes to salvation, Jews are no better nor any worse than Gentiles, nor are Gentiles any better or worse than Jews. All are equally under sin, and all are equally able to be saved.

The same thing holds true for anyone of any other race. Whites are no better off than blacks, nor are they any worse, and vice versa. Pick a race, pick a skin color, and the exact same thing is true: no "we" is any better than any "they."

Romans 3:10 *As it is written, There is none righteous, no, not one:*

Romans 3:10 is a quote from both Psalm 14:1 and Psalm 53:1. Paul reaffirmed in Romans 3:10 the fact that there is none righteous in and of themselves, not even a single one. People think they are righteous on the basis of where they were born, where they live, who their family is, or the works that they do, but there is none righteous, no not one.

Romans 3:11 *There is none that understandeth, there is none that seeketh after God.*

Not only are there none righteous, Paul here asserts the fact that there is no one that even understands, no one that even seeks after God.

When this is said, people who have read their Bibles will immediately have some questions arise in their minds. Please look at a couple of other verses of Scripture:

Isaiah 55:6 *Seek ye the LORD while he may be found, call ye upon him while he is near:*

2 Chronicles 7:14 *If my people, which are called by my name, shall humble themselves, and pray, and seek my face, and turn from their wicked ways; then will I hear from heaven, and will forgive their sin, and will heal their land.*

Psalm 63:1 *O God, thou art my God; early will I seek thee: my soul thirsteth for thee, my flesh longeth for thee in a dry and thirsty land, where no water is;*

How do we reconcile the fact that in Romans 3:10 we are told that there is none that seeketh after God with the fact that in these three passages of Scripture and many others, we are told to seek after God and that people have sought after God?

The reconciliation is simple and biblical. Man on his own does not seek after God, ever. But God draws all men to Himself (John 12:32), and in response to this drawing, some choose to

58

seek Him. But no one *by himself* seeks after God, so "we" are not any better than "they!"

Romans 3:12 *They are all gone out of the way, they are together become unprofitable; there is none that doeth good, no, not one.*

Please notice once again the universal terms used in this passage: "all, together, none, not one." *They are all gone out of the way, they are together become unprofitable; there is none that doeth good, no, not one.*

When verse twelve says that they are all gone out of the way, it tells us that God has laid out a prescribed path for mankind to walk in and that all of mankind has deviated from that path. Since all of mankind has deviated from that path and become unprofitable, "we" are not any better than "they."

Romans 3:13 *Their throat is an open sepulchre; with their tongues they have used deceit; the poison of asps is under their lips:* **14** *Whose mouth is full of cursing and bitterness:*

Paraphrasing three different Psalms and a passage from Jeremiah, Paul here points out the universal standing of mankind in regard to the wickedness of their mouths. Even if no other body part showed us all universally to be under sin, that one does! Jew or Gentile, black or white, the things that people say demonstrate their universal guilt before God.

Romans 3:15 *Their feet are swift to shed blood:*

Quoting Isaiah 59:7-8, Paul observes that not only do people do violence, but mankind is also inclined to be swift to violence. This trait crosses national boundaries and takes in all; everyone is equally on the same level of guilt before God in this matter.

Romans 3:16 *Destruction and misery are in their ways:*

Many years ago, I learned of one of the most unique traits of the common termite. Everyone knows that termites eat wood and do incredible damage to the framing of a house. But what many people do not know is that termites can be perceived even when they cannot be seen. You see, termites travel in a tunnel of mud that they build. They literally leave a trail of destruction!

All of mankind is just like that. Yes, there are individuals in every nation who do good and are kind. But in every nation, there is a sin nature causing destruction and misery. No nationality and no ethnicity is immune.

Romans 3:17 *And the way of peace have they not known:*

It is not just that mankind does not want peace; it is literally that they do not know the way of peace. Mankind crucified the Prince of Peace, and they know nothing of the peace that only He can bring. There is no ethnicity any better or any worse; in this area, mankind is equal in the sense that *the way of peace have they not known.*

Romans 3:18 *There is no fear of God before their eyes.*

No matter what the nationality, *there is no fear of God before their eyes.* Mankind must forever be taught to fear and reverence God, and those who have not been taught this lesson and absorbed this lesson simply do not by nature fear God. No one is born right in this area; we are all born wrong in this area.

"Black is beautiful! White is right! Brown is better all around! Red is as good as a nice warm bed!"

Seriously? Do you think that any "we" are somehow better than any "they?" Don't even think about it!

Don't even think that a person can be justified by the deeds of the law

After such a list as was given in the previous section, the thinking would probably be, "That's bad! Those people need to obey the law; then it would all be fine!" But obedience to the law is merely an external form devoid of any internal power.

Romans 3:19 *Now we know that what things soever the law saith, it saith to them who are under the law: that every mouth may be stopped, and all the world may become guilty before God.*

The law was never designed to make people proud of the fact that they were keeping the law. In fact, the very opposite was true. The law was designed to teach man that he is completely deficient and desperately needs a Savior. It was designed to make people be quiet about how good they are because they are not good at all. It was designed to show us that we are all guilty.

Romans 3:20 *Therefore by the deeds of the law there shall no flesh be justified in his sight: for by the law is the knowledge of sin.*

Though all the words of Scripture are important, when it comes to salvation, this is quite possibly one of the most essential verses in the Bible. Notice the strength of this universal absolute: by the deeds of the law there shall *no* flesh be justified in His, God's sight! Being good, or being moral, or keeping the Ten Commandments, none of these kinds of things have ever saved so much as one single soul. The law does not bring a cure for sin; it merely brings the awareness of sin.

By the way, this verse shows something very important about the book of Romans, something that Martin Luther could not seem to grasp while he was studying the book of James and comparing it to the book of Romans. The book of James speaks of our being justified by the law; the book of Romans clearly says that we cannot be justified by the works of the law. Romans 3:20 shows the perspective that Romans was written from: the perspective of God. In God's sight, no flesh can be justified by the works of the law. James is written from the perspective of man: in man's sight, no man can truly be seen as being saved unless the works of the law are present in his life.

Both perspectives are correct. We cannot work to be saved (Romans 3:20), but if we are saved, we will most certainly have works to prove it.

Do you think that a person can be justified by the deeds of the law? Don't even think about it!

Don't even think that we can take credit for salvation

Romans 3:21 *But now the righteousness of God without the law is manifested, being witnessed by the law and the prophets;*

The righteousness of God was never intended to come by the law. Even the Old Testament Law and Prophets

(Scriptures) testified to that. But now, Paul said the righteousness of God without the law was manifested. He was talking about Jesus Christ, His sacrifice on Calvary, and how we now know that we are saved by that alone, not by the works of the law or any combination of works and grace. Salvation is all of grace through faith in Jesus Christ alone. And far from being a new thing, were they truly to have studied it honestly, they would have found that all of it was *witnessed by the law and the prophets.*

This is why Jesus was able to say in John 5:39, *Search the scriptures; for in them ye think ye have eternal life: and they are they which testify of me.*

Romans 3:22 *Even the righteousness of God which is by faith of Jesus Christ unto all and upon all them that believe: for there is no difference:* **23** *For all have sinned, and come short of the glory of God;*

Verse twenty-one has ended, but the sentence and the thought that it began continues all the way through verse twenty-six.

What was it, then, that was *being witnessed by the law and the prophets*? The fact that righteousness is of God, by faith in Jesus Christ, and that it is equally available to all who believe. Verse twenty-three tells us that *all have sinned, and come short of the glory of God.* All are equally sinners, and all are equally able to be saved. There is no difference!

Romans 3:24 *Being justified freely by his grace through the redemption that is in Christ Jesus:*

Continuing the thought, Paul now shows that all who believe are justified. That word means that they have been judicially declared righteous on the basis of what Jesus did on Calvary. In more colloquial terms, it means that they are "just as if they had never sinned." As far as we are concerned, this happens freely. In other words, we cannot pay for it, and the reason that we cannot pay for it is because Jesus Christ already did! We are redeemed [*apolutrosis*, liberated by the payment of a ransom], we are bought, by Jesus Christ. And since He is the one doing the buying, He has every right to say who He wants to buy. He has quite plainly told us that He wants to redeem Jew and Gentile, man and woman, black and white, boy and girl, everyone! Peter referenced that truth in 2 Peter 3:9, saying that God is *not willing that any should perish, but that all should come to repentance.*

But please understand that since He is the one doing the redeeming, the justifying, the purchasing, that salvation is of Christ and not of us. Yes, we are responsible for accepting Him, but salvation is still not a work on our part. If we think that we can work for salvation, then we really do not understand salvation.

Romans 3:25 *Whom God hath set forth to be a propitiation through faith in his blood, to declare his righteousness for the remission of sins that are past, through the forbearance of God; 26 To declare, I say, at this time his righteousness: that he might be just, and the justifier of him which believeth in Jesus.*

God the Father set forth [*protithemia*, ordained] Jesus Christ to be a *propitiation*. That word is from *hilasmos* and means *that which appeases or satisfies another*. In other words, God the Father would never be satisfied with us, a sacrifice we make, or any work that we do, but He was satisfied with what Jesus Christ did for us on Calvary. And after thousands of years of the law being in place and millions of people trying to keep it, since He was never satisfied with any one of those people, we know beyond a shadow of a doubt that Jesus Christ is the only One He will ever be satisfied with.

Our salvation is through faith in His blood. Why did God choose to do it this way? The remainder of verses twenty-five and twenty-six mean this: God passed over [*remission, aphesis*, a passing over], withheld judgment [forebearance, *anokay*, showed tolerance], on all of those past, Old Testament, pre-Calvary sins. In simple terms, He put them on His own account, promising to pay. Had He not eventually paid, He could not have been either just or a justifier. But He did! He paid the full price for our sins when He died on Calvary.

Romans 3:27 *Where is boasting then? It is excluded. By what law? of works? Nay: but by the law of faith.*

We are observing that we cannot take credit for salvation. And so, it makes perfect sense that Paul begins verse twenty-seven with this question: *where is boasting then?* In other words, what right exactly do we have to brag? The answer is none! Boasting is excluded. By what law is boasting excluded? The law of works? No, if it were by works, we certainly could boast. Boasting is excluded by the law of faith. Because salvation is simply obtained by placing our faith in Jesus Christ, we have no right or reason at all to brag.

Romans 3:28 *Therefore we conclude that a man is justified by faith without the deeds of the law.*

The conclusion of the doctrine of salvation as found in the book of Romans is not found at the end of the book; it is found right here in Romans 3:28. Out of everything that has been said about salvation in this book, and will yet be said about salvation in this book, the conclusion of it all is that a man is justified by faith without the deeds of the law. As the book bounces back and forth from point to point, subject to subject, proposition to proposition, always keep that conclusion in mind: *a man is justified by faith without the deeds of the law.* Romans 3:28 is the pivotal verse in all of the book of Romans.

Romans 3:29 *Is he the God of the Jews only? is he not also of the Gentiles? Yes, of the Gentiles also:* **30** *Seeing it is one God, which shall justify the circumcision by faith, and uncircumcision through faith.*

If salvation is by the law, God would only be the God of the Jews because the law came to them. But since salvation is by grace instead of by the law, God is God both of the Jew and Gentile; He is God of whoever believes. And since salvation is by grace instead of by the law, none of us have any right to claim credit for that salvation. There is only one God and, therefore, one means of justification – faith.

Do you think that you have somehow earned salvation? Do you think that is even possible? Don't even think about it!

Don't even think that salvation by grace minimizes the law

Romans 3:31 *Do we then make void the law through faith? God forbid: yea, we establish the law.*

This is the third time in chapter three we have found the phrase *God forbid*. This is the third time we have found God saying, basically, "Don't even think about it!"

And what is it concerning this time? It is concerning the idea that the doctrine of faith that Paul was espousing minimizes the law. The fact of the matter is, it does not minimize the law. It puts the law in its proper place; it establishes it; it holds it up. You see, the place of the law is to teach us how to live right and, in so doing, teach us that we can never live right enough to be saved. The law is not a bad thing; it is a good thing. Paul and the apostles were not opposed to the law; they were in favor of the law because they knew that the law was designed to bring men to the point of hopelessness and then point them to faith in Christ.

So, what do we learn from this section of Scripture, Romans 3? We learn that the problem with man is not God's word, we learn that God is right in judging us, we learn that we are not better than they, we learn a person cannot be justified by the deeds of the law, and we learn that salvation by grace through faith does not minimize the law. And if you are inclined to think otherwise, "Don't even think about it!"

Chapter Five
E - Examining Imputation

Romans 4:1 *What shall we say then that Abraham our father, as pertaining to the flesh, hath found?* **2** *For if Abraham were justified by works, he hath whereof to glory; but not before God.* **3** *For what saith the scripture? Abraham believed God, and it was counted unto him for righteousness.* **4** *Now to him that worketh is the reward not reckoned of grace, but of debt.* **5** *But to him that worketh not, but believeth on him that justifieth the ungodly, his faith is counted for righteousness.* **6** *Even as David also describeth the blessedness of the man, unto whom God imputeth righteousness without works,* **7** *Saying, Blessed are they whose iniquities are forgiven, and whose sins are covered.* **8** *Blessed is the man to whom the Lord will not impute sin.* **9** *Cometh this blessedness then upon the circumcision only, or upon the uncircumcision also? for we say that faith was reckoned to Abraham for righteousness.* **10** *How was it then reckoned? when he was in circumcision, or in uncircumcision? Not in circumcision, but in uncircumcision.* **11** *And he received the sign of circumcision, a seal of the righteousness of the faith which he had yet being uncircumcised: that he might be the father of all them that believe, though they be not circumcised; that righteousness might be imputed unto them also:* **12** *And the father of circumcision to them who are not of the circumcision only, but who also walk in the steps of that faith of our father Abraham, which he had being yet uncircumcised.*

We do not often think of hillbillies as being great and deep theologians. But there is a word that is frequently used by hillbillies and rarely used by others that is a great theological word. You will often hear them say, "I reckon" or "I reckon not." In Biblical terms, to reckon means to add to an account. The word is used three times in our text in English but eight times in the Greek language. Two of those times, it is translated as *counted*, and three of those times, it is translated as the word *impute*.

So, each time in this text that you see the word count, reckon, or impute, understand that they come from the exact same word, and that word means to add to an account.

You might say that God is in the "spiritual banking business." The way things happen at the First Bank of Heaven is completely different than the way that earthly banks operate. Let's get into this text and examine imputation. It is one of the most important doctrines in all the Bible, especially in regard to salvation.

A fleshly thing found

Romans 4:1 *What shall we say then that Abraham our father, as pertaining to the flesh, hath found?*

The Jews placed great stock in the fact that they were descendants of Abraham. To this day, they still do. That being the case, all that Paul has said in chapters one through three would naturally make them accuse him of teaching that it meant nothing to be a Jew. This is the classic "pendulum swinging."

In other words, if you are not way over here, you must be way over there! For instance, if you are not Calvinist, you will automatically be accused of being Arminian. But the fact of the matter is, both of those positions are extreme and extremely wrong, and there is a truth that is extremely right that bears little resemblance to either of those wrongs.

It did mean something, and it does mean something to be a Jew. Abraham did find something; his physical descendants could be partakers in something very special, but not what they

68

thought. They thought they were partaking in righteousness by birth, but that has never been the case for anyone.

So, what did Abraham find? The answer is in verse eleven. He received circumcision, a sign of the faith that he already had, and the righteousness that faith had already brought.

Abraham received an outward sign of an inward change. He received a symbol of his salvation. He received something that, once they heard about it, said to a lost world, "This man is different!"

That ought to tell us something. God expects us today to manifest outwardly the change He has made inwardly.

And that demonstrates one of the flaws of many popular, culturally acceptable churches. The music sounds just like the music of the world; the appearance looks just like the appearance of the world; the behavior is just like the behavior of the world; there is no visible change whatsoever. When a person truly gets born-again, he will be changed, and that change is something that God expects to see as a visible thing, a testimony to a lost and dying world.

Everybody knew that the Jews practiced circumcision; it was not a secret; it was a known fact.

Faith to faith

Let us begin this section by jumping back to Romans 1:17:

Romans 1:17 *For therein is the righteousness of God revealed from faith to faith: as it is written, The just shall live by faith.*

The phrase *from faith to faith* is an intensive phrase that means "by faith alone." Hold that thought as we begin to look at Romans 4:2-8.

Romans 4:2 *For if Abraham were justified by works, he hath whereof to glory; but not before God.*

Here is a summary of Jewish thought concerning Abraham: "Abraham was a great man because his works justified him before God! Abraham can hold a proud head up before God because of his works."

Paul was answering that erroneous thought in this verse. His answer was *But not before God.* In other words, "That is not the way God sees it." By the way, that is not the way Abraham saw it either. Both Abraham and God knew that Abraham's works came from a believing heart and that this salvation preceded the works.

Abraham was not justified by works, and therefore, he had no right to glory, no right to brag. And if Abraham for all of his greatness was not justified by his works, be quite assured that neither you nor I can be justified by our works either.

Romans 4:3 *For what saith the scripture? Abraham believed God, and it was counted unto him for righteousness.*

Romans 4:3 is a quote from Genesis 15:6:

Genesis 15:6 *And he believed in the LORD; and he counted it to him for righteousness.*

Genesis 15:6 describes the time that Abram, the old man, was given the Abrahamic covenant. Abraham was told by God that he was going to have a son. Despite the fact that he was old, despite the fact that his wife was well past childbearing years, God promised him a son, and He promised that that son would produce offspring as numerous as the stars for him.

When Abraham heard this, he believed God, and God counted that to him for righteousness.

There is a significant element of time to consider here. At this point in time, Abram was less than eighty-six years old. The rite of circumcision that the Jews so highly valued was never even mentioned by God until two chapters later, after thirteen years had elapsed. In other words, Abraham believed God, was justified, was saved, before the "work" of circumcision ever came into existence! No wonder Paul said that Abraham had nothing to glory about, nothing to boast about; Abraham was simply saved by belief. Abraham had righteousness added to his account without the first work on his part.

Romans 4:4 *Now to him that worketh is the reward not reckoned of grace, but of debt.* **5** *But to him that worketh not, but* *believeth on him that justifieth the ungodly, his faith is counted for righteousness.*

When Paul said *now to him that worketh is the reward not reckoned of grace, but of debt,* he was basically saying, "If you are determined to work your way there, all you will receive is that which you have earned, which is never enough to satisfy God."

By contrast, all that you will be given if you humbly and truly believe is grace, that which you could never earn. Specifically, the grace of the righteousness of Christ added to your account, that which is always enough to satisfy God.

He goes on in verse five to point out that God is the justifier of the ungodly. Since God is the justifier of the ungodly, anything that we do to try to help Him is simply getting in His way! Our "help" simply interferes with the process.

When our children were much younger, they were really interested in everything that was going on in the kitchen as my wife cooked. And they wanted more than anything else to "help." My wife never minded having them around, but the fact of the matter is their help only made things worse. Until they finally got out of the way and let her do her job, the dinner would never be done and would certainly never be done right.

When it comes to salvation, there is no help that we can give God; all of the work has already been done; it is simply up to us to believe and to receive the work that He Himself has accomplished on Calvary.

Romans 4:6 *Even as David also describeth the blessedness of the man, unto whom God imputeth righteousness without works,* **7** *Saying, Blessed are they whose iniquities are forgiven, and whose sins are covered.* **8** *Blessed is the man to whom the Lord will not impute sin.*

This section of verses is a quote from Psalm 32:1-2.

Psalm 32:1 *Blessed is he whose transgression is forgiven, whose sin is covered.* **2** *Blessed is the man unto whom the LORD imputeth not iniquity, and in whose spirit there is no guile.*

The occasion of this Psalm was David's great sin with Bathsheba. David desperately wanted things to be set right. David, wise despite his sin, understood enough to speak of God adding righteousness without works. David understood this truth better than most because there were no sacrifices prescribed for the sins of adultery and murder. The penalty for these sins was death, and no works could change that. David was completely at God's mercy, and he knew it. When we finally realize that and realize that He adds righteousness to our account without works, that is "blessedness."

Notice the word impute both in Romans and Psalms. That is the word that we are focusing on. David and Paul both spoke of the fact that when a person's sin is forgiven, the Lord will not impute, will not add iniquity or count iniquity to their account. He certainly could, He would have every right to do so, but He chooses not to do so.

This righteousness, this justification, this blessedness, cannot come from works. It is from faith to faith; it is by faith alone.

First things first

Romans 4:9 *Cometh this blessedness then upon the circumcision only, or upon the uncircumcision also? for we say that faith was reckoned to Abraham for righteousness.*

Go back with me again and remember the thinking of the Jews. "Because we are Jews, descendants of Abraham, Isaac, and Jacob, we are righteous. In addition to that, we also have circumcision, so we know that we are righteous. Everyone else is just out of luck!"

Paul has now very skillfully maneuvered them into a position where they are thinking about themselves (the circumcision) and others (uncircumcision). Then he gave them a teaser, reminding them that he and the other apostles believe that faith was reckoned to Abraham for righteousness, rather than works being reckoned to Abraham for righteousness. Then he took them to verse ten:

Romans 4:10 *How was it then reckoned? when he was in circumcision, or in uncircumcision? Not in circumcision, but in uncircumcision.*

Here is Paul's home run shot, telling them what I told you just a few verses ago. God adding righteousness to Abram's account in response to Abram's belief occurred in Genesis 15:6, which was two chapters and a bare minimum of thirteen years before and possibly as many as twenty-four years before he was circumcised!

In other words, salvation came first; circumcision came much, much, much later.

Salvation always comes first; works of any kind come later!

This contradicts the teachings of many churches and cults. The Church of Christ teaches that baptism proceeds and causes salvation. The Roman Catholic Church teaches that the sacraments give grace and, thereby, bring salvation. The Mormons believe that two years of missionary service and special linen underwear bring salvation.

Abraham would not have believed any of that. Abraham simply listened to what God said, believed it with all his heart, and God reckoned that to him for righteousness. God imputed righteousness to his account before Abraham ever engaged in the work of circumcision.

A father to the faithful

Romans 4:11 *And he received the sign of circumcision, a seal of the righteousness of the faith which he had yet being uncircumcised: that he might be the father of all them that believe, though they be not circumcised; that righteousness might be imputed unto them also:* **12** *And the father of circumcision to them who are not of the circumcision only, but who also walk in the steps of that faith of our father Abraham, which he had being yet uncircumcised.*

Paul had come a long way from the feet of Gamaliel, to the synagogue, to the Damascus Road, to the writing of the book of Romans. Paul used to believe with all his heart that salvation was something he could earn by the deeds that he was doing in his flesh. Paul used to believe that Abraham was his father and that no one other than the Jews had any right to claim any type of kinship with Abraham.

But now Paul was putting pen to paper and writing words that he once upon a time would have considered absolutely heretical. Here was Paul referring to Abraham as the father not just of the circumcised Jews but also of the uncircumcised Gentiles. Here was Paul claiming that anyone could be a descendant of Abraham simply by having the kind of faith that Abraham had!

In sending this message, Paul used two crucial words: *sign* and *seal*. Both indicate an identifying mark. To put that in an easy-to-understand picture, think of a brand on a cow. The brand is not the cow; the brand is merely a visible indicator of who the cow belongs to. For Abraham and any true and understanding believer in those days, circumcision was merely an "evidence of righteousness" by faith, not something that produced or earned righteousness. As Paul pointed out, God counted Abraham as righteous while he was still uncircumcised! And since the faith was what actually would be counted by God for righteousness, righteousness was and is available to any, circumcised or not.

There is a song that we teach our bus kids to sing:

Father Abraham had many sons, and many sons had Father Abraham; I am one of them, and so are you, so let's just praise the Lord...

That song is one hundred percent true. Whoever we are, if we have been born again by the blood of the Lamb, we can truly claim kinship with Abraham. Abraham looked ahead and believed what God said and would do; we are looking back and believe what God said and did. Abraham is our father, and not the father of anyone who is physically descended from him yet does not believe like he believed.

So very, very long ago, God saw the spiritual bank accounts of all of lost mankind. We were running a huge deficit caused by sin. The debt was so large we could never pay, and we were all doomed to die and go to hell for all time.

But God in mercy said, "I will go to Calvary, and I will pay all of that debt for every single one of them:"

1 John 2:2 *And he is the propitiation for our sins: and not for ours only, but also for the sins of the whole world.*

When He did that, it brought everyone's account up to zero because our debt was paid. And as you read those words, red flags are starting to wave in your brain, and you are getting just a little bit worried. You may not know why you are getting worried, but something inside of you instinctively knows that if the story ends there, we are still in a lot of trouble. You see, zero was still not enough. Zero means the debt has been paid, but we still have no way to pay our way into heaven.

So, God did something else. In addition to paying our debt and bringing our account up to zero, God also said, "I have added their sin to my account, but I will also add my righteousness to their account! We will do a complete exchange!"

He then put out the call, *believe on the Lord Jesus Christ and thou shalt be saved.*

In response to that call, some choose to earn what righteousness they can by doing whatever good deeds they can do. And it is never, ever, ever enough. Their account will always read zero.

But some realize the gift that they are being offered and accept it in full belief. At that point, their account is no longer at zero. At that point, the righteousness of Christ is imputed to their account, and God the Father sees them as if every bit of the Son's righteousness belongs to them personally, because it does!

If you try to be good enough, if you try to work your way to heaven, I promise you beyond any shadow of a doubt, it will not ever work. But I also promise you that if you simply repent of your sins and trust Jesus Christ as your Savior, He will take your account, which, because of what He did on Calvary, now stands at zero, and He will add all of His righteousness to you. You will one day stand on the street of gold and then kneel before His throne and kiss His precious feet and thank Him for the day that you learned all about examining imputation.

Chapter Six
F - Faith, Faith, and More Faith!

Romans 4:13 *For the promise, that he should be the heir of the world, was not to Abraham, or to his seed, through the law, but through the righteousness of faith.* **14** *For if they which are of the law be heirs, faith is made void, and the promise made of none effect:* **15** *Because the law worketh wrath: for where no law is, there is no transgression.* **16** *Therefore it is of faith, that it might be by grace; to the end the promise might be sure to all the seed; not to that only which is of the law, but to that also which is of the faith of Abraham; who is the father of us all,* **17** *(As it is written, I have made thee a father of many nations,) before him whom he believed, even God, who quickeneth the dead, and calleth those things which be not as though they were. {before him: or, like unto him}* **18** *Who against hope believed in hope, that he might become the father of many nations, according to that which was spoken, So shall thy seed be.* **19** *And being not weak in faith, he considered not his own body now dead, when he was about an hundred years old, neither yet the deadness of Sara's womb:* **20** *He staggered not at the promise of God through unbelief; but was strong in faith, giving glory to God;* **21** *And being fully persuaded that, what he had promised, he was able also to perform.* **22** *And therefore it was imputed to him for righteousness.* **23** *Now it was not written for his sake alone, that it was imputed to him;* **24** *But for us also, to whom it shall be imputed, if we believe on him that raised up Jesus our*

Lord from the dead; 25 Who was delivered for our offences, and was raised again for our justification.

The African impala can jump to a height of over ten feet and cover a distance greater than thirty feet. Yet these magnificent creatures can be kept in an enclosure in any zoo with a three-foot wall. The animals will not jump if they cannot see where their feet will fall. Faith is the ability to trust what we cannot see, and without it, we are trapped behind a wall that should not be able to hold us.

Paul was a man who tried to be very clear in what he was thinking. To do so, he often used the same word many times in rapid succession. In the previous chapter (Examining Imputation, Chapter 5), the word for "adding to an account" appeared eight times in twelve verses. In this section of thirteen verses, the Greek word *pistos* will appear ten times: six times as faith and four times as believe.

Faith is a genuine heart belief. It is a belief that produces the proper response. **Hebrews 11:1** describes it like this: *Now faith is the substance of things hoped for, the evidence of things not seen.* Verse six goes on to say, *But without faith it is impossible to please him: for he that cometh to God must believe that he is, and that he is a rewarder of them that diligently seek him.*

Because mankind wants to "do" something to be saved, they tend to scoff at salvation by faith alone:

Christian Science - Science and Health with a Key to the Scriptures:

> "Waking to Christ's demand, mortals experience suffering. This causes them, even as drowning men, to make vigorous efforts to save themselves; and through Christ's precious love these efforts are crowned with success. 'Work out your own salvation,' is the demand of Life and Love, for to this end God worketh with you...When the smoke of battle clears away, you will discern the good you have done, and receive

according to your deserving." (Emphasis mine.)
(Eddy, 22)

Mormons, Pearl of Great Price:
Mormonism, however, teaches that–in addition to necessary faith–salvation is earned by works. "The Articles of Faith" states, "We believe that through the Atonement of Christ, all mankind may be saved, by obedience to the laws and ordinances of the Gospel." (Emphasis mine.) (Smith, 60)

Masons
Notes in the Holman Masonic Bible say of the Master Mason, "The conclusion we arrive at is, that youth, properly directed, leads us to honorable and virtuous maturity, and that the life of man, regulated by morality, faith, and justice, will be rewarded at its closing hour, by the prospect of eternal bliss." (Emphasis mine.) (Sickels)

When the world says that faith is "simple," they are right! When they say that it is weak (not strong enough to save), they are dead wrong! Faith can do some things that works can never do.

A promise bought by faith

Romans 4:13 *For the promise, that he should be the heir of the world, was not to Abraham, or to his seed, through the law, but through the righteousness of faith.*

God made Abraham a promise in Genesis 13:14-16. God told him to look north, south, east, and west, and whatever land he saw, God would give it to him. Then God said that He would make Abraham's seed as the dust of the earth. So, in effect, He promised him the world! This promise was not bought by Abraham obeying the law; it was bought by his faith that produced righteousness.

Romans 4:14 *For if they which are of the law be heirs, faith is made void, and the promise made of none effect:* **15**

Because the law worketh wrath: for where no law is, there is no transgression.

Paul begins verse fourteen by speaking of *they which are of the law.* And that introduces a matter of time that Paul speaks of quite often in his writing, namely that the law and those to whom it was given came into existence hundreds of years after Abraham. His argument, then, is that if it is the law that brings the promise, then Abraham's faith (that God Himself spoke so highly of) is void, empty, worthless, and, therefore, the promise God made him based on that faith is rendered powerless, and of no effect.

Paul then uses that mention of the law to delve into a further discussion of it in verse fifteen. His argument there, in simple terms, is that if there is no law present, people do not feel "bound and determined" to break it. But, if you tell someone they cannot do something, it "worketh wrath" or "makes them angry." They will be determined to break it. Their flesh demands it. So, if you say that the law can bring the good promises of God, you have just made faith worthless, and you are also ignoring the effects that the law actually does have.

Romans 4:16 *Therefore it is of faith, that it might be by grace; to the end the promise might be sure to all the seed; not to that only which is of the law, but to that also which is of the faith of Abraham; who is the father of us all,*

Therefore (because of the drawbacks of the law) it (the good promises of God) is of faith, that it might be by grace (a gift) so that the promises might be sure to <u>all</u> the seed. If the seed (those who believe) must also keep the law, some might do worse than others. Because of this, God just says in so many words, "Whether you are a Jew (*of the law*) or a Gentile, believe, have faith, and you shall have the promise, and Abraham will be your father."

Romans 4:17 *(As it is written, I have made thee a father of many nations,)*

This is a parenthetical thought, a quote from **Genesis 17:5** *but thy name shall be Abraham; for a father of many nations have I made thee.* It goes with the last of verse sixteen,

80

showing that saved Gentiles are the spiritual descendants of Jewish Abraham.

Romans 4:17b *...before him* [in the sight of him] *whom he* [Abraham] *believed, even God, who quickeneth the dead, and calleth those things which be not as though they were.*

God *quickeneth the dead.* This does not mean He speeds up the drivers in your country hometown; it means He brings to life those dead in sin.

Why can the sinner not seem to do right? He is dead! He is spiritually dead. He, therefore, has no capacity to truly be right. But God can fix this; He can make something that is not so "so" just by saying it.

Romans 4:18 *Who against hope believed in hope, that he might become the father of many nations, according to that which was spoken, So shall thy seed be.*

Who refers back to Abraham. He had no tangible reason to believe; he *against hope believed in hope.* He and Sarah were both pushing one hundred. Faith is not believing that which you can definitively predict; faith is believing God just because He said it, even when it seems counterintuitive.

Romans 4:19 *And being not weak in faith, he considered not his own body now dead, when he was about an hundred years old, neither yet the deadness of Sara's womb:* **20** *He staggered not at the promise of God through unbelief; but was strong in faith, giving glory to God;*

The facts as Abraham knew them are spelled out here: he was a hundred years old, and Sarah's womb was dead. And yet, he believed anyway.

Two phrases should leap out, two possible reactions to the incredible things God has asked us to believe. The first is *staggered not.* We can stagger at God's promises, such as simple salvation, full payment of sin, eternal security, the reality of heaven, and so much more. The second is *strong in faith.* Concerning the promises of God, we always have these two choices. We can stagger, or we can be strong in faith, absolutely, positively, unshakeable in belief. This latter choice glorifies God.

The promise of God to Abraham of a land and a multitude of descendants was bought by faith.

The promise of God to us of salvation and righteousness is bought by faith.

The following letter was found in a baking powder can wired to the handle of an old pump that offered the only hope of drinking water on a very long and seldom-used trail across Nevada's Amargosa Desert:

"This pump is all right as of June 1932. I put a new sucker washer into it and it ought to last five years. But the washer dries out, and the pump has got to be primed. Under the white rock, I buried a bottle of water, out of the sun and cork end up. There's enough water in it to prime the pump, but not if you drink some first. Pour about one-fourth and let her soak to wet the leather. Then pour in the rest medium fast and pump like crazy. You'll git water. The well has never run dry. Have faith. When you git watered up, fill the bottle and put it back like you found it for the next feller. (signed) Desert Pete. P.S. Don't go drinking the water first. Prime the pump with it, and you'll git all you can hold." (Miller, Larson)

The promises of God come by faith. No faith, no water; no faith, no salvation.

A persuasion bonded by faith

Romans 4:21 *And being fully persuaded that, what he had promised, he was able also to perform.*

There is a difference between what the world would call "persuaded" and what Paul here calls *fully persuaded.* Fully persuaded is from *plerophoreo,* and it means to be absolutely certain of something, not waffling on it in the least. Abraham was fully persuaded of God and His promises, not merely cautiously optimistic.

Israel, in the days of Elijah, was "persuaded" that Baal was God. They were also "persuaded" that Jehovah was God.

82

Such waffling simply will not do! So, Elijah did what preachers today are commonly told not do—he preached a "polarizing" message:

1 Kings 18:21 *And Elijah came unto all the people, and said, How long halt ye between two opinions? if the LORD be God, follow him: but if Baal, then follow him. And the people answered him not a word.*

Joshua looked out at a people who were persuaded that Jehovah was God but also persuaded of the power of the false gods around them, and he also preached a polarizing message:

Joshua 24:15 *And if it seem evil unto you to serve the LORD, choose you this day whom ye will serve; whether the gods which your fathers served that were on the other side of the flood, or the gods of the Amorites, in whose land ye dwell: but as for me and my house, we will serve the LORD.*

It is time we be fully persuaded in our God. It is time we cast aside any shadow of doubt and take Him at every one of His Words.

We are not trusting in ourselves; we are trusting in Him. We are to be fully persuaded that what He has promised, He is able to perform.

For Abraham, it was a physical miracle. For the believers, it is a spiritual, eternal miracle.

When God says, "I can change you; I can unmake what you have always been and make you what you have never been," you need to believe Him. It is a miracle, it is supernatural, but He can do it.

A story is told that one night, a house caught fire, and a man stood on the ground below with outstretched arms, calling to his son, "Jump! I'll catch you." He knew the boy had to jump to save his life. All the boy could see, however, was flame, smoke, and blackness. As can be imagined, he was afraid to leave the roof. His father kept yelling, "Jump! I will catch you." But the boy protested, "Daddy, I can't see you." The father replied, "But I can see you, and that's all that matters."

You may as well jump into the arms of God because even when you cannot see Him, He can see you, and that is all that matters.

A pardon brought by faith

Romans 4:22 *And therefore it was imputed to him for righteousness. 23 Now it was not written for his sake alone, that it was imputed to him; 24 But for us also, to whom it shall be imputed, if we believe on him that raised up Jesus our Lord from the dead; 25 Who was delivered for our offences, and was raised again for our justification.*

The thought now shifts from the physical blessings of Abraham's belief to the spiritual blessings brought by his belief and ours.

Romans 4:22 *And therefore it was imputed to him for righteousness.*

Therefore, because of Abraham's belief in God, God imputed, added righteousness to his account.

Romans 4:23 *Now it was not written for his sake alone, that it was imputed to him;*

Paul now points out that Abraham was not a one-off; the imputed righteousness that God wrote of concerning him way back in Genesis applied far more widely than just to Abraham alone. In fact, it was written for our sakes:

Romans 4:24 *But for us also, to whom it shall be imputed, if we believe on him that raised up Jesus our Lord from the dead;*

These things that were written of Abraham were written so that we could know something about salvation, namely that righteousness will also be added to our account if we believe, have absolute faith in Him that raised up Jesus our Lord from the dead.

Romans 4:25 *Who was delivered for our offences, and was raised again for our justification.*

Who [Jesus] *was delivered* [crucified] *for our offenses* [our sins] *and was raised again for our justification* [our being judicially declared as righteous].

84

Simply put, because Jesus died and rose again, we can be justfied, we can be saved.

He did it; He paid for it. He completed it; all that is left for us is to believe and receive it.

There's something works can never do,
A barrier they cannot break through,
A ceiling of brass, twixt us and the throne,
Impenetrable, hard, and cold as stone.
In vain do works assault this veil,
For naught do pilgrims crawl and wail,
The barrier cannot be broken,
By works and efforts and useless tokens,
They fly against it to fall and shatter,
Nothing but worthless and empty clatter.

But then toward the veil, another rises,
Childlike faith, which God so prizes.
Like a speeding arrow, its force increases,
With every doubt that man releases,
The brazen veil stands not a prayer,
It's shattered and scattered beyond repair,
And the light of Glory descends from above,
Mercy, grace, and infinite love,

Yes, faith alone will make it through,
Something that works can never do.

Bo Wagner 7/21/2001

Chapter Seven
G - Gifts Found Under the Justification Tree

Romans 5:1 *Therefore being justified by faith, we have peace with God through our Lord Jesus Christ:* **2** *By whom also we have access by faith into this grace wherein we stand, and rejoice in hope of the glory of God.* **3** *And not only so, but we glory in tribulations also: knowing that tribulation worketh patience;* **4** *And patience, experience; and experience, hope:* **5** *And hope maketh not ashamed; because the love of God is shed abroad in our hearts by the Holy Ghost which is given unto us.* **6** *For when we were yet without strength, in due time Christ died for the ungodly.* **7** *For scarcely for a righteous man will one die: yet peradventure for a good man some would even dare to die.* **8** *But God commendeth his love toward us, in that, while we were yet sinners, Christ died for us.* **9** *Much more then, being now justified by his blood, we shall be saved from wrath through him.* **10** *For if, when we were enemies, we were reconciled to God by the death of his Son, much more, being reconciled, we shall be saved by his life.* **11** *And not only so, but we also joy in God through our Lord Jesus Christ, by whom we have now received the atonement.*

Over and over in the first four chapters of Romans, Paul has driven home this thought: every human being is separated from God by his sinful birth and by his sinful choices. That being the case, no one is able by his own efforts to fix the problem. Because we cannot <u>be</u> righteous, God made a way through faith in His Son that we can be <u>declared</u> righteous, justified.

The greatest truth that mankind can ever grasp is that God will judiciously declare us righteous based on what Christ did on Calvary if we will simply believe.

However, simply memorizing the definition of justification does not do it justice. There are so many more things that justification does for us than just save us. Justification is similar to a beautiful Christmas tree in this regard: you can sit for hours and hours and admire the tinsel, lights, decorations, etc. But there are some gifts underneath that tree! Paul, in this passage, is going to give us a list of gifts that cannot be found under the tree of works, the tree of efforts, or the tree of morality. They can only be found under the "justification tree."

Peace

Romans 5:1 *Therefore being justified by faith, we have peace with God through our Lord Jesus Christ:*

Whether they would admit it or not, the world is at war with God. The world regards God as an adversary. But what many people may not know is that, in spite of the fact that God "so loved the world," that love does not stop Him from being an adversary right back:

Psalm 7:11 *God judgeth the righteous, and God is angry with the wicked every day.*

This is not just an Old Testament truth. All through the Old Testament, God loved sinners but was still angry with them because of their sin. All through the New Testament and beyond, God loves sinners and yet is still angry with them because of their sin. God is the adversary of the sinner the entire time that He is trying to win the sinner to Himself.

People struggle with this, but it actually makes perfect sense. You see, God does not desire to be an adversary of the sinner. God desires to be an ally of the sinner. God does not desire for there to be enmity between the sinner and Himself; God desires for there to be peace between the sinner and Himself. And the only way that peace will ever come is through justification. The only way that justification will ever come is through our Lord Jesus Christ.

God can either be the greatest adversary you ever have or the greatest ally that you ever have. It can either be a war between you and God or peace between you and God.

When a person gets saved, God moves from being an adversary of that person to being an ally of that person. He establishes peace between the two based solely on what the Lord Jesus Christ did on Calvary.

If you are saved, when you got justified it did not just result in your salvation. It resulted in a change of attitude from God toward you. God now looks at you with the same peaceful look that He looks at his own Son with.

The old song goes, "When He sees me, He sees the blood of the Lamb. He views me as worthy and not as I am. He sees me in garments that are white as the snow, for the Lamb of God is worthy, and He's washed me this I know."

Access

Romans 5:2a *By whom also we have access by faith into this grace wherein we stand,*

The picture presented in this portion of Scripture is staggering. God is on the throne in His holiness, as seen in Isaiah 6. He is high and lifted up. His train, the edge part, the bottom fringe of His garment is so massive that it fills the Temple. The seraphim are praising His purity, shouting, "Holy, holy, holy is the Lord God Almighty."

Isaiah sees this in his vision. But we have, since birth, been unworthy to enter this awesome scene. Our sin has barred us from it. Access has been denied; there is a veil that stands thick and imposing between us and the Holy of Holies.

But suddenly, something has changed. That something is that we have now been justified. We are standing without, not knowing that we are welcome within. We have been held back for so long that our fear prevents us from stepping across the threshold.

But then Jesus Christ Himself takes us by the hand and brings us into the throne room! You see, the word *access* is from the word *prosagojay,* and it means *an introduction, a leading one into something.*

So now we find ourselves standing in the throne room, before the throne of God itself, before God Himself. We know that we should rightfully fall on our faces, as Isaiah did, and cry out, "Woe is me!"

But as you step back and view the scene, Romans 5:2 says that we are *standing* in this grace!

The first thought that must go through our minds is, "That is arrogance!" No, it is not arrogance; it is boldness:

Hebrews 4:16 *Let us therefore come boldly unto the throne of grace, that we may obtain mercy, and find grace to help in time of need.*

We are there standing before the throne. But no one, no seraphim, no cherubim, dares question our boldness. They clearly see that the hand holding ours has nail prints! But furthermore, the Lord Jesus Christ Himself is making an introduction on our behalf before the throne. He is presenting us to the Father and the Father to us.

Can you just imagine that: "Father, here is John. I bought him and paid for him with what I did on Calvary, and he has accepted me. John, this is my Father. And since He is my Father, He is now your Father. I thought the two of you should get to know each other!"

He is bringing two formerly separated parties together, and He is doing so based on the fact that He is our go-between who paid our sin debt.

And those seraphims and cherubims? Not only do they hear that introduction, but they also clearly see that our garments have been washed white in the blood of the Lamb. We are standing before the throne because we have the right to stand before the throne, not because of anything that we have done, but because the justification we have received through the sacrifice of Christ has granted us this access.

Rejoicing

The world often has a picture of Christians as miserable, moping, down-in-the-mouth people. Maybe the reason they have that picture is because so many saved people are, in fact, just like that!

But if a saved person is like that, he is like that in spite of justification, not because of it. Justification, if allowed to do so, produces rejoicing:

Romans 5:2b *...and rejoice in hope of the glory of God.*

The first thing that justification allows us to rejoice in is the *hope*, the "earnest expectation" of the glory of God. In other words, we rejoice because we know that He is coming back, and we know all of the things we are going to get and see and experience when He does.

When a child first begins to believe in a mythical obese character dressed in red, who engages in chronic breaking and entering once a year, they begin to rejoice in the expectation of what that mythical character and that special day will bring.

We who are saved have something so much better than that. From the moment we believed in Him unto salvation, we have been able to rejoice in the fact that He is real, and that He is really coming back, and that it is going to be really wonderful when He does come back!

No more sickness, no more sorrow, no more pain, no more aging. A mansion, a street of gold, gates of pearl, a river of life. A reunion with our saved loved ones who have gone before us.

All of this is something that we can rejoice over, and we can rejoice over it because it is a byproduct of our justification.

But if our justification only allowed us to rejoice in the good, it would not be that impressive. Our justification also allows us to rejoice in the seemingly negative things as well:

Romans 5:3 *And not only so, but we glory in tribulations also: knowing that tribulation worketh patience;*

Even the world does not have much trouble believing that we can rejoice in the hope of His glory. But this, the idea that we can rejoice in tribulation, comes as a real shock! So much so that Paul will spend seven verses explaining it. Here is why we can rejoice in tribulation:

We can, first of all, rejoice in tribulation because, according to verse three, tribulation works (produces) patience.

When we look at old people who have been through so very much, people like Corrie Ten Boom, who survived the horrors of a concentration camp and yet maintained a sweet spirit and a patient attitude for all of her latter years, we see that people like that are nearly universally admired. Everyone wants to be that kind of patient, level-headed, sweet-spirited person.

But that kind of patience carries a price tag. The cost of patience is tribulation.

But when we say it that way, we are really focusing on the negative rather than the positive. Let's try like this: the reward for tribulation is patience. When children of God go through the fire, they come out on the other side of it a more purified product. And that which has been burned away will usually be the impatience that was in us before the fire. But please remember, all of this is a byproduct of justification. For a person who has never been justified, there is no reason to expect that their tribulations will produce patience in them. They are still sinful individuals on the inside, wrapped in sinful individuals on the outside, and as such, tribulations are more likely to produce anger and bitterness in them rather than patience.

Romans 5:4 *And patience, experience; and experience, hope:*

The second reason that we, the justified, can rejoice in tribulation is because tribulation produces patience, and that patience then produces experience in us. Experience is from the word *dokimay,* and it indicates a proving, a testing. It brings to mind an acid test used to determine whether or not something is, in fact, gold or a cheap substitute.

When a child of God has gone through tribulation patiently, it will reveal to them the character that God has built into them from the day that they were justified. A Christian will go through tribulation that he or she cannot begin to understand while the tribulation is going on. But almost inevitably, when the storm of tribulation clears and the sun shines again, that child of God will be able to look back in amazement at how well they themselves did through the tribulation. When the tribulation was going on, they felt like they were failing on every hand and doing miserably. But when they come out on the other side and can look back clearly, they will see that they did far better than they thought they were doing and that it was a result of the fact that they were justified, they were a child of God, and therefore, they largely behaved themselves as such.

The third reason that we can rejoice in tribulation is because the tribulation that produces patience and the patience that produces experience then produces hope.

Hope in the Bible is not merely a "wishful thinking," it is a confident expectation. The more that we, the justified, have experienced tribulation, and had the tribulation produce patience in us, and have that patience produce experience in us, the more we have all of that work together to produce hope in us.

People who are justified tend to be a much more hopeful people than the lost, depressed, downtrodden people of the world who do not know Christ as their Savior.

The accusation may then arise, "If you are so hopeful, so confident that God will come through, you may end up being embarrassed! Maybe God won't really save you; maybe He won't be there when you need Him." To that, Paul responds that we will never worry about that, that we will never have to be ashamed:

Romans 5:5 *And hope maketh not ashamed; because the love of God is shed abroad in our hearts by the Holy Ghost which is given unto us.*

Notice that Paul did not just make the claim that we would not be ashamed, he also gave the reasons for that claim. The justified, the child of God, will never have to be ashamed, first of all, because the love of God is shed abroad, poured out in our hearts. This love is poured out in our hearts by none other than the Holy Ghost Himself.

A child of God has no need to be ashamed of what he believes since he can spend every day feeling the love that God has for us deep down in our hearts.

The uncertain may then wonder how can we know that the feeling that we have in our heart, that feeling that God loves us, is actually correct. Paul answers that musing in verses six through eight.

Romans 5:6 *For when we were yet without strength, in due time Christ died for the ungodly. 7 For scarcely for a righteous man will one die: yet peradventure for a good man some would even dare to die. 8 But God commendeth his love toward us, in that, while we were yet sinners, Christ died for us.*

We know that God loves us because when we were still wicked, godless, lost sinners, God loved us enough to die for us. So if He loved us enough to die for us while we were yet sinners, how much more does He love us now that we have been justified!

When verse six says that Christ died for the ungodly in "due time," it means the "fit or proper time." Commentator Albert Barnes said:

> "All experiments had failed to save men. For four thousand years the trial had been made under the law among the Jews; and by the aid of the most enlightened reason in Greece and Rome; and still it was in vain. No scheme had been devised to meet the maladies of the world, and to save men from death. It was then time that a better plan should be presented to men." (Barnes, 111)

Just when it was the exact right time, the Lord Jesus Christ came and died, not for good people, not for a righteous person like some would doubtless be willing to do, but for abject sinners. And once again, if He loved sinners that much, then when you who are justified feel the love of God being poured into your heart, you can trust that feeling because if He paid that price for you while you were lost, you know that He loves you even more now that you have been justified.

In examining the amazing thought of Christ dying for the ungodly, Paul gives comparisons in verses seven and eight to demonstrate just how amazing it is. Look at those verses again:

Romans 5:7 *For scarcely* [*molis,* very rarely] *for a righteous man will one die: yet peradventure* [*tacha,* perhaps, maybe]for *a good man some would even dare to die.* **8** *But God commendeth* [*sunistao,* proves, demonstrates] *his love toward us, in that, while we were yet sinners, Christ died for us.*

In a nutshell, very rarely will a human being ever be willing to die for anyone else, even if that someone else is a very good person. But God demonstrated His great love toward all of us by dying for us while we were still yet sinners.

Romans 5:9 *Much more then, being now justified by his blood, we shall be saved from wrath through him.* **10** *For if, when we were enemies, we were reconciled to God by the death of his Son, much more, being reconciled, we shall be saved by his life.*

These two verses bring the thought of verses six through eight full circle. We were lost, but now we are saved. Now we are justified. That being the case, Paul said, *much more then,* being justified through His very blood, *we will be saved from wrath through Him.* God is no longer angry at the saved; all of His anger was poured out on Christ on our behalf. We have nothing more to fear.

He goes on to say that if when we were enemies, if when we were lost abject sinners, God loved us enough to reconcile us to God by the death of His Son, much more now, being already reconciled, we shall be saved by His life.

In other words, if the death of God was good for the sinner, how much more beneficial is the resurrection and eternal life of God to the justified! We got saved by His death; we stay saved by His life. He interceded with the Father on our behalf as He died on Calvary, but now He ever lives to make intercession for us at the throne.

What possible response to this could be more appropriate than rejoicing? People ask, "Why do you make such a fuss? Why do you get so happy in the Lord? Why do you shout? Why do you raise your hand? Why do you wave hankies?"

A better question might be, if you are saved, why don't you do any of those things? What possible response to our justification, even in the midst of tribulation, could be more appropriate than rejoicing?

But there is one more thing that Paul tells us that we can rejoice in. We can rejoice in God Himself:

Romans 5:11a *And not only so, but we also joy in God through our Lord Jesus Christ,*

It is easy to rejoice in what God does for us. But being justified, we can rejoice in God, even apart from what He does for us. We can rejoice in who He is. We can bask in everything we learn of Him. We can rejoice in His presence.

We who are justified get to experience, at least in a measure, the presence of God Himself. We do not have to wait until we get to heaven for that experience. There are times when God will make Himself very well known to us. It may be during a time of prayer that He just overwhelms us with His presence; it may be during a service when the glory of God comes down; it may be a specific answer to prayer that no one even knew we were praying. However He does it, it is good and pleasant, those times where we can rejoice just in His presence, in who He is.

Atonement

Romans 5:11b *...by whom we have now received the atonement.*

What does justification bring? Not just a cleansing but also a covering. This is the only time in the entire English New Testament that the word atonement is used. In other places, the word it came from appears as the English word reconciled. God could have chosen to preserve it here as reconciled, but instead, He chose the word atonement. This brings back the picture of what took place all throughout the Old Testament: sin being covered by blood. But the New Testament blood of Christ takes it a step further.

The word atonement literally means *a covering*. Because of that, people have often railed on this verse and claimed that the word is mistranslated. "This should have more properly been translated as reconciled," they will say.

But God knew exactly what He was doing. There was a specific picture that He wanted to paint. You see, in the Old Testament, it was sin being covered by blood. But in the New Testament, it is the sinner being covered by blood! It is not our sin that has received the atonement; it is we ourselves, former sinners, that have received the atonement.

Because we have been covered by that blood, not only has that blood washed our sin away, but that blood remains on us as a covering, thereby preventing any further contamination!

That is one reason why Ephesians 4:30 says that we are *sealed* unto the day of redemption. The blood has taken care of all of our sin—past, present, and future.

That ought to help Christians get a good night's sleep!

All of this, this peace, this access, this rejoicing, and this atonement are the byproducts of justification. These four things are just gifts that we find under the justification tree.

Chapter Eight
H - How Can Two Men Be More Different?

Romans 5:12 *Wherefore, as by one man sin entered into the world, and death by sin; and so death passed upon all men, for that all have sinned:* **13** *(For until the law sin was in the world: but sin is not imputed when there is no law.* **14** *Nevertheless death reigned from Adam to Moses, even over them that had not sinned after the similitude of Adam's transgression, who is the figure of him that was to come.* **15** *But not as the offence, so also is the free gift. For if through the offence of one many be dead, much more the grace of God, and the gift by grace, which is by one man, Jesus Christ, hath abounded unto many.* **16** *And not as it was by one that sinned, so is the gift: for the judgment was by one to condemnation, but the free gift is of many offences unto justification.* **17** *For if by one man's offence death reigned by one; much more they which receive abundance of grace and of the gift of righteousness shall reign in life by one, Jesus Christ.)* **18** *Therefore as by the offence of one judgment came upon all men to condemnation; even so by the righteousness of one the free gift came upon all men unto justification of life.* **19** *For as by one man's disobedience many were made sinners, so by the obedience of one shall many be made righteous.* **20** *Moreover the law entered, that the offence might abound. But where sin abounded, grace did much more abound:* **21** *That as sin hath reigned unto death, even so might grace reign through righteousness unto eternal life by Jesus Christ our Lord.*

If I asked you how many humans were present in the Garden of Eden, you would say two. If I asked you how many people ate the forbidden fruit, you would say two. And in both of those answers, you would not be entirely correct. You see, Adam was carrying in himself the genetic material that would become Cain, Abel, and Seth, and then the entire human race! There was literally part of Adam in those boys. Likewise, there is a part of Adam in the sons and daughters and grandsons and granddaughters of those boys. When it gets right down to it, every one of us is related. Acts 17:26 says that we are all of one blood. Every one of us, literally, to this day, carries the genetic material and descended blood of Adam and Eve, his wife, made of his flesh, blood, and bone, within us.

We all came physically from Adam, so it would be perfectly accurate to say that there were billions of people in that garden. It is perfectly accurate to say that we all partook of that fruit. The sinful man named Adam that God cursed, after he was cursed, reproduced himself into a bunch of different children. As unique and kind of thrilling as it is to realize that we are all physically descended from Adam, when we begin to realize the spiritual implications of it, it presents us with a sobering realization.

The first Adam got us all into a world of trouble. But Jesus, whom 1 Corinthians 15:45 describes as the *last Adam,* is completely different from the first. It is He alone who can undo the damage done by the first Adam.

Let us work our way through this passage and examine the staggering differences between the first and the last Adam. You see, one of these two Adams must represent you! All flesh is descended from Adam. So, whether you choose to follow Buddha, or Mohammed, or Charles Taze Russell, or yourself, you have chosen Adam, the first Adam. The only other choice is Christ, the last Adam.

Adam was a failure; Jesus was a success

Romans 5:12 *Wherefore, as by one man sin entered into the world, and death by sin; and so death passed upon all men, for that all have sinned:*

Paul begins verse twelve with a *wherefore*. It means *because of all of this* and refers back to everything he has said about salvation in the previous verses. He is using all of that to spring ahead into this discussion of how badly Adam messed up and how thoroughly Christ fixed it.

And Adam did mess up. He is the *one man* spoken of here who allowed sin to enter into the world and death to enter along with it.

Anyone with eyes, ears, a brain, and even a modicum of honesty has to admit that this world is saturated with abject wickedness.

The U.S. Postal Service recently issued a commemorative stamp for a man named Harvey Milk. Who, you ask, was Harvey Milk? A pedophile. A truly evil man. And the U.S. Postal Service just honored him with his very own stamp.

Each day, women are raped, children are abused, pornography is celebrated, drunkenness is epidemic, and self-centeredness is the order of the day. And as much as we would like to blame people in our modern-day for that wickedness, and they do indeed bear part of the responsibility, the origin and root of all of it was the man Adam.

I doubt if Adam had any idea just how bad things were going to get, just how filthy, based on his choice to engage in that first sinful act. Adam is responsible for opening the floodgate of every evil that exists and giving it access to our world.

Therefore, Romans 5:12 says, all must die! Why? Because God promised Adam that if he sinned, he would die, and we were all still in him when he sinned. Therefore, all mankind must die.

Romans 5:13 *(For until the law sin was in the world: but sin is not imputed when there is no law.*

Verses thirteen through seventeen form a parenthesis of thought dealing with the effects of Adam's sin.

It is not that people before Moses "broke the law and then died." Yes, people from the time of Adam up until the time of Moses still sinned. But here is the salient point: verse twelve told us that it was sin that caused death. The law spoken of in verse thirteen did not come till the time of Moses. Some 2,500 years or so of humanity had all lived and then died before there ever was a written law of God to break.

That tells us that it was not the sin of breaking the law that brought about death. Verse thirteen tells us that even though there was sin in the world, that sin was not imputed; it was not added to man's account until the law was written down and given to Moses. In other words, God was not going to impute something to someone's legal account for something that He had not even officially told them was wrong yet, even though they already knew in their conscience that things like murder and adultery were wrong.

So, if people did not die for breaking the law that was not yet written down, if they did not die for breaking what they had not been told was a commandment, why then did they die? Why did millions of people before the time of Moses and the law live and then die?

They died for breaking the commandment that they did know about: "Thou shalt not eat of the tree of the knowledge of good and evil."

You say, "But that was Adam, not me!" No, please remember, it was Adam, and you in Adam. The genetic material that is you came from Adam and Eve. Every fiber of your being came from Adam and Eve. And because of Adam, your father, you will die. You were in him when he sinned. Look at 1 Corinthians 15:22:

1 Corinthians 15:22 *For as in Adam all die, even so in Christ shall all be made alive.*

The sin of breaking the Ten Commandments is not the first thing being imputed to you, causing you to die and go to hell; the sin of eating that fruit in the garden is.

Romans 5:14 *Nevertheless death reigned from Adam to Moses, even over them that had not sinned after the similitude of Adam's transgression, who is the figure of him that was to come.*

Nevertheless, even though there were no Ten Commandments, and even though you did not *sin after the similitude of Adam's transgression,* in other words, even though you yourself did not put that fruit to your lips like Adam did, death still reigned all the way from Adam to Moses. Once again, that is because we were all in Adam when he sinned.

The last part of verse fifteen makes a unique statement about Adam. It says that he was the figure, the picture of Him that was to come. We will soon see that what that phrase is talking about is Jesus. Adam is a flawed picture of Jesus, and Jesus is an unflawed picture of Adam. Jesus and Adam compare and contrast with each other, and that is the way that God designed it.

Romans 5:15 *But not as the offence, so also is the free gift. For if through the offence of one many be dead, much more the grace of God, and the gift by grace, which is by one man, Jesus Christ, hath abounded unto many.*

This verse begins to show the blessed contrast between Jesus and Adam. Adam is seen in the word *offence*, and Jesus is seen in the phrase *the free gift.* Adam was a failure; he brought the offence of sin; he blew it for himself and all of us. But by contrast, Jesus was a success! He brought the free gift, salvation by grace through faith; He was a success for Himself and all of us.

All who have been born of Adam, described as *many* in the first part of verse fifteen, have fallen with him; they are all either dead or dying. But all who are born of Christ, the last *many* seen in verse fifteen, those who have received *the grace of God, and the gift by grace,* have been raised with Him. They may die physically, but they will never die spiritually, and then one day, they will live both spiritually and in a glorified physical body forever.

Adam brought a fall; Jesus brought salvation

Romans 5:16 *And not as it was by one that sinned, so is the gift: for the judgment was by one to condemnation, but the free gift is of many offences unto justification.*

The unfamiliar phrasing of the first part of fifteen, in modern vernacular, would be something like *and far differently from what we have from the one that sinned on the one hand, we have the gift on the other hand.*

The word *one* occurs twice in this verse. The second *one* in this verse refers to Adam's one sin. It only took that one sin of Adam to condemn us all. You would think that Adam would have to have been a murderer or rapist or pedophile to have caused the universal condemnation of all mankind, but no! God is so holy, so anti-sin, that it only took that one bite of fruit to place all mankind under the condemnation of God.

Please remember this the next time you hear someone say or infer that God is okay with us just the way we are. If God were okay with us just the way we are, He would not have had to die for us. It only took one sin to separate us from a perfectly holy God.

We have already seen Jesus and Adam contrasted; now we see what they did contrasted. The offense of Adam, the one sin, caused all mankind to fall under condemnation. But the free gift of Jesus looked at that one sin, and all of the other *many offences* of mankind, all of the things that Adam did, and all the things that we have done, and it caused Jesus to go to the cross and die so that we could be saved.

Jesus and Adam could not be more different; what they did could not be more different.

Adam brought fatality; Jesus brought superiority

Romans 5:17 *For if by one man's offence death reigned by one; much more they which receive abundance of grace and of the gift of righteousness shall reign in life by one, Jesus Christ.)*

The word *one* was the focus of the last verse. The focus of this verse is the word *reign*. We are reminded that by one man's offense, in other words, by Adam's sin, death reigned.

Since the time of Adam, sinners have been slaves to a very cruel taskmaster, death. A sinner is a slave to death, his master. A sinner is born on his way to the grave, and when he gets there, he is never getting out.

But there is another *reign* in this verse. The sinner has death reigning over him, but the saved, the righteous, will reign in life by one, by only one, by Jesus Christ. That is a picturesque way of saying that while death reigns over the sinner, the saint reigns over death.

There is a glorious truth to the saved. Death is, in a way, our servant. God has given death the task of handing us off from here to there. God has given death the task of ushering us into His presence. We have a natural fear of death, but one split second after death, we will wonder why we did.

Adam brought fear; Jesus brought security

The parenthetical thought that began in verse thirteen is now complete. So, let's look at verses twelve and eighteen together as we begin to consider verse eighteen.

Romans 5:12 *Wherefore, as by one man sin entered into the world, and death by sin; and so death passed upon all men, for that all have sinned:*

Romans 5:18 *Therefore as by the offence of one judgment came upon all men to condemnation; even so by the righteousness of one the free gift came upon all men unto justification of life.*

The focus of this verse is the continued contrast between justification/condemnation that comes from Jesus/Adam.

Paul observes here at the outset that Adam's one offense in the garden has caused judgment to come upon all men to condemnation [*katakrima*, damnation].

Nothing is more frightening than the thought of being condemned. Imagine standing in a courtroom on trial for your life. You have been accused of murder. The prosecuting attorney has laid out mountains of evidence that sounds so convincing. He has called you horrible names. The looks on the faces of the jury tell you that they probably believe what he has said about you. The judge says to the foreman, "Has the jury reached a verdict?" The foreman says, "Yes, your honor, we have. We, the jury, find the defendant..."

What is going on in your mind right now? How do you feel? Is your heart racing? Are you holding your breath? You are scared to death, and rightfully so! Nothing is more frightening than the thought of being condemned. And that is what Adam did for us. He placed us in a position where we will one day have to stand before a holy God and have Him pronounce us guilty and worthy of hell.

But if nothing is so scary as being condemned, nothing is so secure as being justified. I want you to put yourself back in that courtroom for just a moment. You are on trial for your life. You have been accused of murder. The prosecuting attorney has laid out mountains of evidence that sounds so convincing. He has called you horrible names. The looks on the faces of the jury tell you that they probably believe what he has said about you.

But then suddenly something happens. Suddenly the judge interrupts the proceedings, and he says, "This case is dismissed..."

You are probably feeling pretty good right about now. But then he says something that makes it even better. After the words, "This case is dismissed," he adds the words, "with prejudice."

When a judge says, "This case is dismissed with prejudice," it will change the entire ballgame, not just temporarily, but absolutely forever. When something is dismissed with prejudice, it means that it can never again even be brought up in a court of law. It means you can never be charged with that crime again. It means you can never be accused of it again. It means that you can walk out of that courtroom holding your head up high, and no bailiff can stop you, no officer can stop you, no lawyer can stop you. It means that you can go about your life as if you had never even been to court.

When Romans 5:18 says that we have been given justification of life, in effect, it means pretty much the same as "dismissed with prejudice." It means that when Jesus took our sin upon Himself, we were declared righteous and forever set free. It means that everything you ever did is no longer even an issue with God. It means that the devil can accuse in railing terms over all of the bad things you have ever done, but it is not going to get him anywhere because God is not even listening to him.

Adam fell; Jesus stood

Romans 5:19 *For as by one man's disobedience many were made sinners, so by the obedience of one shall many be made righteous.*

There is one thing we know for certain that both Adam and Jesus had in common. Both of them were tempted by the devil in an attempt to get them to sin. Adam was tempted in the garden; Jesus was tempted in the wilderness.

But as far as temptation goes, that is where the comparison ends and the contrast begins. The first part of this verse reminds us that when Adam was tempted, he disobeyed God; he fell. But the last part of this verse reminds us that when Jesus was tempted, when the devil tried to short-circuit His path to the cross, He obeyed God, He went all the way through with everything; He stood.

The first part of this verse tells us that when Adam disobeyed and fell, many were made sinners. That word *many* includes everybody who ever lived (Romans 5:12, Romans 3:23). But the second part of this verse tells us that because Jesus obeyed and stood, many shall be made righteous. That word *many* includes everybody who ever lived who accepts what Jesus did for them (Romans 13:10, John 1:12).

Our falling under the condemnation of Adam's sin was completely involuntary; we had no choice in the matter. Our receiving the righteousness of Jesus's obedience is completely voluntary; we have every choice in the matter!

Adam brought that which was formidable; Jesus brought that which is sovereign

Romans 5:20 *Moreover the law entered, that the offence might abound. But where sin abounded, grace did much more abound: 21 That as sin hath reigned unto death, even so might grace reign through righteousness unto eternal life by Jesus Christ our Lord.*

Search your Bible very carefully, and you will find that no one was ever saved by the deeds of the law. But if that is the case, then why was there even a law to begin with? Verse twenty tells us, painting much the same picture that the book of Galatians does in reference to sin.

The law entered, that the offence might abound.

We should begin by defining a key word, the word *entered.* In verse twelve, when speaking of sin, it was from *eiserchomai,* and it simply means to enter right on in. Here in verse twenty, though, when speaking of the law, it has a prefixed attached to it, *para,* and the whole word is now *pareiserchomai.* That little addition changes the meaning to something like *to bring in from the side.* As Qurollo observed of this, "Law did not have a supreme place in God's plan. God introduced the law as a side issue in order that sin might be shown to be what it really is." (94)

When you add that definition to what follows, you see that this verse does not claim that the law is the thing that causes sin. Again, mankind sinned before there ever was a law. But when the law came, it both made sin to abound (caused more of it both because mankind was now responsible for what was written and because they chafed at having to obey and refused to do so) and made it to appear much more obvious.

When it came, the law drew a perfectly straight line that was visible for everybody to see. And since that line was perfectly straight and visible for everyone to see, any deviation from that line was very clearly seen as well.

Many years ago, when we were building the Sunday school rooms in the back of our old church building, we framed up three interior walls that would separate the big back room into three smaller rooms. At this point in my life, I am very experienced in building things. But back then I knew very little. I grabbed a two-by-four, held it up against the wall, and got ready to nail it into place. A friend of mine was there that was a very experienced carpenter.

He said, "Uh, preacher, what are you about to do?"

I said, "I'm going to nail this board to the wall to get our framing started."

He said, "Don't you think you should level it up?"

I said, "It looks pretty straight to me!"

He said, "No offense to your eyes, Preacher, but why don't we put a plumb line on it and check."

Then he pulled a metal plumb bob out of his bag, attached a string to it, got up on a ladder, and held it right near to the board that I was holding. When he did, suddenly, my board did not look so straight after all! It took something perfectly straight to show me how bad what I thought was straight really was.

That is exactly what the law was designed to do. God gave man the law not to cause him to sin but so that he could see how very sinful he already was. That is what this verse means when it says the law entered that the offense might abound.

But that is not the end of the story. The next thing you read is that *where sin abounded, grace did much more abound*! God used the law to show us how sinful we were and to bring us to the point of helplessness and hopelessness, and then He, in His grace, sent us the one and only solution that would work. His name was Jesus.

You say, "But preacher, we didn't deserve something that good." You are exactly right. But where sin abounded, grace did much more abound. Where we were giving God what He did not deserve—grief and sorrow and heartache because of our sin—God turned right around and gave us what we do not deserve—salvation through faith in the shed blood of the Lord

Jesus Christ. And no amount of sin was too great; the abounding of grace was, and is, and always will be far greater than the abounding of sin.

Sin was strong, the law was strong, but grace is even stronger!

In the last verse of this chapter, we are reminded that sin reigned unto death. Sin was the undefeated, undisputed champion. It was formidable; it took everyone out.

But whenever a better fighter comes along and knocks the head off of that formerly undefeated fighter, everyone tends to forget about the first guy and sing the praises of the second. Sin had reigned, but when grace showed up, it really was not even a good contest:

...even so might grace reign through righteousness unto eternal life by Jesus Christ our Lord.

Sin reigned – past tense. Grace now reigns *even so*, even to the degree that sin once did. And while sin reigned unto death, grace now reigns forever through righteousness unto eternal life.

Look how Paul described it to the Colossians:

Colossians 2:13 *And you, being dead in your sins and the uncircumcision of your flesh, hath he quickened together with him, having forgiven you all trespasses;* **14** *Blotting out the handwriting of ordinances that was against us, which was contrary to us, and took it out of the way, nailing it to his cross;* **15** *And having spoiled principalities and powers, he made a shew of them openly, triumphing over them in it.*

Jesus was not biting His nails hoping that He could win; it was a grand slam home run victory. Grace reigns through righteousness unto eternal life by Jesus Christ our Lord. Grace is large and in charge. The grace of God can cleanse every sin, remove every stain, redeem any sinner, and defeat every plan that the devil ever had for you.

───────────────〜─────────────

Spiritually, you and I are in a representative system. We are either going to have Adam representing us or Jesus representing us. Some people choose to have Adam Buddha representing them, some people choose to have Adam Mohammed representing them, some people choose to have Adam the pope representing them, some people choose to have Adam themselves representing them. But no matter who you choose, it all boils down to the fact that if you are trusting anyone other than Jesus you are trusting in Adam. All of those men were descended from Adam just like you, and therefore they are no better than you. You were born a sinner, and so was Mohammed. You were born a sinner, and so was Buddha. You were born a sinner, and so was the pope. If you are trusting anyone other than Jesus, then you are just like a drowning man out in the ocean grabbing ahold of another drowning man for help.

I have seen the effects of what the first Adam caused. I have no desire to trust any Adam, myself or any other one. The only person worthy of my trust and the only person worthy of your trust is the Lord Jesus Christ who alone can fix what Adam broke.

Chapter Nine
I - If You Are Saved, Live Like It!

Romans 6:1 *What shall we say then? Shall we continue in sin, that grace may abound?* **2** *God forbid. How shall we, that are dead to sin, live any longer therein?* **3** *Know ye not, that so many of us as were baptized into Jesus Christ were baptized into his death?* **4** *Therefore we are buried with him by baptism into death: that like as Christ was raised up from the dead by the glory of the Father, even so we also should walk in newness of life.* **5** *For if we have been planted together in the likeness of his death, we shall be also in the likeness of his resurrection:* **6** *Knowing this, that our old man is crucified with him, that the body of sin might be destroyed, that henceforth we should not serve sin.* **7** *For he that is dead is freed from sin.* **8** *Now if we be dead with Christ, we believe that we shall also live with him:* **9** *Knowing that Christ being raised from the dead dieth no more; death hath no more dominion over him.* **10** *For in that he died, he died unto sin once: but in that he liveth, he liveth unto God.* **11** *Likewise reckon ye also yourselves to be dead indeed unto sin, but alive unto God through Jesus Christ our Lord.* **12** *Let not sin therefore reign in your mortal body, that ye should obey it in the lusts thereof.* **13** *Neither yield ye your members as instruments of unrighteousness unto sin: but yield yourselves unto God, as those that are alive from the dead, and your members as instruments of righteousness unto God.* **14** *For sin shall not have dominion over you: for ye are not under the law, but under grace.* **15** *What then? shall we sin, because we are not* *under the law, but under grace? God forbid.* **16** *Know ye not, that to whom ye yield yourselves servants to obey, his servants ye are to whom ye obey; whether of sin unto death, or of obedience unto righteousness?* **17** *But God be thanked, that ye were the servants of sin, but ye have obeyed from the heart that form of doctrine which was delivered you.* **18** *Being then made free from sin, ye became the servants of righteousness.* **19** *I speak after the manner of men because of the infirmity of your flesh: for as ye have yielded your members servants to uncleanness and to iniquity unto iniquity; even so now yield your members servants to righteousness unto holiness.* **20** *For when ye were the servants of sin, ye were free from righteousness.* **21** *What fruit had ye then in those things whereof ye are now ashamed? for the end of those things is death.* **22** *But now being made free from sin, and become servants to God, ye have your fruit unto holiness, and the end everlasting life.* **23** *For the wages of sin is death; but the gift of God is eternal life through Jesus Christ our Lord.*

The story is told of an elderly widow who had a son in the military. He was in a position that he did not really need his government check. Each week he sent it home to his mother. But the mother did not recognize them and did not know what they were; she thought they were just souvenirs from her son! So, each one that came in, she put it in a drawer and kept it.

When the son came home on furlough, he found his mother's home in disrepair, and she was eating crackers and water! He asked her what had happened to all the money he sent to her. She was shocked to find out that she had been living far below her means.

This scene is often repeated in the Christian life. God the Son has made elaborate preparations for us to be able to live as He desires. Yet we often live like spiritual paupers, wallowing in the poverty of sin.

In this passage, Paul will forcefully drive home a thought that we should all take to heart: if you are saved, live like it!

In Romans 5:20, Paul made a profound statement. *Where sin abounded, grace did much more abound.* Among other important things, this also means we cannot possibly out-sin God's grace; there is no number of sins too high for grace to handle and no depth of sin too low for grace to go deeper than. That is a powerful and blessed truth but also an extremely dangerous one. When we make that statement, you know how the lost mind or how the mind of a carnal Christian will react. "If grace is such a good thing, and if sinning more brings more grace, let's just keep on sinning!"

It is that exact wicked mindset that Paul has in mind as he begins chapter six.

A question about the abounding of grace

Romans 6:1 *What shall we say then? Shall we continue in sin, that grace may abound?*

After using the words *What shall we say then?* to tie what he has just said to what he is about to say, Paul asks a very unique, rhetorical question as the chapter begins. Who would ever imagine a preacher of the gospel asking if we should continue to sin? Preachers, through the years, have generally tended to frown upon that sort of thing, mostly because God's Word itself frowns on that sort of thing.

But he had a very good reason for asking. His reason for asking was that he knew people. Anytime someone thinks they have a license to do wrong, you can pretty much chalk it up that they are, in fact, going to do wrong. And Paul knew that the cleansing power of grace was going to be taken and twisted by some into a very powerful license to sin.

So Paul begins this chapter with the question: if you cannot out-sin God's grace, and if more sin brings more grace, shouldn't we just keep on sinning so that God can keep on sending more grace?

The question has been asked, but with a question like that, it certainly was not going to take Paul long to get around to answering it:

Romans 6:2 *God forbid. How shall we, that are dead to sin, live any longer therein?*

It took Paul exactly two words to answer the question: God forbid! In Greek it is *May Ginoito,* may it never ever be, God forbid it entirely forever, do not even think of such a foolish thing. It is an extremely firm and harsh negative both in Greek and in English. And the reason he gave for God forbidding such a thought was that we who are saved are dead to sin and are no longer to be living therein.

The idea that grace gives us a license to sin is absolutely disgusting and abominable to a person who truly loves God. And more people than you realize hold that idea even if they do not put it in those exact words.

Usually, they put it in words something like this: "I have eternal security; I can live however I want!"

Pay very close attention. The Bible teaches eternal security, and some people are truly saved and truly do have eternal security. But do you know a good way to test whether or not someone actually does have eternal security? If they make indefensible and unbiblical statements like, "I have eternal security; I can live however I want!" that is a pretty good indication that they are as lost as a ball in high weeds and do not have salvation or security of any kind, eternal or otherwise. Look how Paul put it in another place:

2 Corinthians 5:17 *Therefore if any man be in Christ, he is a new creature: old things are passed away; behold, all things are become new.*

If you are still what you used to be and still do the things you used to do, you are no more born-again than the devil himself. One who is truly saved is dead to sin. Does that mean that he is sinlessly perfect? No, absolutely not, and we will cover that in much greater detail as we progress through this book. It does mean, though, that he is very different from what he once was and how he once lived.

Please bear in mind as you go through the book of Romans and the other writings of Paul that it is generally not hard to figure out what Paul had in mind when he wrote any particular part of Scripture. Just look for key words or key concepts to be repeated over and over. In this case, you will find in this chapter a repetition of life and death. We have already seen death occur once in verse two, and both it and life will recur throughout this chapter.

Romans 6:3 *Know ye not, that so many of us as were baptized into Jesus Christ were baptized into his death?*

When a person becomes a born-again child of God, they are spiritually baptized into Christ:

1 Corinthians 12:13 *For by one Spirit are we all baptized into one body, whether we be Jews or Gentiles, whether we be bond or free; and have been all made to drink into one Spirit.*

After that birthing again, that spiritual baptism into Christ, a person who is obedient is then baptized in water. This is a picture of the death, burial, and resurrection of Christ and of the death, burial, and resurrection spiritually of the sinner. When we are put under the water, it is a symbol of the fact that we have died, been buried, and have been raised a brand-new creature that we have never been before.

At this particular moment, though, Paul is focusing on the death part. If we have been saved, the old us is dead, just as Christ died. If that is the case, then we are not to be living like the "old us" any longer.

Romans 6:4 *Therefore we are buried with him by baptism into death: that like as Christ was raised up from the dead by the glory of the Father, even so we also should walk in newness of life.* **5** *For if we have been planted together in the likeness of his death, we shall be also in the likeness of his resurrection:*

We know that salvation was to bring us life, but first, it was to bring us death, the death of our old man. We are *buried with him by baptism into death.* But the story does not end there.

When Jesus died, it was not to prove that He could die; it was to prove that He could not help but live! He came out of that grave and walked in *newness of life. Even so* [*houtoe*, in the same manner] we who have been raised up spiritually are also to be walking in newness of life; since *we have been planted together in the likeness of his death,* we are guaranteed one day to be raised in the likeness of His resurrection.

But Paul is not merely stating that as a wonderful promise to look forward to. Again, from all the way back to the very first verse of the chapter, his point is that we are to be living right today. We are right now to be walking in the likeness of His resurrection.

Do you know what that means? When Jesus was resurrected, He was different than before. He walked through walls. He appeared and then disappeared. His body had been glorified. Was He able to do the things that He used to do in His unglorified body? Yes. He made a point of eating some fish and honeycomb in their presence to let them know that it was Him, not a ghost. He was able to do the things He used to do; He just did not do the things He used to do. In fact, previously, He had voluntarily limited Himself to teach us some things. He got hungry and tired and thirsty. He was limited; there were some things He could not do. Yes, since He was fully God, those limitations were voluntary. But they were real, and they were designed to teach us some things.

When we got saved, we not only received the promise of a future resurrection and a forever home, we presently became different than we were before. In our old flesh, we were limited. We literally could not help but sin in some way, shape, or form pretty much all the time. But now that we are saved, now that we have been resurrected as a new creature in Christ, we do not have to sin anymore. We can now live like a child of God. We have a choice that we did not previously have. When I, as a pastor, look out to my congregation and say, "Live like a child of God," do you know what I know? I know that every one of them who is truly saved can live like a child of God if they choose to do so! I also know that they can choose not to live like a child of God.

Romans 6:6 *Knowing this, that our old man is crucified with him, that [hina, in order that] the body of sin might be destroyed, that henceforth we should not serve sin.*

Here is the point-blank explanation of what Paul said in verse two. Our *old* man was crucified with Christ the moment we got saved in order that the body of sin [the body which is characterized by sin] might be destroyed. Our old man not only had a constant desire for sin, he had little or nothing inside of him keeping him from it. He was on his own with nothing more than a vacillating conscience to help him do right.

If we were ever going to overcome sin, that old man had to die. It is the only way we could ever stop serving sin. When we died at the altar, that body of sin died; if we sin now, we are serving a dead man who has no power over us.

Romans 6:7 *For he that is dead is freed from sin.*

In the concentration camps of World War II, people had no choice but to obey their taskmasters. Until they died, that is. At that point, those taskmasters could crack the whip all they liked, but that dead body would serve them no more. They were free!

When Betsie Ten Boom died in Ravensbruck concentration camp, here is what her sister, Corrie, wrote. "There lay Betsie, her eyes closed as if in sleep, her face full and young. The care lines, the grief lines, the hunger, and disease were simply gone. This was the Betsie of Harlem, happy and at peace..." (Ten Boom, 213)

Now, on one hand, it is evident that death is an excellent way to "win over sin." But on the other hand, death is a pretty gloomy thought until you realize, that is, that God brings life out of death. Look at the next verse:

Romans 6:8 *Now if we be dead with Christ, we believe that we shall also live with him:*

Our old man is dead the moment we get saved. But let's be honest, there are some sacrifices to that. There are some things that my flesh would like to do and some things that your flesh would like to do that we know that we can no longer do. But when you consider the end result of our being dead with Christ, it makes that seem like a pretty small sacrifice. If we are dead with Christ, we shall also live with Him. That refers both to the life that we have in Christ now, this joyful, amazing thing we call the Christian life, and it refers to the eternal life that we will have with Him in heaven. When you put that on one side of the scale and the things that you are leaving behind on the other side of the scale, it is not balanced at all. It is overwhelmingly in favor of getting saved and living for Christ and going to heaven forever. I can do without the alcohol and the drugs and the filth and foolishness of earth in light of all that I have waiting for me on the other side!

Romans 6:9 *Knowing that Christ being raised from the dead dieth no more; death hath no more dominion over him.* **10** *For in that he died, he died unto sin once: but in that he liveth, he liveth unto God.*

Christ died exactly one time, and it will never happen again. Death had only one shot with Him. He is alive, and alive forevermore. And the point of all that is that we who are saved are also alive, and alive forevermore. Just like Jesus will never be physically dead again, we who are saved will never be spiritually dead again. Jesus did not live then die, then live then die, then live then die, and a person who gets saved also does not live then die, then live then die, then live then die spiritually. Jesus died once, came back to life, and is alive forevermore. A sinner gets saved once, comes to life as a child of God, and is alive as a child of God forevermore.

Romans 6:11 *Likewise reckon ye also yourselves to be dead indeed unto sin, but alive unto God through Jesus Christ our Lord.*

Every door must have a hinge of some type that it swings on. Every passage of Scripture is much the same. We have spent ten verses covering the fact that we are not what we used to be, that we are, in fact, "dead to sin." But if that is the case, why does all of this even have to be discussed? If we are dead to sin, then we obviously cannot sin anymore, and if we have been raised a new creature in Christ, obviously, we will always do right, right?

But I know better than that, and you know better than that, and even Paul, who was writing this, knew better than that. Look at what he said in another passage:

Romans 7:18 *For I know that in me (that is, in my flesh,) dwelleth no good thing: for to will is present with me; but how to perform that which is good I find not. **19** For the good that I would I do not: but the evil which I would not, that I do. **20** Now if I do that I would not, it is no more I that do it, but sin that dwelleth in me. **21** I find then a law, that, when I would do good, evil is present with me. **22** For I delight in the law of God after the inward man: **23** But I see another law in my members, warring against the law of my mind, and bringing me into captivity to the law of sin which is in my members. **24** O wretched man that I am! who shall deliver me from the body of this death?*

Even Paul struggled with sin. So, how does that reconcile with the fact that we are dead to sin?

The hinge of this chapter is verse eleven, and one word in verse eleven in particular, the word "reckon." Look at it again.

Romans 6:11 *Likewise reckon ye also yourselves to be dead indeed unto sin, but alive unto God through Jesus Christ our Lord.*

You know by now that to reckon means to impute, to add something to an account. In other words, it is there; we just have to apply it. Just like that military mother had all of that money, but it was not doing her any good because she was not applying it, we have the ability now to live right, we have the ability to act on the fact that we are dead to sin, we just have to apply it. We could not do it before because it was not available to us, but we can do it now because it is available to us.

Romans 6:12 *Let not sin therefore reign in your mortal body, that ye should obey it in the lusts thereof.*

Before you got saved you had very little choice in the matter; sin did reign in your mortal body, and you did obey it in the lusts thereof. But if you are born-again, you now have a choice whether or not to let sin reign in your mortal bodies and whether to obey it in the lusts thereof. You can choose to do right, thanks to the Holy Ghost of God living inside of you, you now have the power to do so. And the more you act on that, the stronger you get at it.

121

If you are saved and sin has dominion over you, it is because you are letting it have dominion over you.

I grew up with horses, and the two horses that we had the longest were Dixie and Bambi. Dixie was Bambi's mother. When Dixie got very old, twenty-five years old, in fact, she did the unthinkable. She broke through the barbed-wire fence one snowy winter day and ran off through the woods. You would think a horse would be easy to track in the snow, and you would be wrong. We absolutely could not find that horse. After several months, we assumed that she was dead.

But then one day we got a call. Someone from several miles away called to let us know that our horse was on his property tangled up in some wire. We went over there and got her out and brought her home.

Now, a unique thing about horses is that there will always be one that rules the pasture. Dixie had ruled the pasture for twenty-five years. But in the months that she had been gone, obviously, Bambi ruled the pasture. When Dixie came home, she was old and worn and beaten and weak. She was malnourished; she had no strength. Bambi, though, was still young and strong and thriving.

When we put Dixie into that pasture and let her go, it did not take but a matter of minutes before there was a stare-down. Dixie and Bambi were going head-to-head to determine who would rule the pasture. Physically, there was no contest. Bambi could have killed her easily. But the most amazing thing happened; Dixie won that stare-down and went right back to ruling the pasture.

Bambi had the power to beat her, but she did not reckon on that power. You and I, who are saved, have the power to rule over sin in our lives; it is just a question of whether we are going to have the discipline and will to do so.

Romans 6:13 *Neither yield ye your members as instruments of unrighteousness unto sin: but yield yourselves unto God, as those that are alive from the dead, and your members as instruments of righteousness unto God.*

Another key word occurs in this verse, the word *yield*. We can either yield our members, the parts of our body, as instruments of unrighteousness unto sin, or we can yield those very same instruments to God to be used as instruments of righteousness. Either way, we are yielding. And these are the only two things a child of God really has the option to yield to. You who are saved will either willingly yield the members of your body to do that which is wrong, or you will, as those that are alive from the dead, yield them to the Lord and do that which is right with the members of your body.

Yield, in both uses in this verse, is from a very picturesque word, the word *paristaymi,* and it means "to place at someone's disposal." When it gets right down to it, you will either place your body parts at the devil's disposal or at God's disposal; those are your two options.

If you are saved, you can live right; it is a matter of yielding yourself to do so.

Romans 6:14 *For sin shall not have dominion over you: for ye are not under the law, but under grace.*

When Paul says that sin shall not have dominion over you, please notice that he did not say, "Do not let sin have dominion over you." He simply made the blanket statement that *sin shall not have dominion over you.* It is no longer possible. In other words, it is never true when a child of God says, "I know I sinned; I just couldn't help myself."

Yes, you most certainly could. Sin does not have dominion over you anymore. If you sin, it is because you have yielded yourself to sin. You are no longer a lost person under the law who does not have the ability to keep the law. You are now a saved person under grace who has the divine and supernatural ability in you to do right.

This verse is often used to remind people that we do not have to keep the Law of Moses anymore. And that is certainly true. But it does not mean that we no longer have to do right. The moral aspects of the Mosaic Law are for all times and were all restated either explicitly or implicitly in the New Testament for Christians. Grace never gives us an excuse to sin. These days, it is normally used that way by liberal theologians, but they are completely wrong and utterly twisted in their view of grace. Take a look at another passage, and let me show you what grace does for a child of God:

Titus 2:11 *For the grace of God that bringeth salvation hath appeared to all men,* **12** *Teaching us that, denying ungodliness and worldly lusts, we should live soberly, righteously, and godly, in this present world;* **13** *Looking for that blessed hope, and the glorious appearing of the great God and our Saviour Jesus Christ;* **14** *Who gave himself for us, that he might redeem us from all iniquity, and purify unto himself a peculiar people, zealous of good works.*

Grace does not give us a license to sin; it teaches us not to sin! Any view of grace that results in an impure life rather than a pure life is a warped and twisted and unbiblical view of grace.

When you were lost, you were under the law. The law said, "Don't do it! You're on your own." Because of this, sin had dominion over us because we ourselves could not overcome it. Now that we are saved, we are under grace. Grace says, "Don't do it! I'll help you." So, while we are no longer bound to all of the civil and ceremonial aspects of the Mosaic Law, the demand for righteousness is still the same. The difference is now we actually can be righteous.

Therefore, because you are dead to sin, because you are now alive to God, since you are now a Christian, live like it!

That is the answer to the question about the abounding of grace.

A question about the authority of grace

Romans 6:15 *What then? shall we sin, because we are not under the law, but under grace? God forbid.*

It should not have escaped your notice how very similar this verse is to verse one:

Romans 6:1 *What shall we say then? Shall we continue in sin, that grace may abound?*

Just as verse one was a rhetorical question, verse fifteen is as well. And just as the answer to the first question was, *God forbid*, the answer to the second question is also *God forbid*. And just as Paul gave a reason for that first *God forbid*, he will, in verses sixteen through twenty-three, give the reasons for this second *God forbid*, and his argument can be summed up in the word "servant."

Romans 6:16 *Know ye not, that to whom ye yield yourselves servants to obey, his servants ye are to whom ye obey; whether of sin unto death, or of obedience unto righteousness?*

There is sin, and there is righteousness. You will serve one or the other. If you yield yourself to righteousness, you are the servant of righteousness. If you yield yourself to sin, you are the servant of sin.

If you are saved, every single time you are ever confronted with sin you have this exact same choice: "What will I serve?" I, for one, do not want to be the servant of sin.

Romans 6:17 *But God be thanked, that ye were the servants of sin, but ye have obeyed from the heart that form of doctrine which was delivered you.* **18** *Being then made free from sin, ye became the servants of righteousness.*

The people that Paul was writing to were saved! They were released from their former master because they obeyed from the heart. That is verse seventeen. But verse eighteen is the follow-up truth. Yes, they were made free from sin, but they then chose to become the servants of righteousness. Those two things are not the same thing. There are actually a goodly number of people who are made free from sin, they are saved, they have the ability to do right, but they never yield themselves to become the servants of righteousness.

Do not stop with just salvation. If you are saved, yield your bodies to the Lord; become the servants of righteousness.

Romans 6:19 *I speak after the manner of men because of the infirmity of your flesh: for as ye have yielded your members servants to uncleanness and to iniquity unto iniquity;*

even so now yield your members servants to righteousness unto holiness.

When Paul says that he speaks after the manner of man, he is in no way indicating that what he is saying is not inspired. He is telling them that he is speaking in human terms and using a physical illustration (servants and servitude) to help them understand it because their flesh is infirmed and weak and has trouble understanding it.

Adam Clarke paraphrased it this way, saying, "I make use of metaphors and figures connected with well-known natural things; with your trades and situation in life; because of your inexperience in heavenly things, of which ye are only just beginning to know the nature and the names." (Clarke, 79-80)

Our flesh, including the mind, is weak, infirmed, and crippled by sin. Because of that, it is wise for God's man to take great care to be understandable. If I do not make my preaching and teaching and writing understandable, then I am not doing a good job. There is no glory to be found in words that are too big for people to understand.

In verse nineteen, Paul reminded them that they had at one point yielded their members as servants to uncleanness. He follows with an odder phrase, though, *and to iniquity unto iniquity.* This means that they were so engrossed with sin that they went from one sin to the next to the next in rapid succession. Then he said even so, just like you used to do that, now yield your members as servants *to righteousness unto holiness,* go from one godly act to the next to the next to the next. In other words, just like you used to go all out for sin, if you are saved, now you need to go all out for God!

Romans 6:20 *For when ye were the servants of sin, ye were free from righteousness. 21 What fruit had ye then in those things whereof ye are now ashamed? for the end of those things is death.*

That is a very unique phrase in verse twenty. When you were the servants of sin, you were *free from righteousness.* When you were lost, you never had to worry about all of that "religious junk," like going to church and reading your Bible and tithing and soul-winning and living right.

But, if you look back like verse twenty-one tells you to do, you will find that your life produced fruit. Just like a righteous life produces good fruit, an unrighteous life produces bad fruit. A person who truly gets saved will look back at their former life, and they will be ashamed of how they used to live because the end of the way they used to live is death, not life; it is bad, not good.

Romans 6:22 *But now being made free from sin, and become servants to God, ye have your fruit unto holiness, and the end everlasting life.*

Look at how verse twenty-two contrasts with verse twenty-one. Now that you are free from sin and have become servants of God, you have fruit in this life also, but this fruit is good fruit. This fruit is *unto holiness, and the end everlasting life.* The deeds of the saved are *unto* [*eis*, towards, going the direction of] holiness. And at the end of the way, we walk right into eternal life.

If you compare the results of a saved life and a lost life, there is no comparison. The results of a saved life are better than the results of a lost life all day, every day.

Romans 6:23 *For the wages* [*opsonion*, pay, allowance, earnings] *of sin is death; but the gift of God is eternal life through Jesus Christ our Lord.*

Verse twenty-three paints that contrast that we just spoke of more clearly than anything I can imagine. Sin always gives people what they deserve: death. But the gift of God is eternal life through Jesus Christ our Lord. If you are saved, then, if you truly have eternal life, you have no business doing things that will earn you the wages of sin in any way, shape, or form.

Therefore, because you can choose every day to yield yourself to serve unrighteousness or righteousness, since you are a Christian, live like it!

That is the answer to the question about the authority of grace.

A saved person who does not live like a Christian has no excuse. He also has no beneficial impact on the lost world around him. Let us live our lives so that when we arrive in heaven, we turn to find a host of others following us safely there.

Chapter Ten
J - Jeopardy from the One Closest to Us

Romans 7:1 *Know ye not, brethren, (for I speak to them that know the law,) how that the law hath dominion over a man as long as he liveth?* **2** *For the woman which hath an husband is bound by the law to her husband so long as he liveth; but if the husband be dead, she is loosed from the law of her husband.* **3** *So then if, while her husband liveth, she be married to another man, she shall be called an adulteress: but if her husband be dead, she is free from that law; so that she is no adulteress, though she be married to another man.* **4** *Wherefore, my brethren, ye also are become dead to the law by the body of Christ; that ye should be married to another, even to him who is raised from the dead, that we should bring forth fruit unto God.* **5** *For when we were in the flesh, the motions of sins, which were by the law, did work in our members to bring forth fruit unto death.* **6** *But now we are delivered from the law, that being dead wherein we were held; that we should serve in newness of spirit, and not in the oldness of the letter.* **7** *What shall we say then? Is the law sin? God forbid. Nay, I had not known sin, but by the law: for I had not known lust, except the law had said, Thou shalt not covet.* **8** *But sin, taking occasion by the commandment, wrought in me all manner of concupiscence. For without the law sin was dead.* **9** *For I was alive without the law once: but when the commandment came, sin revived, and I died.* **10** *And the commandment, which was ordained to life, I found to be unto death.* **11** *For sin, taking occasion by the commandment,* *deceived me, and by it slew me.* **12** *Wherefore the law is holy, and the commandment holy, and just, and good.* **13** *Was then that which is good made death unto me? God forbid. But sin, that it might appear sin, working death in me by that which is good; that sin by the commandment might become exceeding sinful.* **14** *For we know that the law is spiritual: but I am carnal, sold under sin.* **15** *For that which I do I allow not: for what I would, that do I not; but what I hate, that do I.* **16** *If then I do that which I would not, I consent unto the law that it is good.* **17** *Now then it is no more I that do it, but sin that dwelleth in me.* **18** *For I know that in me (that is, in my flesh,) dwelleth no good thing: for to will is present with me; but how to perform that which is good I find not.* **19** *For the good that I would I do not: but the evil which I would not, that I do.* **20** *Now if I do that I would not, it is no more I that do it, but sin that dwelleth in me.* **21** *I find then a law, that, when I would do good, evil is present with me.* **22** *For I delight in the law of God after the inward man:* **23** *But I see another law in my members, warring against the law of my mind, and bringing me into captivity to the law of sin which is in my members.* **24** *O wretched man that I am! who shall deliver me from the body of this death?* **25** *I thank God through Jesus Christ our Lord. So then with the mind I myself serve the law of God; but with the flesh the law of sin.*

It has rightly been said that almost anyone can withstand jeopardy from a distance. But the far greater danger is jeopardy from those closest to you. An enemy soldier is not in nearly as good a position to do harm to a country as an enemy spy is. An enemy of the church is not in nearly as good of a position to do damage to a church as a wolf in sheep's clothing is. And in like measure, a spiritual enemy on the outside of you is not in nearly as good of a position to do damage as the enemy that you carry with you everywhere every day. The devil and the world are certainly formidable enemies. But the greatest danger that you will ever carry, even as a child of God, is the danger in your very own flesh.

A marriage after death

As we begin to examine this passage, please pay attention to the fact that it is not about divorce. In fact, divorce is never even mentioned. This passage is about our former relationship to the law and our new relationship with the Lord Jesus Christ. The illustration Paul uses is not an illustration about divorce; it is an illustration about a marriage ending due to the death of a spouse. So, remove any thoughts from your mind of divorce and remarriage when studying this passage.

Romans 7:1 *Know ye not, brethren, (for I speak to them that know the law,) how that the law hath dominion over a man as long as he liveth?*

In chapter six, we saw again and again that our old man died with Christ. When we got saved, the old sinful person that we were died, and we are now a new person that we were not before. So, as Paul begins chapter seven, he uses that thought to remind his readers that according to the law, as long as a man lives, he is under the dominion of the law. And he addresses this truth to brethren, which here means those who are saved. The law he speaks of, then, at least in this verse encompasses much more than merely the Mosaic law; most all known law in his day matched the descriptions he will give in this passage.

He begins with the truth that as long as our old man was alive, in other words before we got saved, we were bound under the chains of the law.

Romans 7:2 *For the woman which hath an husband is bound by the law to her husband so long as he liveth; but if the husband be dead, she is loosed from the law of her husband.*

As we saw in the last chapter, it is our death spiritually that removed us from the dominion of the law. A dead person is not going to get a speeding ticket; he is not going to be summoned for jury duty; he is not going to be a witness in a court case; he is not subject to the law.

The illustration Paul used in verse two is that of the legal bonds of marriage. A woman is bound by the law to her husband. But that legal bond ends with the grave.

As long as Mr. So-and-so is alive, he is not going to let Mrs. So-and-so marry someone else. If Mrs. So-and-so comes home one day and says, "Guess what! I got another husband today!" There will most certainly be trouble. Mr. So-and-so is not going to allow that, and the law is not going to allow that.

But if Mr. So-and-so passes away, everything changes. Once Mr. So-and-so passes away, that legal bond is broken, and Mrs. So-and-so is free to marry someone else.

Romans 7:3 *So then if, while her husband liveth, she be married to another man, she shall be called an adulteress: but if her husband be dead, she is free from that law; so that she is no adulteress, though she be married to another man.*

Paul pointed out something very obvious to people who, in those days, had much better sense than many people today have. If a woman with a living husband goes and marries someone else, she has committed adultery. She has sinned. She has done wrong. God's plan for marriage always has been and always will be one man for one woman for one life. The same holds true if a man with a living wife marries someone else.

However, once either of those two lives ends, the remaining spouse does not have to stay away from a member of the opposite sex anymore. A person with a living spouse cannot date someone else, court someone else, like someone else, or even flirt with someone else.

If my wife decides to run off and marry another man now, it is going to be a great irritation, because digging a twenty-foot hole to put another man's body in takes a while even with an excavator. (Calm down, please; I am kidding!) But if I am lying in a casket and some man says to my wife, "Hey, are you free Friday night?" That would certainly be in very poor taste and very poor timing, I would think, but as far as the law is concerned, she actually has perfect liberty to say, "That depends; you're not a preacher, are you?"

Romans 7:4 *Wherefore, my brethren, ye also are become dead to the law by the body of Christ; that ye should be married to another, even to him who is raised from the dead, that we should bring forth fruit unto God.*

With the word *wherefore*, Paul now begins to let his readers know what he was driving at by use of this illustration of marriage. And what we find puts a very unique twist on Paul's illustration. Paul basically said that the one who died gets remarried to another one who used to be dead and that together they have "fruit."

Before we got saved, we were married to the law. We had to obey the law. We were bound to the law. And it was a brutal, cold, hard, lifeless type of existence. But when we got saved, we died to the law, thereby breaking our relationship with it. And then, when we were raised up to newness of life, we found ourselves married to the Lord Jesus Christ, who Himself had already died and risen from the dead. That marriage relationship between Christ and the saved produces fruit. It produces spiritual children. It produces spiritual possessions. It produces spiritual goals. And where our former relationship with the law was a brutal, cold, hard, lifeless type of existence, our new relationship with Christ is a loving, kind, enjoyable existence. So much so, that we produce spiritual fruit with Him.

Romans 7:5 *For when we were in the flesh, the motions of sins, which were by the law, did work in our members to bring forth fruit unto death.*

When we were in the flesh, when we were lost, the motions of sins, and that word *motions* means the passions of our sins, produced fruit. So please understand that whether you are lost and married to the law or whether you are saved and married to Christ, that relationship is going to produce fruit. But whereas the relationship with Christ brings forth good fruit, being lost, according to verse five, produces fruit unto death. That is an eloquent way of saying that nothing good comes from being lost. The lost person produces evil things here and now and experiences the effects of their sin now, and then after this life has to spend an eternity apart from God in hell. That certainly qualifies as fruit unto death.

Romans 7:6 *But now we are delivered from the law, that being dead wherein we were held; that we should serve in newness of spirit, and not in the oldness of the letter.*

133

I love those first two words, *but now*. There used to be a time when we were in the flesh, under the law, and the things we did produced fruit unto death. But now, we are delivered from the law.

The second phrase of verse six, though, is very telling. Paul has already told us that once we die we are delivered from our former bonds. But the second phrase in verse six reminds us that even while we were under the law, in one way, we were actually already dead. We were not free; we were basically "dead while living." We may have been alive, but all we were doing was existing, not really living. And that is all the law has the capacity to produce. The law never does produce happy, joyful, vibrant, living, loving, thriving type of people.

But now that we are delivered from that, now that we do not have to serve the law, what do we do? We still serve! A real Christian will serve God now more than he ever served the law previously. The difference is that now we serve in the newness of the Spirit and not in the oldness of the letter.

You have heard of people observing "the letter of the law." They are rigid and hard and unhappy. I am not trying to be in any way derogatory or denigrating, but you do not normally see any strict Orthodox Jews laughing and smiling and cutting up and having a good time. Even though the Temple and the Holy of Holies and the sacrifices are gone, they are still trying their best to serve in the oldness of the letter, and it is not producing any joy or life or vibrancy within them.

But when a person gets saved, all of that changes. We now serve and love doing it! We love coming to church, we love feeding the hungry, we love giving, we love worshipping, we love cutting the grass for those who are shut in, we love reading the Bible, we love praying, we love running buses and bringing boys and girls to Jesus. There is now a life to what we do, and it is all because we have a marriage after death.

A misuse of the law

Romans 7:7 *What shall we say then? Is the law sin? God forbid. Nay, I had not known sin, but by the law: for I had not known lust, except the law had said, Thou shalt not covet.*

Both the Lord Jesus Christ and the apostles had an accusation that was very commonly leveled against them. They were accused of being against the law of Moses and of trying to overturn it. Paul was certainly aware of this, and even though it was not true, he quite often took time to clarify and explain his position on the subject. And this is one of those times.

After using terms like "delivered from the law," he knew that people might think that he thought that the law was evil, that it maybe even was sin! And so, for the sixth time in the book, he took time to say, "God forbid." He will end up saying this five more times in the book of Romans. There are certain things that he wanted all of us to clearly understand. And one of those things was that the law was not a bad thing but a good thing.

Did Paul write then and have I written here about the law being a harsh thing? Yes, we did. But God designed it to serve an essential purpose. He designed the law to help us know sin and our own sinfulness. It was that very law that taught us just how incredibly wrong and wicked we were and let us know just how desperately in need of help we were.

According to verse seven, mankind really cannot know sin as an internal matter. In other words, there is nothing inside of us that can infallibly identify that which is wrong. We needed an outside source to tell us what was wrong. You see, all of mankind's internal sources vacillate and change. There was a time when mankind thought it was perfectly acceptable to have slaves. Most people do not think that way anymore. There was a time in Nazi Germany when the bulk of a modern nation believed that it was acceptable to murder six million people. Even people in Germany do not believe that anymore. It used to be that Americans had enough sense to know that it was wrong to harm a baby, but since about 1973 in our nation, it has somehow been viewed as acceptable to murder tens of millions of innocent babies. So again, I say there is nothing inside of us that can infallibly identify that which is wrong because all of our internal sources vacillate and change. We need an external source, a moral authority to let us know on an infallible basis what is right and what is wrong, and that is what Paul was talking about when he said *I had not known sin, but by the law: for I had not known lust, except the law had said, Thou shalt not covet.*

Our external moral authority is God, and the code of behavior that He set down for us prior to Calvary was the law.

Romans 7:8 *But sin, taking occasion by the commandment, wrought in me all manner of concupiscence. For without the law sin was dead.*

Everything that God ever made or built, our sin nature has sought to twist and warp. Sin, our sin nature, uses the commandments of God to say, in effect, "If God is telling you no, it must be really good, so let's do it!" It is the old "don't stick your hand in the cookie jar" dilemma. You have to tell the children not to get in the cookie jar, but as soon as you tell them that, their mind is now focused on the cookie jar.

Paul said that sin, taking occasion [*Aphormayn labousa,* seizing an opportunity] by the commandment, wrought in me all manner of concupiscence. Not many of us run around using the word "concupiscence" anymore. It is from the word *epithumia*; it is often translated as the word lust, and in this case, it means *an extreme craving for that which is wrong.* Without the law, sin was dead. In other words, before there was a law, there was not that moral authority written down to give life to and stir up our desires for those things that were wrong. But once the law was spelled out for us, our sin nature began to automatically crave all of the things that God had placed off limits to us.

Romans 7:9 *For I was alive without the law once: but when the commandment came, sin revived, and I died.*

Romans 7:9 is an essential verse of Scripture that is hardly ever mentioned. But I want you to get it and the truth that it teaches because there are some foundational things found in this verse.

Paul said that there was a time once when he was alive without the law. I have a question: when was that? Any guesses?

There is only one time in a person's life when he is alive without law. That is when they are alive without the ability to understand right and wrong. In other words, infants or people who are severely mentally impaired. Those individuals are alive without an understanding of the law, and therefore, they are not responsible before God for the keeping of the law. They are not saved, but they are *safe*.

There is a very good phrase that we use that is not found in the Bible, but the teaching of it is found in the Bible. That phrase is "the age of accountability." Just like the word rapture, and the word Trinity, and the word grandfather for that matter, the words "the age of accountability" are not found in Scripture, but the doctrine is. There is such a thing biblically as the age of accountability. Paul was once alive without the law, and you and I were once alive without the law. But Paul said there came a day when the commandment came, sin revived, and he died. He died to innocence and found himself alive under the law, which made him dead while he lived.

For these precious babies that we have in our midst, there will come a day when they will grow up enough to understand right and wrong and their need to accept Christ as their Savior. At that point, the seeds of sin that they have had within them since conception "revive," they literally "come to life," and they, at that point, become spiritually dead.

This is not a biological age. The Bible does not specify whether the age of accountability comes at age fifteen or seventeen or twenty-one, or any age in particular. It is not a biological age; it is a mental and spiritual age. It is the age of understanding to a degree of being fully responsible for what you now know and having the Holy Spirit through that convict your heart of your sinfulness and your need before God.

Romans 7:10 *And the commandment, which was ordained to life, I found to be unto death.*

The specific commandment that Paul mentioned in verse seven, and every other one that went with it as well, was *ordained to life*, meaning that they had life as their ultimate goal. This encompassed how they were to live and that if they kept the commandments, they would be allowed to keep on living. And in theory, if anyone could ever have kept the law perfectly, it would have led to eternal life. I say "in theory" because such a theoretical human never did exist and never could exist, and that was very much the point the entire time. So, instead of life, because of our sinfulness, the commandments that were aimed toward life ended up condemning us to death.

Romans 7:11 *For sin, taking occasion by the commandment, deceived me, and by it slew me.*

Verse eleven takes us right back to the illustration of the cookie jar. Our sin, seeing that the commandment not to do something has produced in us a desire to do it, tricks us into doing it by telling us how wonderful it will be and then destroys us. It did that to all of us through the sin of Adam, and it continues to do it to all of us through our own individual sins as well.

Romans 7:12 *Wherefore the law is holy, and the commandment holy, and just, and good.*

Has the law done anything wrong? No. There is nothing wrong with the law. The law is fine. The law could not help to save us, but the law also did nothing wrong. All of it, in general, is holy, and the specific commandment he just mentioned in verse seven (thou shalt not covet) and elaborated on in verses eight through eleven is holy and also just and good. The law did not make us sin; our sin merely used the law as a lure to tempt us to sin.

Romans 7:13 *Was then that which is good made death unto me? God forbid. But sin, that it might appear sin, working death in me by that which is good; that sin by the commandment might become exceeding sinful.*

That which is good in verse thirteen is the exact same good thing he was talking about in verse twelve, the law. Paul knew that, in saying what he just said, people would object that the law, which God designed for life, had become the source of death for Paul, meaning that God somehow messed up pretty badly in His plans. To that, Paul once again objects with *God forbid!* He then goes on to point out that it was sin, not the law, that brought death; the law merely shined the light on all of it, making it to *appear sin* and *become exceedingly sinful.*

The purpose of the law was not to harm us. The purpose of the law was to present such a stark contrast between holiness and non-holiness that we would immediately be able to recognize the exceeding sinfulness of sin. When we look at all of the commandments of God, especially through the Old Testament, we cannot escape the fact that we are a lot more sinful than we think we are. And the fact that the law teaches us that is actually a very good thing.

A man with a problem

Romans 7:14 *For we know that the law is spiritual: but I am carnal, sold under sin.*

It is at this point in the text that Paul does a very remarkable thing. Paul had no problem with preaching to and at others, but he is now, along with pointing the finger at others, pointing squarely at himself.

The law is not wicked. The law is spiritual. The law is right. Paul basically said, "The law is not the problem; **I am**." Paul said that he, and we, by the way, are carnal, sold under sin. The word carnal means *fleshly.* My biggest problem is me, and your biggest problem is you. We fleshly people are *sold under sin.*

Paul was saved! But here he said that even as a saved man, he is presently carnal, presently sold under sin. He did not say that he was; he said that he is. Sold under sin is a pretty stark term; it indicates being sold as a slave under the bondage of another.

Has Paul not very clearly, up to this point in the book of Romans, made it known that he is a saved person, that he is no longer under the law but under grace, and that he is redeemed and justified? Yes, he most certainly has. But do you know what every saved person is? A person with a problem. Our inner man has been redeemed and set free; our outer man, though, is still struggling with a master who does not want to let go.

There is some good news. The problem that we presently have is much smaller than the problem that we used to have. The fact that we are right now having to struggle against sin in our lives is a much smaller problem than the fact that we used to not be struggling at all and were merrily making our way to hell! Nonetheless, it is a problem, and it does need to be dealt with.

Romans 7:15 *For that which I do I allow not: for what I would, that do I not; but what I hate, that do I.*

Let's take a second and define a word in this verse so that we do not misunderstand it, and that word is the word *allow*. When we think of the word allow, we think of *to permit*. But there is another usage of the word allow. The old-timers would often say something to the effect of, "I'll allow you that." What they meant was, "I understand that."

That is the way the word is used here. It is from the word *ginosko,* which means to understand or to perceive. Paul was saying, "I don't understand the things that I do!" He said, "The things that I want to do, I don't do, but the things that I hate the very thought of, I do."

This is a man with a problem. And every one of us are just like him. The fact that we have been born again does not change the fact that we, like Paul, are carnal, sold under sin. Paul still had his flesh to deal with, and we still have our flesh to deal with. Once again, our biggest jeopardy is not jeopardy from without, it is jeopardy from within.

Romans 7:16 *If then I do that which I would not, I consent unto the law that it is good.*

The fact that since salvation Paul did not want to do the bad things that he ended up doing but wanted to obey God's law instead was a testimony to the fact that the law is good, and he knew it, and we know it. We, as Christians, struggle with sin in our lives. Do you know how that makes us different from those who are not Christians? They do not struggle at all! A sinner can point-blank sin, and as long as there are no immediate consequences to it, they are usually fine with it.

Romans 7:17 *Now then it is no more I that do it, but sin that dwelleth in me.*

There is another very essential doctrine found in this often-overlooked verse of Scripture. A person who is saved is a person who has a dual nature. Paul was not just Paul; he was at the same time Paul the justified and Paul the flesh.

In a rather unique way, things become more complex for us after salvation. Before we are saved, we have only one nature. Our body is lost, our soul is lost, our spirit is lost. Another way to put it is we are lost both on the outside and on the inside. But when we get saved, our inner man, our soul and spirit, gets saved. Our flesh, though, stays lost. We who are saved are now a saved inner man wrapped in a lost outer man. We now have a struggle in this area of sin. Again, it did not use to be a struggle at all because we were okay with sin both on the outside and on the inside. But now that we are saved, there is at least a struggle. Now that we are saved, there is at least a part of us that wants to do right. When we do sin, just like Paul, it is *no more I that do it,* it is *sin that dwelleth in me,* in my flesh.

Romans 7:18 *For I know that in me (that is, in my flesh,) dwelleth no good thing: for to will is present with me; but how to perform that which is good I find not.*

Paul the apostle was one of the greatest, godliest, most spiritual men who ever lived, yet his evaluation of his own flesh was that there was not one good thing in it. If there was not any good thing in Paul's flesh, then there is also nothing good in my flesh or in your flesh. Simply put, you better not trust yourself as far as you can throw yourself. You may be saved, but you are going to have to struggle against the desires of your flesh until the day that you breathe your last breath and wake up in heaven without that putrid sin nature. You may want to do right; Paul did. He said, *To will is present with me.* But he then said, *how to perform that which is good I find not.*

Every child of God carries his or her own worst enemy with them wherever they go. Not to skip too far ahead in the book Romans, but it is that exact reason that Paul said this:

141

Romans 13:14 *But put ye on the Lord Jesus Christ, and make not provision for the flesh, to fulfil the lusts thereof.*

Paul was a very spiritual man, and he believed in justification. But he was also a very practical man, and he understood the necessity of boxing in our flesh and not giving ourselves a chance to do wrong.

Romans 7:19 *For the good that I would I do not: but the evil which I would not, that I do.* **20** *Now if I do that I would not, it is no more I that do it, but sin that dwelleth in me.*

It is very clear that Paul's desires changed once he got saved. Some of the old desires still cropped up and gave him trouble, but there was a war against them where there used to be no fight at all. And when he lost that fight, as he surely did from time to time, he recognized, according to verse twenty, that it was not even him that did it anymore, but sin that dwelt in him. Your inner man (your redeemed soul and spirit), that "new you" that you became upon salvation, never does actually sin. It is always that old you contained in your flesh that does the sinning.

Romans 7:21 *I find then a law, that, when I would do good, evil is present with me.*

There is a bit of a riddle in this verse, and it would do us good to work our way through it. Paul said that whenever he wanted to do good, evil was present with him. In other words, if he was on top of a mountain and wanted to do good, evil was present with him. But if he left the mountain and went down to the sea and wanted to do good, evil was still present with him. But if he left the sea and went into the middle of the desert and wanted to do good, evil was still present with him. So here is the riddle: how is that even possible?

The only way it is possible is that he was carrying that evil with him everywhere he went. And he was. As a matter of fact, he was walking around in it, and you are as well. Anywhere that you go and take your body with you, you are taking evil with you.

This lets us know that you could lock yourself away in a monastery without any television, internet, radio, computer, or literature and still find a way to sin. Are we not supposed to be boxing in our flesh like we just said? Yes, absolutely. But we are not then to think that we are automatically guaranteed victory over sin in our lives. We will not have ultimate and final victory until we are removed from these sinful bodies and given a glorified, non-sinful body.

That may not sound very encouraging, but there is one part of this verse that I personally find extremely encouraging. Paul said that this was a *law*. In other words, it is something that is true for everybody. Do you struggle against sin and often get discouraged because you feel like you are losing? Let me suggest something to encourage you. The next time you go to church, look to your right… look your left… and realize that you are not alone. Other people are struggling just like you are. And by the way, that ought to serve as a really good motivation to pray for one another.

Romans 7:22 *For I delight in the law of God after the inward man:*

Here is the crucial difference between the lost person and the saved person. Both the lost and the saved have a sinful flesh. But what the saved has that the lost does not have is an inward man who delights in the law of God, an inward man who desires to always do right no matter what the circumstances. That is the supernatural product of being born again.

Romans 7:23 *But I see another law in my members, warring against the law of my mind, and bringing me into captivity to the law of sin which is in my members.*

Paul delighted in the law of God in his inner man. But in verse twenty-three, he harkens back once again to what he mentioned in verse twenty-one, the fact that in his members, in his flesh, there was an entirely different law, warring against the law of his mind and bringing him into captivity to the law of sin which was still in his members, in his flesh, in his body.

In other words, brethren, you are redeemed and pure on the inside, but your flesh is not redeemed, and it has not gotten the memo that the battle is over, so it is just going to keep on fighting. Does that sound a bit discouraging? If it does, realize that you are not the only one that felt that way:

Romans 7:24 *O wretched* [*talaiporos*, absolutely miserable] *man that I am! who shall deliver me from the body of this death?*

Anyone who is so foolish as to believe the false doctrine of sinless perfection cannot possibly be paying attention to what Paul has said. Paul did not call himself sinlessly perfect; he called himself wretched! He called his flesh *the body of this death*! He recognized that even though he was saved, he was going to be in a battle against sin for the rest of his life. He knew that he was justified; he knew that he was going to heaven no matter what. But that salvation, that justification, produced in him a desire to live holy and pure and sinless now. And anyone that claims to be saved is going to be just like that. There is a word we can use to accurately describe a person who claims to be saved and yet does not have the desire to live holy and pure and right and does not despise it when they do wrong. That word is "lost."

Romans 7:25 *I thank God through Jesus Christ our Lord. So then with the mind I myself serve the law of God; but with the flesh the law of sin.*

You may think that after twenty-four verses of battling and battling and battling that Paul would be down in the dumps and discouraged. But he ended this chapter by saying, "I thank God…"

What was he so thankful for? What did he even have to be thankful for? What he had to be thankful for was the clear understanding that the main battle had already been won. His inner man (which he here calls the mind) and outer man had been separated, and even though he would always have to fight to keep the outer man pure, the fight for the inner man was over. Paul knew he was saved, he knew he was going to heaven, and he knew that nothing that he did in his flesh could change that.

Did that result in him living wickedly? Study his life! No one believed in the doctrine of eternal security any more firmly than Paul did, no one believed in complete justification any more than Paul did, but no one lived any more pure than he did either.

144

Your biggest problem and my biggest problem will always be what we carry around with us, our flesh. That is the bad news; we will always have our flesh to fight with and to deal with until we get to heaven. But it is also the good news. The inner man has already been justified, the battle for salvation is over, and no matter what happens from here on out, even if we slip and fall, one day, we are going to be just fine.

Chapter Eleven
K - Kinship with Christ and Its Effects

Romans 8:1 *There is therefore now no condemnation to them which are in Christ Jesus, who walk not after the flesh, but after the Spirit.* **2** *For the law of the Spirit of life in Christ Jesus hath made me free from the law of sin and death.* **3** *For what the law could not do, in that it was weak through the flesh, God sending his own Son in the likeness of sinful flesh, and for sin, condemned sin in the flesh:* **4** *That the righteousness of the law might be fulfilled in us, who walk not after the flesh, but after the Spirit.* **5** *For they that are after the flesh do mind the things of the flesh; but they that are after the Spirit the things of the Spirit.* **6** *For to be carnally minded is death; but to be spiritually minded is life and peace.* **7** *Because the carnal mind is enmity against God: for it is not subject to the law of God, neither indeed can be.* **8** *So then they that are in the flesh cannot please God.* **9** *But ye are not in the flesh, but in the Spirit, if so be that the Spirit of God dwell in you. Now if any man have not the Spirit of Christ, he is none of his.* **10** *And if Christ be in you, the body is dead because of sin; but the Spirit is life because of righteousness.* **11** *But if the Spirit of him that raised up Jesus from the dead dwell in you, he that raised up Christ from the dead shall also quicken your mortal bodies by his Spirit that dwelleth in you.* **12** *Therefore, brethren, we are debtors, not to the flesh, to live after the flesh.* **13** *For if ye live after the flesh, ye shall die: but if ye through the Spirit do mortify the deeds of the body, ye shall live.* **14** *For as many as are led by the Spirit of*

147

God, they are the sons of God. **15** *For ye have not received the spirit of bondage again to fear; but ye have received the Spirit of adoption, whereby we cry, Abba, Father.* **16** *The Spirit itself beareth witness with our spirit, that we are the children of God:* **17** *And if children, then heirs; heirs of God, and joint-heirs with Christ; if so be that we suffer with him, that we may be also glorified together.* **18** *For I reckon that the sufferings of this present time are not worthy to be compared with the glory which shall be revealed in us.*

You cannot be related to someone without it having some effects. I have blessings, benefits, and even quirks from being related to my wife, Dana, and her family.

There are effects to kinship. And there are definitely many and marvelous effects due to our kinship with Christ.

This passage, fourteen times growing stronger and stronger, references the fact that through salvation, we are now related to Christ. In verse one, we are *in Christ Jesus.* In verse nine, we are *in the Spirit.* In verse four, *the Spirit dwells in you.* In verse ten, it is *Christ in you.* In verse eleven, we find that *the Spirit that raised Jesus from the dead dwells in you.* In verse eleven, again, we read of *the Spirit in you.* In verse fourteen, *we are the sons of God.* In verse fifteen, we have *received the Spirit of adoption.* In verse fifteen again, we cry *Abba, father.* In verse sixteen, we are *the children of God.* In verse seventeen, we are *children.* In verse seventeen, we are *heirs.* In verse seventeen, we are *heirs of God.* In verse seventeen, again, we are *joint heirs with Christ.*

Let's hear it for being in God's family!

Kinship with Christ has effects on condemnation

Romans 8:1 *There is therefore now no condemnation to them which are in Christ Jesus, who walk not after the flesh, but after the Spirit.*

This is one of the most remarkable verses and remarkable promises in the entire Bible. This is apples of gold in pictures of silver. This is a small taste of the riches that we have through our salvation.

A marvelous two-part description is here given, and we who are saved are the ones being described.

We who are saved are first of all described as being in Christ, and therefore uncondemned. There is no more secure spot anywhere in the universe.

During the Cold War, it was fashionable for people who had wealth to build themselves nuclear fallout bunkers. These were big concrete underground chambers designed to protect a family from the end-of-the-world cataclysm of nuclear war. But I have often wondered why people, even back then, could not see a huge flaw in the thinking behind it, namely that you have to come out sometime! There is no bunker in the world big enough to sustain the family in food and water and air forever, and when you come out, you are going to be destroyed by the nuclear fallout.

But when a person is in Christ, they never have to come out, and every need is supplied.

You can be in a church without being in Christ. You can be in a state of relative morality without being in Christ. You can be in the United States of America, the greatest nation on earth, without being in Christ. You will find there is no real security in being in church, or in a state of relative morality, or in America. The only certain security that you will ever have is to be in Christ, and that only happens when a person is born again.

We who are saved are in Christ.

We are secondly described as those who walk not after the flesh but after the spirit.

A saved person walks in conformity to what God expects. A lost person walks according to what his flesh desires. A saved person's final authority is God's Word. A lost person's final authority is his or her own opinion.

We who are saved are right now at this very moment forever and completely delivered from condemnation. A lost person right now, this very moment, is under the condemnation of God because they have no kinship with Christ.

The saved are free! We are forever secure, forever safe because we are forever set free from condemnation (John 5:24).

149

Before moving on, we should say a word about how the second half of this verse is to be regarded. It must either be regarded as an expectation to be met or as a position in which we reside. In other words, it either means that our freedom from condemnation is dependent on walking right and doing right, or it means that since we are in Christ Jesus and free from condemnation, we will walk right and do right.

With Scripture interpreting Scripture, there is no question as to which of the two uses is correct. Good works never produce salvation (Ephesians 2:8-9, Titus 3:5), but salvation always produces good works (Titus 2:11-14). Furthermore, what one-half of the verse is referring to must also be what the second half of the verse is referring to; there is no justification for making them refer to different things. In other words, either our good works produce a state in which we are in Christ Jesus and are therefore uncondemned, or the fact that we are in Christ Jesus and uncondemned produces good works.

Both of the descriptions given of a child of God in this verse are a result of the fact that we are in kinship with Christ. The fact that we have been saved means that we are uncondemned and that we walk not after the flesh but the Spirit.

From the rest of Scripture, especially the rest of the book of Romans, we know that the first half of that equation is absolutely perfect and complete, while the second half of that equation is a daily ongoing process. Paul regarded himself as completely saved, but he also lamented the fact that his flesh still behaved in an unsaved manner from time to time. Nonetheless, the general behavior of his life, and of everyone who is truly born again, will be a pure and righteous behavior.

Romans 8:2 *For the law of the Spirit of life in Christ Jesus hath made me free from the law of sin and death.*

Verse two begins to explain how the truth of verse one is even possible. Being in Christ has resulted in us being subjected to a higher law. We were in the lower court of sin and death when we were lost. Being saved, we are now found uncondemned in the highest court possible, the law of the Spirit of life in Christ Jesus. Everyone who is lost stands in the lower court condemned to die. But everyone who is saved stands in the highest court uncondemned and can never be sent back because the debt has been paid in full, and we are in Christ who paid the debt! Once the higher court has decided a matter, the lower court has no more jurisdiction.

Romans 8:3 *For what the law could not do, in that it was weak through the flesh, God sending his own Son in the likeness of sinful flesh, and for sin, condemned sin in the flesh:*

The old law's weakness is the fact that we, in our sinful flesh, could not keep it. Because of our sin, the old law condemned us. But since God the Son died for us, we are not condemned, our sin is! We and our sin used to be one— inseparable. God on the cross performed Holy Ghost surgery. He cut us apart from our sin, condemned the sin by taking it on Himself and taking it to Calvary with Him, and justified us.

Perhaps one of the most appropriate descriptions of sin to our modern minds would be that of a cancer growing inside of our body. It is not supposed to be there, and it is eventually going to grow to the point that it kills us. A surgeon will identify that cancer, open the body, and remove it, destroy it, and set us free.

But with sin, there is one essential difference. Sin was not able to be destroyed outside of a body, it had to be destroyed inside of a body, and to do that, the body had to be destroyed along with it. Therefore, the Lord Jesus Christ took our sin, our cancerous spiritual growth, cut it out of us, put it inside His own body, and then destroyed it on Calvary. Our immune system was flawed and weak and incapable of handling this but His was perfect; He was able to destroy our sin in His own body and yet live again.

Romans 8:4 *That the righteousness of the law might be fulfilled in us, who walk not after the flesh, but after the Spirit.*

In our sinful flesh, we could not fulfill the law as God demanded. God took our sin, gave us His righteousness, thus fulfilling the law's demands in us.

If the devil were to argue with God about this arrangement, it might go something like this:

Devil: They are not pure, God. Therefore, they must die!

God: They may not be pure, but they have purity.

Devil: Wait a minute, that is not their purity; that's your purity – I would recognize it anywhere!

God: But it is theirs now; I gave it to them!

The righteousness of the law can never be accomplished in us, but it can be *fulfilled* in us.

All of this means one essential thing: our kinship with Christ has affected our condemnation. In fact, it has affected it to such a degree that we are no longer condemned!

Our kinship with Christ has affected our carnality

Romans 8:5 *For they that are after the flesh do mind the things of the flesh; but they that are after the Spirit the things of the Spirit.*

There is a word that is in this verse twice, once spelled out and once implied, as opposed to a word that we might expect to appear in its place. I am talking about the word "do" as opposed to the word "should."

This verse says *For they that are after the flesh DO mind the things of the flesh; but they that are after the Spirit* [do mind] *the things of the spirit.*

We would expect it to say, "For they that are after the flesh SHOULD mind the things of the flesh; but they that are after the Spirit (should mind) the things of the spirit." Actually, to be even more precise, most people would expect it to say different things at each point, even though there is no logical or grammatical reason for it to do so. In other words, most people, even Christians, would expect the verse to read like this:

For they that are after the flesh DO mind the things of the flesh; but they that are after the Spirit [SHOULD mind] *the things of the spirit.*

But the fact that the verb in the first half of the verse is not stated in the second half of the verse, according to the laws of grammar, means that it is implied in the second half of the verse and must be exact. In other words, we have to understand the word *do* in both halves of the verse.

152

They that are after the flesh mind the things of the flesh, period. In other words, they set their minds on, they are intent on, the things of the flesh. A person who consistently follows the desires of the flesh is **lost**, period!

But they that are after the spirit, the saved, set their minds on, are intent on, the things of the Spirit. A saved person does what he or she never could truly do before; they follow after the desires of God because they are now His kin.

People, by their very nature, instinctively favor family. There is a lot of truth to the statement "blood is thicker than water."

When a person is truly born again, his closest family relation is to the Lord Jesus Christ, period. That is why a saved person normally lives in a spiritual manner rather than a carnal manner.

Romans 8:6 *For to be carnally minded is death; but to be spiritually minded is life and peace.*

There are certain things in Scripture that look so much alike that we need to be very careful to distinguish between them. One example of that is just how much a lost person and a saved carnal person look alike. Carnal, by the way, means fleshly, oriented to the desires of the body.

We know that it is entirely possible for a person who is genuinely born again to still be a carnal person because in 1 Corinthians 3:3, Paul spoke to the *brethren*, the saved, and he said to them, *"Ye are yet carnal."* That is why I said two paragraphs above that a saved person "normally" lives in a spiritual manner.

It is possible for a Christian to grow cold on God, be backslidden, give in to the desires of the flesh, and, therefore, behave him or herself in a carnal manner. When he does, he will look very much like a lost person. That being the case, when we come to Romans 8:6, we need to find out which of these two types of people Paul is talking about.

When Paul says, *For to be carnally minded is death*, he is not talking about a Christian who has backslidden into a state of carnality; he is talking about a lost person. Chapter eight begins by clearly describing the difference between a saved person and a lost person; the entire chapter deals with the difference between saved people and lost people; the entire chapter emphasizes the blessings and benefits that we have by being saved as opposed to the blessings and benefits that the lost do not have because they are not saved.

Once we understand that, we can begin to grasp what verse six is teaching.

When Paul says, *For to be carnally minded is death; but to be spiritually minded is life and peace,* he is letting us know that the very way a lost person thinks will lead them to death, not just any death, but spiritual death, death that is contrasted with the life and peace produced by one who is spiritually minded.

In other words, a lost person ends up going to hell because they think like a lost person. They think they can be good enough on their own; they think they can be moral enough to please God. They think they are evolving upward into godhood; they think there is no such thing as literal judgment. They think, they think, they think, and most of the things they think are wrong. The things that they think and that they are so certain of keep them from accepting Christ as their Savior.

But when a person gets saved, they become spiritually minded, and that produces life and peace—peace right now, abundant life now, followed by eternal life forever (John 10:10).

Romans 8:7 *Because the carnal mind is enmity against God: for it is not subject to the law of God, neither indeed can be.*

We established just one verse ago that when we are speaking of the carnal person in this passage, we are talking about a lost man. But please understand that the principles apply pretty well to the backslidden carnal Christian also. Those two look alike, and they think alike.

In verse seven, Paul begins to describe something about the carnal mind. The carnal mind, especially in the lost person, is opposed to God. The carnal mind is not only not subject to the law of God, it cannot be subject to the law of God. You can argue with a lost person until you are blue in the face, and they will still never be able to fully submit themselves to the desires of God. Their mind rebels against it.

Take your Bible and sit down with a homosexual sometime, go through the very clear passages of Scripture showing how opposed God is to that lifestyle, and see just how willing they are, see how able they are, to submit themselves to the will of God on this matter.

Take your Bible and sit down with an adulterer some time, go through the very clear passages of Scripture showing how opposed God is to that lifestyle, and see just how willing they are, see how able they are, to submit themselves to the will of God on this matter.

Take your Bible and sit down with a drunk sometime, go through the very clear passages of Scripture showing how opposed God is to that lifestyle, and see just how willing they are, see how able they are, to submit themselves to the will of God on this matter.

The carnal mind is not friendly toward God or toward His word or toward His house or toward His man or toward His beliefs or toward His authority. The carnal mind is enmity against God. Until a person submits to God in salvation, they will not likely submit in much of anything else.

Romans 8:8 *So then they that are in the flesh cannot please God.*

The truth of this verse is hated and despised by modern religious sinners. You see, religion is actually very popular among sinners. There are churches left and right where a charlatan minister will stand before hundreds and perhaps even thousands of people, open the Bible, twist it like a pretzel, and tell people that every sin they are engaging in is wonderful as long as they love Jesus. Now, they clearly do not love Jesus, but they actually believe that they are trying to please God.

They will give to the poor... They will feed the hungry... They will tend to the sick... But the one thing they cannot do is actually please God. Without being born again, you are still in

155

the flesh, and no matter how good you think you are, you cannot please God.

You see, as long as you are in the flesh, as long as you are unsaved, then the one thing you have not done is to place yourself under God. And God will not have any rivals.

Romans 8:9 *But ye are not in the flesh, but in the Spirit, if so be that the Spirit of God dwell in you. Now if any man have not the Spirit of Christ, he is none of his.*

The last several verses have been necessarily negative and harsh. And that makes me so glad for the little three-letter conjunction that starts verse nine.

You who are saved may battle *with* your flesh, but you are not *in* the flesh. Your problems may be the same, but your position is definitely not the same. Paul said you are not in the flesh, but in the Spirit, if so be that the Spirit of God dwell in you.

We need to stop there for just a moment.

Do you understand the earth-shattering truth that is taught here? The Spirit of God, capital S, the third member of the Trinity, lives inside of a Christian. In fact, the last part of this verse tells us that if the Spirit of Christ is not inside a person, that person does not even belong to God; he is not saved.

There is a foundational doctrinal truth in this verse that you need to grasp and that is the truth of the indwelling of the Holy Spirit of God.

The scoffer will say that there is no Holy Spirit. But this verse says that there is a Holy Spirit and that if you do not have Him living inside of you, you are not saved.

The charismatic will tell you that after you are saved you then need to receive the Holy Ghost. But this verse says that if you have not already received the Holy Ghost, you are not even saved.

The moment you get born again, the Holy Ghost of God indwells you. You may not realize it, you most definitely will not fully understand it, but there will be something inside of you that changes your outlook and your desires and your direction. That something, or Someone rather, is the Holy Ghost of God.

156

And when the Holy Ghost of God comes to live inside of you, when Jesus the Son of God gives you His Holy Spirit, He will begin the push to change your behavior from that of a carnal person to that of a spiritual person.

Our kinship with Christ has affected our corruption

Romans 8:10 *And if Christ be in you, the body is dead because of sin; but the Spirit is life because of righteousness.*

All through this chapter, we continually see the contrast between flesh and spirit. We see it again in this verse, only this time, Paul uses the word body when he is talking about our flesh. He begins by saying *and if Christ be in you*, and that lets us know that he is still talking to people who are saved and telling them what has happened because they got saved.

If Christ be in you, the body, the flesh, the old you, is dead because of sin. In other words, the old you could not remain alive, and you still get born again. God does not let a person remain alive as the sinner that he was and yet be a child of God. When you got saved, the old you died because of the sin that you had been living in.

But by contrast, when you got saved, Paul says that the Spirit is life because of righteousness. In other words, that Holy Spirit that verse nine says came to live inside of you when you got saved produces life in you because of righteousness. Not because of our righteousness, we did not have any of that, but because of Christ's righteousness.

A simple way of putting all of this is that when you got saved, you got changed. And if you did not get changed, you did not get saved. Obviously, the change will be far more drastic and notable in an adult drunk than in a child who was raised in church, but there will be a change, nonetheless.

Romans 8:11 *But if the Spirit of him that raised up Jesus from the dead dwell in you, he that raised up Christ from the dead shall also quicken your mortal bodies by his Spirit that dwelleth in you.*

Once again, in this verse, we see the foundational doctrinal truth that we saw in verse nine, namely the truth of the indwelling Spirit of God. Twice in the space of three verses, God clearly taught the doctrine of the indwelling Spirit of God. Do not ever let anyone talk you out of your rock-solid belief in the indwelling Spirit of God in the heart of every believer.

In verse ten, Paul mentioned the body being dead. He was using that as somewhat of a metaphor, which is certainly true, but that metaphor would absolutely get them and us thinking about literal physical death. Getting saved does not mean that you are not going to die. And truthfully, even though it is wonderful news that our inner man, our spirit, has been made alive, we all have to admit that we have gotten attached to this "skin stuff."

And that makes verse eleven very good news to us. The same Spirit of God that raised Jesus Christ physically and bodily from the dead and that lives in your heart will also raise your physical body from the dead. Look how Paul put it when writing to the believers in Corinth.

1 Corinthians 15:50 *Now this I say, brethren, that flesh and blood cannot inherit the kingdom of God; neither doth corruption inherit incorruption.* **51** *Behold, I shew you a mystery; We shall not all sleep, but we shall all be changed,* **52** *In a moment, in the twinkling of an eye, at the last trump: for the trumpet shall sound, and the dead shall be raised incorruptible, and we shall be changed.* **53** *For this corruptible must put on incorruption, and this mortal must put on immortality.* **54** *So when this corruptible shall have put on incorruption, and this mortal shall have put on immortality, then shall be brought to pass the saying that is written, Death is swallowed up in victory.*

God was not just interested in our souls but also in our bodies. Again, when you got saved and when I got saved, the Holy Ghost of God came to live inside of our bodies. Here is something else Paul said to the Corinthians that supported what he was saying here to the Romans:

1 Corinthians 6:19 *What? know ye not that your body is the temple of the Holy Ghost which is in you, which ye have of God, and ye are not your own?* **20** *For ye are bought with a* *price: therefore glorify God in your body, and in your spirit, which are God's.*

Since the Holy Ghost of God has been living inside our bodies, it stands to reason that He actually thinks highly of our bodies! As such, He is going to do something very special for and with our bodies. He is going to raise our bodies back from the dead, make them perfect and flawless and eternal, put our soul and spirit back into them, and we are going to get to enjoy all of eternity as a soul and spirit living forever inside a perfect, healthy, flawless body.

The corruption that seizes our body and causes it to die and decay is handled by our kinship with Christ. We have a benefit that the lost person does not have. The lost person is going to have to endure an eternity in hell feeling the things that a body would feel but not actually having a body. Their body is corrupt and is going to decay back to dust, and it is going to stay dust. But because of our kinship with Christ, we get to have a body forever.

Romans 8:12 *Therefore, brethren, we are debtors, not to the flesh, to live after the flesh. 13 For if ye live after the flesh, ye shall die: but if ye through the Spirit do mortify the deeds of the body, ye shall live.*

In verse twelve, Paul addresses the concept of us being debtors to our flesh. In case that sounds a bit odd, let me give you an illustration that will help you understand it. Each time that you sit down to watch television and you see a commercial where someone is guzzling a beer and the commercial says something along the lines of, "You owe yourself a really good beer," what you are being told is that you are a debtor to your flesh and that you have to live after the flesh.

But if you are a born-again child of God, you owe your flesh nothing! You and I owe everything to God and nothing to our flesh.

A lost person will live according to the desires of his or her flesh. A saved person, though, through the power of the Holy Ghost living in us, will mortify, he will put to death, the deeds

159

of the body. A person who does this does so because they are saved, and they will live like it.

Kinship with Christ has effects both on physical and spiritual corruption.

Our kinship with Christ has affected our communication

Romans 8:14 *For as many as are led by the Spirit of God, they are the sons of God.*

There is a clear and noticeable difference between those led by their own flesh and those led by the Holy Spirit of God. If a person is submitting himself to the Spirit of God, his life will line up with the Scripture; he will be clearly identifiable as a son of God. You cannot be lost and be led by the Spirit, because you have no kinship with Christ, and therefore, no communication with the Holy Spirit.

When you begin to consider this concept of being related to God, that sounds fairly intimidating. In fact, it sounds like we should be cowering back, scared to death to be around this God of all power. Who can imagine having God the Father as your father? But look at what the next verse says.

Romans 8:15 *For ye have not received the spirit of bondage again to fear; but ye have received the Spirit of adoption, whereby we cry, Abba, Father.*

When a person is lost and yet desperately trying to please God and stay out of Hell, it is the spirit of bondage, and it is a frightening kind of life. Who knows whether your good deeds are eventually going to outweigh your bad deeds? Who knows if you are going to die in one of those moments when you are doing good or in one of those moments when you are doing bad? That is a frightening way to live.

But that is not what we were given when we got saved. When we got saved, we were given the Spirit of adoption. We were brought into God's family just like we were a precious child that He went somewhere to pick out. We can now refer to him as our Abba, Father. That word Abba is a term of tenderness.

160

It is something a child would say as he or she was crawling up into a daddy's lap.

My daughter, Karis, began to speak very early. When she was just a little thing of maybe fourteen or fifteen months, I was sitting back in a lounge chair, and without any fear whatsoever, she crawled up into the chair with me, laid on my chest looking up at me and said, "What's up?"

I was old enough and big enough and strong enough to crush that child. But that thought never even crossed my mind. She had no reason to be afraid whatsoever because she was my baby, and I was her abba, father. She was able to communicate with me that freely and that fearlessly because of our kinship. You and I are able to communicate just that freely and just that fearlessly with God because of our kinship with Christ.

Romans 8:16 *The Spirit itself beareth witness with our spirit, that we are the children of God:*

We have been for a few verses now dealing with the fact that our kinship with Christ has affected our communication. A very essential form of that communication is found in verse sixteen. This is an incredibly important verse of Scripture, and there is an incredibly important truth taught within it.

Paul said that *the Spirit itself beareth witness with our spirit, that we are the children of God.* There is a minor matter in this verse and a major matter in this verse. The minor matter that we should deal with is the neuter pronoun. In this verse, the Spirit is referred to as an "it." But we are very clearly talking about the Spirit of God, the third member of the Trinity. Because this verse uses that neuter pronoun in regard to the Holy Spirit, many of the cults say that the Holy Spirit of God is not the third member of the Trinity. In fact, they say that He is just some impersonal force; He is not actually a person. He is just an it.

There is only one of two possible options concerning why the cults say this. Those options are as follows: they are either ignorant or dishonest. Anyone willing to do even the slightest amount of study in the grammar of this verse will very quickly be able to find out why the Holy Spirit of God is called an "it" here, while He is in other places referred to as a person.

161

The Greek language utilizes three genders for words: masculine, feminine, and neuter.

The word spirit is a neuter word. That is the only reason the word *it* is used here. It does not in any way indicate that the Holy Spirit of God is not, in fact, a person. We find in the Bible that the Holy Spirit can be lied to; we find in the Bible that the Holy Spirit can be grieved; we find that the Holy Spirit makes intercession for us; we find that the Holy Spirit told men what to write when it came to the writing of Scripture; the Holy Spirit of God clearly proved Himself to be a person over and over and over in Scripture.

The major matter in this verse, though, is what the Holy Spirit of God does for us. It may even be better to put it this way: the major matter in this verse is what the Holy Spirit of God does along with us.

Look at this verse one more time.

Romans 8:16 *The Spirit itself beareth witness with our spirit, that we are the children of God:*

Verse fifteen showed us calling God our Abba, Father. He painted a picture for us of a child with enough confidence to crawl up into the lap of his or her father. It is in the context of that thought that the Bible says that *the Spirit itself beareth witness with our spirit, that we are the children of God.*

Many years ago, when I was in Bible College, a good and well-meaning preacher came through to preach chapel. He preached that day on the assurance of salvation. He said that he wanted to help people who were doubting their salvation to be able to not doubt it if, in fact, they actually had it. He listed a great many biblical proofs of salvation, and all of them were right. Until, that is, he got to this exact verse.

When he got to this verse, he proclaimed that this was the most important of all the assurances of salvation. He said that it would be possible to make a mistake on all the others, but that this is one that we could never make a mistake on, because it is just too perfect. He said that this verse teaches that the Holy Spirit of God that lives inside of us will tell us that we are saved.

That sounds very good, but would you please look with me at the exact wording of this verse:

Romans 8:16 *The Spirit itself beareth witness* **with** *our spirit, that we are the children of God:*

This verse did not say that the Spirit bears witness *to* our spirit, it says that He bears witness *with* our spirit. What does the verse just previous to this one say that we are doing? It says that we are already calling God our Abba, Father. It says that we have already received the Spirit of adoption. Does there appear to be any doubt in that verse that would lead to our needing any assurance? No, none at all.

If we take this verse to mean that we draw our assurance of salvation from the Spirit that is inside of us talking to the spirit that is inside us, do you know what that boils down to? A feeling.

Do you really want to depend on a feeling? This is your eternal soul we are talking about; this is heaven or hell we are talking about. Do you really want to depend on a feeling or an emotion or something inside of you saying something to something inside of you?

This verse does not say that the Holy Spirit bears witness to us; it says that He bears witness *with* us. The implication is that we already have the assurance of our salvation based on something else entirely and that the Holy Ghost of God is adding to our witness before someone else. The word that it comes from, *summartureo*, means to bear witness along with another. It means to stand and testify to what someone else is standing and testifying of. Can the working and the leading and the fruit-producing of the Holy Spirit in our lives add an additional measure of the assurance of salvation to us? Certainly. One cannot have the third member of the Trinity living inside of him without noticing the effects.

But in this verse, the Holy Spirit of God is not testifying of our salvation to us; He is testifying of our salvation to God the Father, into whose lap we are so boldly crawling! Does God the Father not already know? Certainly, He does, but that does not stop the Holy Ghost from testifying on our behalf anyway.

Let me ask you this: does God the Father not already know that we have been redeemed and that our sins have been forgiven? Then why does **1 John 2:2** say that *we have an advocate with the father, Jesus Christ the righteous*? Why would we need an advocate if God the Father already knows?

What it boils down to is this: each member of the Godhead plays a role, or maybe even multiple roles, in our salvation, and They will fulfill those roles perfectly. The role of the Son was to pay for our salvation. The role of the Spirit, among other things, is to convict us so that we can be saved, to seal us once we have been saved, and to testify before the Father that we are saved.

My salvation and your salvation is something that we can be assured of, but not based on any internal feeling. You cannot trust your feelings, nor can I. Many people have been quite certain that the Holy Ghost of God was telling them to do something when clearly the Holy Ghost of God had absolutely nothing to do with it. What they were doing was trusting the feeling and assuming that that feeling came from the Holy Ghost.

My salvation and your salvation is something that we can be assured of based one hundred percent on what Scripture says. God is not a liar, has never been a liar, and will never be a liar. If we do it the Bible way, then we can trust what the Bible says on the subject. If you got saved the way that the Bible tells you that you had to get saved, and if you became that new creature in Christ that 2 Corinthians 5:17 talks about, you have all the proof you will ever need of your salvation.

By the way, John 16 tells us that it is the Holy Ghost's job to reprove the world of sin, and that word reprove means to convict or to convince of a fact. It does not mean that it is His job to cause a person to have nagging doubts. If the Holy Ghost of God is really convicting you of the fact that you are lost and need to be saved, then you will know for certain that you are lost and need to be saved.

There is someone I know who is in the business of causing nagging doubts. That would be the devil. The very first thing he ever did when he confronted Eve was to place a doubt in her mind, "*Did God really say...*"

Let me tell you what I expect. I expect people who have truly been born again, I mean people who have repented of their sins and asked Jesus into their heart, not holding back, being honest about it, and truly having received Him into their heart, and having then the evidence in their life that they have truly been saved, I expect those people at some point to have nagging doubts. That is just the way the devil operates.

The smartest thing a Christian can ever do is make up his or her mind that he or she is going to study God's Word on the subject, and whatever the written Word of God says, they are going to believe it and place their confidence in it.

When you do that, you will find yourself so confident that you will be crying Abba, Father, and in a spiritual sense, crawling up into His lap and hugging Him. And it is at that point, when you do, that the Holy Spirit of God that is living inside of you will be standing right there with you before the Father saying, "Yes, Sir, he is right; he is, in fact, a child of Yours."

That is some pretty good communication.

Our relationship with Christ has affected our comparison

Romans 8:17 *And if children, then heirs; heirs of God, and joint-heirs with Christ; if so be that we suffer with him, that we may be also glorified together.*

Much of Romans deals with our legal standing before God. A short summary of that legal standing is this: our legal standing is identical to that of Christ.

We are children; we already saw that in verses fourteen, fifteen, and sixteen, and we see it again here. The Father of the Lord Jesus Christ is now our Father as well. We are also heirs; we have an inheritance coming to us. Our inheritance is not coming from some rich uncle somewhere; we are actually heirs of God. And not only are we heirs of God, we are joint heirs with Christ. His inheritance is also our inheritance. I cannot begin to wrap my mind around everything that entails, and I guarantee you that you cannot either, but we know it is going to be good.

Halfway through the verse, though, you can almost hear a balloon popping. Paul has just told us that we are joint heirs with Christ, and the very next thing he mentions is that we are going to suffer along with Christ.

This is not a qualification for us to be joint-heirs with Christ; it is an outgrowth of the fact that we are joint-heirs with Christ. In other words, in some way, shape, or form, a person accepting Christ as their Savior is somehow, someway, at some point going to directly lead to suffering. He suffered for us, and we are going to have the privilege of suffering for Him. Not everyone is going to burn at the stake, but every child of God who lives long enough after they have gotten saved is at some point going to suffer for Christ. And the longer you live after you have gotten saved, and the more conformed you become to the image of Christ as you live, the more suffering you are likely to endure.

But the verse does not end there. The sufferings of Christ led to Him being glorified, and our sufferings for Christ will also lead to us being glorified along with Him.

There will never be a person who suffers anything for the cause of Christ without Christ Himself noticing it. There will never be a person who is persecuted or slandered or ridiculed for the cause of Christ, that Christ does not glorify him because of it. When we get to heaven, the greatest heroes will be the ones who loved Christ enough to continue living for Him even while being persecuted and suffering because they were living for Him.

Romans 8:18 *For I reckon that the sufferings of this present time are not worthy to be compared with the glory which shall be revealed in us.*

There is that beautiful word "reckon" again that we have seen so many times thus far in the book of Romans. Paul said, "*I reckon...*"

It still means what it has always meant. It means to add it to an account, to bank on it. You could think of it in this verse as intentionally having confidence in it even when you do not really feel like it.

Paul, who suffered more for Christ than any of us will ever suffer for Christ, who was beaten and shipwrecked and stoned and tortured and then martyred for Christ, said, "As far as I am concerned, the things that I am going through are not even worth comparing to the glory that I have coming to me..."

People who are undergoing suffering tend to focus on the suffering that they face.

But they are not worthy to be compared with the glory we will receive! We used to have to compare our troubles on earth with the hell that we were doomed to face. Now we can compare our troubles on earth with our glory in heaven and realize that there is no comparison.

The old song says, "It'll be better by and by," and believe me, brethren, it will be better by and by.

Our kinship with Christ has affected so many things. It has affected our condemnation, it has affected our carnality, it has affected our corruption, it has affected our communication, and it has affected our comparison. It is worth it to be in kinship with Christ; it is worth it to be saved. I wonder, do you have that kinship?

Chapter Twelve
L - Looking Ahead

Romans 8:19 *For the earnest expectation of the creature waiteth for the manifestation of the sons of God.* **20** *For the creature was made subject to vanity, not willingly, but by reason of him who hath subjected the same in hope,* **21** *Because the creature itself also shall be delivered from the bondage of corruption into the glorious liberty of the children of God.* **22** *For we know that the whole creation groaneth and travaileth in pain together until now.* **23** *And not only they, but ourselves also, which have the firstfruits of the Spirit, even we ourselves groan within ourselves, waiting for the adoption, to wit, the redemption of our body.* **24** *For we are saved by hope: but hope that is seen is not hope: for what a man seeth, why doth he yet hope for?* **25** *But if we hope for that we see not, then do we with patience wait for it.* **26** *Likewise the Spirit also helpeth our infirmities: for we know not what we should pray for as we ought: but the Spirit itself maketh intercession for us with groanings which cannot be uttered.* **27** *And he that searcheth the hearts knoweth what is the mind of the Spirit, because he maketh intercession for the saints according to the will of God.* **28** *And we know that all things work together for good to them that love God, to them who are the called according to his purpose.* **29** *For whom he did foreknow, he also did predestinate to be conformed to the image of his Son, that he might be the firstborn among many brethren.* **30** *Moreover whom he did predestinate, them he also called: and whom he called, them he also justified: and whom he justified,* *them he also glorified. 31 What shall we then say to these things? If God be for us, who can be against us? 32 He that spared not his own Son, but delivered him up for us all, how shall he not with him also freely give us all things? 33 Who shall lay any thing to the charge of God's elect? It is God that justifieth. 34 Who is he that condemneth? It is Christ that died, yea rather, that is risen again, who is even at the right hand of God, who also maketh intercession for us. 35 Who shall separate us from the love of Christ? shall tribulation, or distress, or persecution, or famine, or nakedness, or peril, or sword? 36 As it is written, For thy sake we are killed all the day long; we are accounted as sheep for the slaughter. 37 Nay, in all these things we are more than conquerors through him that loved us. 38 For I am persuaded, that neither death, nor life, nor angels, nor principalities, nor powers, nor things present, nor things to come, 39 Nor height, nor depth, nor any other creature, shall be able to separate us from the love of God, which is in Christ Jesus our Lord.*

Not much is as depressing as a person always looking back, never ahead. Paul was one who believed that Christians ought to be looking ahead, and he demonstrates that quite thoroughly in this passage of Scripture. Note the terms of looking ahead found in this text. In verse nineteen, we find the words *expectation* and *waiteth for*. In verse twenty, we find the phrase *in hope*. In verse twenty-one, we see the phrase *shall be delivered*. In verse twenty-three, we find the phrase *waiting for*. In verses twenty-four and twenty-five, we find the word *hope* listed five times. In verse twenty-five, we also find the phrase *wait for*.

It is evident that since Paul got saved, he was constantly and joyfully looking ahead.

The focus of our looking ahead

It is one thing to tell people not to dwell on the past; it is another thing entirely to tell them the things that they actually have to look forward to in the future. Notice the things that we have to look forward to in verses nineteen through twenty-five.

First is the manifestation of the sons of God.

Romans 8:19 *For the earnest expectation* [*apokarodokia*, a deep-seated, confident desire] *of the creature waiteth for the manifestation of the sons of God.*

Manifestation is from the word *apokolupsis*. It is related to our English word apocalypse, and it is where we get the word *revelation* from. It has to do with making something publicly known.

If you are saved, you are the *creature* being referenced in this verse. You are already a son of God right now, and one day, you will be *revealed* as such. The world looks at Christians these days as if they are three-eyed aliens at best or some kind of evil creatures at worst.

But that should not surprise you because that is pretty much how they looked at the Lord Jesus Christ as well. And just as He will one day be manifested as the Son of God, at that exact same time, we will be manifested as sons of God.

Romans 8:20 *For the creature was made subject to vanity, not willingly, but by reason of him who hath subjected the same in hope,*

The opening word of verse twenty, *for*, lets us know that we must consider verses nineteen and twenty together. In doing so, we see that through this curse, we, the saved, are *not yet revealed* as the sons of God—but we will be when that curse is removed.

"Creature" is mentioned for a second straight verse. It will be mentioned in the next two verses as well, though, in verse twenty-two, it will be rendered as *creation*. All four words are from the same word, *ktisis*. While it refers to saved individuals in verse nineteen, here, the context expands its usage to all that God has created. Because of the fall, God put all of creation under a curse, here called vanity. *Vanity* is from the word *mahtayotace*, and it means perversity, depravity, and frailty. In short, we opened the door for disaster, and now God has subjected us to the consequences of that disaster, namely a broken and filthy world. We were unwilling; creation was unwilling; mere moments after it happened, Adam and Eve would have done anything to turn back the clock. But God is in charge. Yet even in this, He left us hope, the earnest expectation of better things to come!

Romans 8:21 *Because the creature itself also shall be delivered from the bondage of corruption into the glorious liberty of the children of God.*

The *creature* here is all of creation, including us, but mainly the creation below us. It is now in the bondage of corruption because the curse is in effect, and Satan and his crowd are in charge. One day, it will be delivered when we are manifested. In other words, things one day are going to get a whole lot better than what they are now. Take your very best day when it seems like the sky is at its bluest and the air is at its sweetest and circumstances at their best, and even that day does not begin to compare to how good things will be when the Lord Jesus Christ is in charge publicly and openly on this earth.

Creation will no longer be under a curse (*the bondage of corruption)* but will instead be perfect as it moves *into the glorious liberty of the children of God.* What a day that will be!

Romans 8:22 *For we know that the whole creation groaneth and travaileth in pain together until now.*

Has it ever seemed to you like the earth itself is crying out in pain? The truth of the matter is, it is. All of this world is creaking and aching and groaning because of how it is falling apart due to the curse of sin. This planet that we live on is aching and hurting, but when God comes back, everything will be set right, including the removal of the curse of sin from off of this planet.

We are going to be revealed as the sons of God, the world is going to be set right, and we have some great things to look forward to!

The second part of the focus of our looking ahead is the redemption of the body mentioned in verse twenty-three:

Romans 8:23 *And not only they* [all of the things of lower creation, animals, plants, etc.]*, but ourselves also, which have the firstfruits of the Spirit, even we ourselves groan within* *ourselves, waiting for the adoption, to wit, the redemption of our body.*

We know that creation is groaning, but this verse points out that we also groan. We who are the children of God and have the first fruits of the Spirit (meaning the Spirit as the first taste, the first part, the evidence of our salvation) are groaning within ourselves, waiting for what this verse calls the adoption, the redemption of our body.

Our outside does not match our inside.

Our inside has been set right; we have been sanctified and justified and sealed unto the day of redemption. In God's sight, we are perfect and flawless in our inner man. But how often do you wake up in the morning feeling perfect and flawless, with no pains, no aches, no joints creaking and popping, and no stress?

Our souls and spirits are redeemed, but our bodies are not yet redeemed.

But we have something to look forward to. One day, our bodies will be as perfect on the outside as we are on the inside.

Romans 8:24 *For we are saved by hope: but hope that is seen is not hope: for what a man seeth, why doth he yet hope for?* **25** *But if we hope for that we see not, then do we with patience wait for it.*

When the Bible speaks of the word hope, it means something quite different than what most people mean today when they use the word hope. The word hope today means something that may or may not happen. In fact, it usually is used for things that probably won't happen. People hope they will win the lottery. People hope some long-lost relative will leave them a fortune in their will. People hope that the individuals they elect to office will not turn out to be liars and thieves and crooks.

But when the Bible speaks of the word hope, it means "an earnest expectation of something that we are quite confident in."

Please understand that when verse twenty-four says that we are saved by hope, it is not talking about salvation from sin. That kind of being saved occurs by grace through faith, not by hope. In the context of the verses we have been studying, it means that we are saved from giving up in these present terrible trials of body and earth. We are able to keep on hanging on and keep on doing right and keep on going day by day by day because we have hope; we have an earnest expectation of how much better things are going to be when both the earth and our bodies are redeemed and set right.

Once that happens, we will be able to see it, and we will not have to hope for it anymore. But right now, since it has not yet happened, and we cannot yet see it, we hope for it, and that hope keeps us going.

The faith of our looking ahead

With so much to hope for, with such a great focus to look at, we might want to ask if there is any reason or reasons why we should have so much of a great focus, and why we should be so confidently looking ahead. The answer is yes, and verses twenty-six through thirty give three reasons.

The first thing that Paul mentions is that of the Spirit's intercession.

Romans 8:26 *Likewise the Spirit also helpeth our infirmities: for we know not what we should pray for as we ought: but the Spirit itself maketh intercession for us with groanings which cannot be uttered.* **27** *And he that searcheth the hearts knoweth what is the mind of the Spirit, because he maketh intercession for the saints according to the will of God.*

If we find that we have something great going for us here and now in the midst of all of our trials, we are going to have that much more confidence in the promise of things eventually being set right and made perfect both in creation and in our bodies. And we most definitely have something great going for us now.

We have the Holy Spirit of God, the third member of the Trinity, helping our infirmities. Paul segued into a discussion of our prayer life at this point and pointed out a weakness in all of our prayer lives. None of us really even know what we should pray for as we ought to. That might help to explain why it often

174

seems like so few of our prayers get answered the way we think they ought to get answered.

Do you remember times when you were quite sure that you knew exactly what God ought to do about a particular situation? You prayed and asked Him to do it, but He absolutely did not do it?

Do you also remember some point, maybe even years later, when you saw what He did instead and were able to look back and say, "Wow, God knew what He was doing a lot better than I did!"

When we pray, the Holy Spirit of God, the third member of the Trinity, takes those prayers that we are not getting right, and He makes them right as He presents them to the Lord. The Holy Spirit of God acts as a sort of filter on our prayer life and a translator of our prayers. It seems as though we will often go to prayer maybe with the wrong type of attitude or the wrong type of spirit from not having full information, and the Holy Spirit of God will take those prayers and do something remarkable with them. He presents them to the Father in the form of *groanings which cannot be uttered.* That is from the two-word phrase *stenagmois alalaytois.* It means "deep sighs that cannot even be expressed with words."

When we get to heaven, we are probably going to find out we had a lot more of our prayers answered than we thought we did because the Holy Spirit of God fixed those prayers before they ever got to the ears of the Father!

When verse twenty-seven speaks of *he that searcheth the hearts,* it is talking about God the Father. The Father *knoweth what is the mind of the Spirit, because he* [the Holy Spirit] *maketh intercession for the saints according to the will of God.*

Those groanings which cannot be uttered? They do not need to be; the Father perfectly understands the deep, heartfelt sighs of the Spirit.

When you tie all of that together, you find us praying our feeble, disjointed prayers, the Spirit taking those prayers and presenting them Himself before the Father, Him always doing so according to the will of the Father, and the Father understanding them perfectly because He perfectly knows the mind of the Spirit.

It is not so much that you cannot get a prayer answered, it is more that you cannot help but have *all* of your prayers answered because, by the time they get to God, they are all perfect, perfectly in His will, and will ultimately be perfectly satisfying to us.

A second reason he gives that we can be confident in our looking ahead is because of God's superintending of events.

Romans 8:28 *And we know that all things work together for good to them that love God, to them who are the called according to his purpose.*

This is perhaps the most famous promise in all of the Word of God. It is not a promise that everything will *be* good in our lives; it is a promise that God will take all of the ingredients of our lives and mix them together to bring good out of them. God is a masterful mixer of ingredients to those who love Him and are called according to His purpose. His purpose, by the way, is to seek and to save that which was lost according to Luke 19:10, so this is another way to say those who are saved. Those who are saved and love Him can expect Him to bring good out of all of the situations of their lives.

And if God is going to do that here and now in our lives, if He is going to take that which it would seem to be impossible to bring any good out of and make good come out of it, we can have full confidence in the things that we are looking ahead for, the redemption of the earth and the redemption of the body.

A third reason he gives that we can be confident in our looking ahead is because of God's full plan.

Romans 8:29 *For whom he did foreknow, he also did predestinate to be conformed to the image of his Son, that he might be the firstborn among many brethren.* **30** *Moreover whom he did predestinate, them he also called: and whom he called, them he also justified: and whom he justified, them he also glorified.*

The promises in these two verses are simply amazing. God foreknew us. He looked through time and knew who was going to accept Him as his personal Savior. Those that He saw doing that, He predestinated to be conformed to the image of His Son. It was the plan and purpose of God to have one only begotten Son, Jesus, but for that one and only begotten Son to be the firstborn among many brethren. In other words, He planned on us.

And His plan was not just to save us, it was also day by day and step by step to make us more like Christ. Every day that you live, God the Father is actively trying to mold you like a potter would mold a lump of clay. Every day that you live, He is trying to make you and me less like you and me and more like Jesus.

Verse thirty tells us that those that He predestinated, He called. But He did not just call us, He also justified us. He made our sins go away. He judicially declared us righteous based on what Jesus did. But not only did He justify us, He also glorified us.

That is a future reality, but it is so certain of a thing that it is spoken of here as a present truth. It harkens back to the promise that our very bodies are going to be redeemed and made perfect.

You will often hear one human say to another human, "I have big plans for you." Let me tell you, nobody has any bigger plans for you than God does.

The finality of looking ahead

When we see all of this, we can be absolutely certain of it because it is clear from the verses that we are about to look at that God sees it as being just as certain as if it had already happened.

Romans 8:31 *What shall we then say to these things? If God be for us, who can be against us?*

What shall we say then basically means "What conclusion should we draw from the above premises?" The conclusions are going to be very good, beginning with the fact that if God is for us, no one can really be against us.

That may come as quite a surprise. In fact, as children of God it almost seems like the exact opposite is true, and that almost everyone is against us and very few are for us.

Here is what this phrase means. Sinners may be against us, and so may the great enemy of our souls, but their power to destroy us is taken away. If you have people who are against you, but they have no power to destroy you whatsoever, then you may as well just go ahead and say that no one can be against you.

There is an electrical symbol, the Greek letter Omega with a lightning bolt going through it. It is a symbol that means "no resistance."

It may not seem like it, but when you got saved it is as if God basically stamped you with the no resistance symbol. The devil can try all he likes, the world can try all it likes, and circumstances can try all they like, but you are not going down, you are going up!

Romans 8:32 *He that spared not his own Son, but delivered him up for us all, how shall he not with him also freely give us all things?*

When you think of the price that God the Father paid for us all, giving up His Son to death for us, it should let you know that He has no intention of holding out on you. Whatever good thing you need, God is going to give it to you. And that includes the good things of the future that we are looking ahead to, the restoration of this world and the redemption of the body.

Romans 8:33 *Who shall lay any thing to the charge of God's elect? It is God that justifieth.* **34** *Who is he that condemneth? It is Christ that died, yea rather, that is risen again, who is even at the right hand of God, who also maketh intercession for us.*

When we talk like this, when we speak of how much God loves us and all of the good things that we have waiting for us, a class of people will inevitably rear their ugly heads and say, "You're just a bunch of hypocrites; you are every bit as dirty as everyone else!"

Paul answers that very nicely in these verses. Who exactly is it that can lay anything to the charge of God's elect, meaning God's chosen ones? No one has a right to put any black mark on your record; God has justified you. There is only one person who has the right to condemn, and that is the Lord Jesus Christ. And He died and rose again just so that you could be saved, and He is even now at the right hand of the Father interceding on your behalf. He is pleading your case and telling the Father just how justified and sinless and pure and righteous you are!

Romans 8:35 *Who shall separate us from the love of Christ? shall tribulation, or distress, or persecution, or famine, or nakedness, or peril, or sword?* **36** *As it is written, For thy sake we are killed all the day long; we are accounted as sheep for the slaughter.*

There is a reciprocal nature in this verse that usually goes overlooked. When it speaks of us and of the love of Christ, it is not just talking about His love for us or the fact that our salvation is secure. It is also talking about the fact that we love Him, and He loves us. It is talking about the two-way street of our relationship.

Adam Clarke explained it this way: "The apostle is referring to the persecutions and tribulations to which genuine Christians were exposed through their attachment to Christ, and the gracious provision God had made for their support and final salvation. As in this provision God had shown his infinite love to them in providing Jesus Christ as their sin-offering, and Jesus Christ had shown his love in suffering death upon the cross for them; so, here, he speaks of the love of the followers of God to that Christ who had first loved them." (Clarke, 104)

Every genuine Christian is going to undergo trials, and some may even be jaw-dropping trials. We are going to experience tribulation and distress and persecution; we may even experience famine or nakedness or peril or the sword. As far as this world is concerned, we are nothing but sheep for the slaughter.

But that persecution will never stop the Lord from loving us, nor will it stop us from loving the Lord. When the Lord looks at it, He looks at all of this as a done deal. In other words, even on your worst day when you are going through such incredible trials that you do not feel like you love Him and maybe even claim that you do not love Him, He still looks at it the way it is actually going to be in heaven once all of the trials are done. He still looks at you as loving Him just like you will love Him the moment that your feet touch the street of gold and all trials are behind you!

Romans 8:37 *Nay, in all these things we are more than conquerors through him that loved us.*

It would be marvelous beyond measure for us just to be conquerors, but according to this verse, we are actually even **more** than conquerors through Him that loved us.

How is it possible to be even more than a conqueror?

A conqueror is simply a person who wins, even by the skin of his teeth. We are going to do a whole lot more than just win. Staying saved forever qualifies as being more than a conqueror. Getting a glorified body qualifies as being more than a conqueror. Never having to go to hell qualifies as being more than a conqueror. Getting to spend all of eternity with our saved loved ones qualifies as being more than a conqueror. Having our own mansion and getting to see Jesus face to face qualifies as being more than a conqueror.

Romans 8:38 *For I am persuaded, that neither death, nor life, nor angels, nor principalities, nor powers, nor things present, nor things to come,* **39** *Nor height, nor depth, nor any other creature, shall be able to separate us from the love of God, which is in Christ Jesus our Lord.*

Paul had had a lot of time to think all of this through. And when he was done with all of that thinking, he said, *I am persuaded.* There was absolutely no doubt at all in Paul's mind about what he was going to say.

Death cannot separate us from the love of God which is in Christ Jesus our Lord.

Life, all of the things that we go through on a daily basis, cannot separate us from the love of God which is in Christ Jesus our Lord.

Angels, even if they wanted to, and the fallen ones certainly do, cannot separate us from the love of God which is in Christ Jesus our Lord.

Principalities and powers, meaning high and lofty demonic rulers in the world of men, cannot separate us from the love of God which is in Christ Jesus our Lord.

Things present, the things you are dealing with right now at this moment on this day, cannot separate us from the love of God which is in Christ Jesus our Lord.

Things to come, the things you will be facing tomorrow and next week and next month and next year, cannot separate us from the love of God which is in Christ Jesus our Lord.

Height or depth, things over your head or under your feet, cannot separate us from the love of God which is in Christ Jesus our Lord.

That list really does cover everything, but just in case somebody may think that somehow, somewhere in those words, there is a loophole, Paul concluded by saying, *Nor any other creature shall be able to separate us from the love of God which is in Christ Jesus our Lord.*

It is a done deal, a done deal, a done deal. If you are saved, you are going to get to see this world remade into the perfect thing it was before, and you are going to have a glorified, perfect body of your own, and you are going to get to enjoy heaven, and you are going to be manifested and declared righteous as a son of God. You may as well not spend your days looking back in mourning over what has been; we have way too much to look forward to for that.

Chapter Thirteen
M - My Greatest Desire

Romans 9:1 *I say the truth in Christ, I lie not, my conscience also bearing me witness in the Holy Ghost,* **2** *That I have great heaviness and continual sorrow in my heart.* **3** *For I could wish that myself were accursed from Christ for my brethren, my kinsmen according to the flesh:* **4** *Who are Israelites; to whom pertaineth the adoption, and the glory, and the covenants, and the giving of the law, and the service of God, and the promises;* **5** *Whose are the fathers, and of whom as concerning the flesh Christ came, who is over all, God blessed for ever. Amen.*

The book of Romans is the greatest doctrinal treatise on salvation ever written. It was written by the Apostle Paul, one of the greatest soul winners who ever lived. Paul himself was chosen by God to bring the gospel to the Gentile world:

Romans 11:13 *For I speak to you Gentiles, inasmuch as I am the apostle of the Gentiles, I magnify mine office:*

1 Timothy 2:7 *Whereunto I am ordained a preacher, and an apostle, (I speak the truth in Christ, and lie not;) a teacher of the Gentiles in faith and verity.*

2 Timothy 1:11 *Whereunto I am appointed a preacher, and an apostle, and a teacher of the Gentiles.*

Paul fulfilled that God-given mission with all of his might, passion, and power. He spent his life taking the gospel into Gentile lands. This was something that constantly got him in hot water with the Jews, even Jews who had become Christians.

The Jews had it in their minds that if a person had anything to do with the Gentiles, that they really did not love the Jewish people. But nothing could be farther from the truth. Jesus, who Himself was a Jew, died for the entire world including all of the Gentiles, yet has never ceased for a moment to love the Jewish people, His own people.

And Paul was just like that. Yes, he was the apostle to the Gentiles. But in spite of that there was something he wanted more than anything else on earth, and it dealt with his own people, the Jews.

The sorrow of Paul

Romans 9:1 *I say the truth in Christ, I lie not, my conscience also bearing me witness in the Holy Ghost, 2 That I have great heaviness and continual sorrow in my heart.*

Done right, the ministry is a very hard life. The hours are long, one never gets to clock out, and the emotional load is heavy beyond accurate description.

But if it is hard now, imagine how much harder it was for someone like the apostle Paul. He went through physical agony, legal trials, emotional weight, brutal untrue accusations, and a great deal more.

But the main thing that got to Paul, the main thing that broke his heart was the fact that he loved people, and those people were on their way to hell.

Paul used two terms in these two verses to describe how bad it was for him. He said that he had *great heaviness* and *continual sorrow* in his heart.

When he said that he had great heaviness, it was his way of painting a picture of having an emotional weight bearing down on him. The constriction in the chest... The tossing and turning at night... The waking up in the morning and automatically having it wash over you all over again...

Even on his good days, when he was smiling and laughing, he had both the *heaviness* and *continual sorrow* in his heart. Paul never did have a day where it was all happiness with him. He never could be completely joyful without there also being that mixture of sadness in with that joy.

When Paul said all of this, he knew how extreme it sounded. That is why he began by saying what he said in verse one, *I say the truth in Christ, I lie not, my conscience also bearing me witness in the Holy Ghost.*

Adam Clarke said:

"This is one of the most solemn oaths any man can possibly take. He appeals to Christ as the searcher of hearts that he tells the truth; asserts that his conscience was free from all guile in this matter, and that the Holy Ghost bore him testimony that what he said was true. Hence, we find that the testimony of a man's own conscience, and the testimony of the Holy Ghost, are two distinct things, and that the apostle had both at the same time." (Clarke, 108)

When Paul said that he was sorrowful, you need to understand and you need to believe that he was truly, deeply, incredibly sorrowful and burdened down by what was on his mind and what was on his heart.

If you have been alive for any decent period of time, then you have learned something. The thing that gets a child of God to be sorrowful and heavy in their spirit quicker than anything else is someone that they love who is not doing right.

The stunning wish of Paul

Romans 9:3 *For I could wish that myself were accursed from Christ for my brethren, my kinsmen according to the flesh:*

Paul started off his life as a Jew to the very core of his being:

Philippians 3:4 *Though I might also have confidence in the flesh. If any other man thinketh that he hath whereof he might trust in the flesh, I more:* **5** *Circumcised the eighth day, of the stock of Israel, of the tribe of Benjamin, an Hebrew of the Hebrews; as touching the law, a Pharisee;* **6** *Concerning zeal,* *persecuting the church; touching the righteousness which is in the law, blameless.*

But then Paul got saved and his priorities changed:

Philippians 3:7 *But what things were gain to me, those I counted loss for Christ.* **8** *Yea doubtless, and I count all things but loss for the excellency of the knowledge of Christ Jesus my Lord: for whom I have suffered the loss of all things, and do count them but dung, that I may win Christ,*

When he went that way, his Jewish brethren not only turned their backs on him, they tried to kill him on multiple occasions:

Acts 9:22 *But Saul increased the more in strength, and confounded the Jews which dwelt at Damascus, proving that this is very Christ.* **23** *And after that many days were fulfilled, the Jews took counsel to kill him:* **24** *But their laying await was known of Saul. And they watched the gates day and night to kill him.*

Things were most definitely not "peachy keen" between Paul and his people, the Jews. They completely changed how they felt about him.

But the most important thing that they needed to know, and that you and I need to know, is that even though they completely changed how they felt about him, he never for a single moment changed how he felt about them.

Not only did he still love them, he loved them even more after he became a follower of Christ than he did before he was a follower of Christ. Look again at what he said in this passage:

Romans 9:3 *For I could wish that myself were accursed from Christ for my brethren, my kinsmen according to the flesh:*

There is no possible way to overstate how serious and drastic of a statement this was.

A lot of times we say things in the English language having only some general concept of what they mean. For instance, people often use the word "anathema." We say, "Oh, so and so is anathema to him" or "That thing is anathema."

We seem to have some general idea that anathema is something that is bad. And that is certainly true. The reason I bring it up at this point is because when Paul said that he could wish himself *accursed* from Christ for his people, the word he used was the word *anathema*.

It will be impossible for him to use a stronger and more dramatic word because there was and is no such word.

Throughout the years, the Jewish people would often give something to God by completely destroying it. They would do so by pouring oil on it and completely burning it until there was nothing left of it. That is what is meant by the word anathema. It was a word for something that was utterly destroyed in the most violent of fires. When Paul used it of himself, everyone understood automatically that he was not talking about the fires of oil; he was talking about hell.

Lenski said, "Paul's personal love for the Jews would drive him, namely, if such a thing were possible, he would buy the salvation of his nation at the price of his own salvation." (Lenski, 583)

Literally, if it were possible, Paul would have died and gone to hell for eternity if it meant that his people the Jews, would be saved and get to go to heaven for eternity.

Let that sink in.

I wonder if any of us could claim that depth of a burden for souls?

I believe the answer is no. The good news, obviously, is that what Paul could wish was not possible. But the lesson to be learned from it is that everyone is supposed to have an almost unfathomable burden to see the people that they love won to Christ. Hold that thought; we will come back to it.

The sacred blessings of Paul's people

Romans 9:4 *Who are Israelites; to whom pertaineth the adoption, and the glory, and the covenants, and the giving of the law, and the service of God, and the promises;* **5** *Whose are the fathers, and of whom as concerning the flesh Christ came, who is over all, God blessed for ever. Amen.*

Look at these phrases one at a time and notice the sacred blessings in them:

Who are Israelites: the Jews were descended from Jacob, whose name was changed to Israel, "Prince of God." Paul's people were royalty to God.

To whom pertaineth the adoption: The Jews were all taken into the family of God and were called his sons and first-born, Exodus 4:22; Deuteronomy 14:1; Jeremiah 31:9; Hosea 11:1.

To whom pertaineth the glory: God actually appeared to them in the Shekinah glory, the pillar of fire by night and the pillar of cloud by day. No other nation experienced His glory like that before or since.

To whom pertaineth the covenants: God made sacred covenants with the Jews through Abraham and Moses and others, covenants that pertained to their status as the chosen race, and to the physical promises of the land that He would give them.

To whom pertaineth the giving of the law: while the world was wallowing in darkness, God appeared to the Jewish people and gave them the light of the law of God.

To whom pertaineth the service of God: this was the entire system of worship that He gave them, this system that so beautifully pointed to the sin of man and the holiness of God in the coming Messiah.

To whom pertaineth the promises: the entire Old Testament is filled with promises that pertain just to the Jewish people.

Whose are the fathers: Adam Clarke gives a good explanation of this phrase:

> Abraham, Isaac, Jacob, Joseph, the twelve patriarchs, Moses, Joshua, Samuel, David, &c., &c., without controversy, the greatest and most eminent men that ever flourished under heaven. From these, in an uninterrupted and unpolluted line, the Jewish people had descended; and it was no small glory to be able to reckon, in their genealogy, persons

of such incomparable merit and excellency. (Clarke, 109)

But the very greatest of their blessings was one that Paul understood that they themselves did not:

...and of whom as concerning the flesh Christ came, who is over all, God blessed for ever. Amen.

Not only are the Jewish people more blessed than most of the rest of the world knows, but they are also more blessed than they themselves know. When the Lord Jesus Christ, the Son of God, chose to come down to this wicked old world and robe Himself in flesh, He did so as a Jew. Jesus did not come as an American or as an Englishman or as a German or as a Spaniard or as a Chinaman or as a Russian or as an Arab or as an Australian or as a Japanese. Jesus came as a Jew.

But when that greatest of blessings came, it was not received as it should have been.

John 1:11 *He came unto his own, and his own received him not.*

And that is exactly why Paul felt like he felt and said what he said in these five verses.

Paul saw his people, his nation, his flag-waving crowd, lost and on their way to hell, and that thought broke him.

Paul's greatest desire was to see his people saved. Nothing else even came close.

I wonder, what is **your** greatest desire?

Chapter Fourteen
N - Neithers and Nots to Notice

Romans 9:6 *Not as though the word of God hath taken none effect. For they are not all Israel, which are of Israel:* **7** *Neither, because they are the seed of Abraham, are they all children: but, In Isaac shall thy seed be called.* **8** *That is, They which are the children of the flesh, these are not the children of God: but the children of the promise are counted for the seed.*

It would be truly wonderful if we could always be positive. Being negative seems so, well, negative! But stating things from a positive viewpoint will only tell half of the story and rob us of a valuable way to illustrate truth. For instance, to state that Fred is married to Lilly is the positive side of the story. Because they are married, they get to do all kinds of wonderful things that single people cannot rightfully do. But that is only half of the story. The negative side of the truth is that because they are married, they cannot do those things with others. Considering both the positive and the negative aspects gives us the complete story.

This is the shortest section we will consider in the book. But it is foundational for one of the most essential-to-understand portions in the book.

<u>Not</u> as though the word of God hath taken none effect

Romans 9:6 *Not as though the word of God hath taken none effect. For they are not all Israel, which are of Israel:*

This verse begins a conclusion of what Paul has been discussing in the previous verses. Everything that he has said in verses one through five has led him to the thought that begins in verse six.

In verses one and two, we find that Paul was completely broken-hearted. In verse three, he said that he could wish himself accursed because of his brethren, Israel, who were lost. Paul was literally willing, if it were possible, to die and go to hell so that his children of Israel brethren could go to heaven.

He then mentioned all of the things that Israel had been given by God: the adoption as a nation, the glory, the covenants, the law, the service of God, the promises of God, the fathers, the bloodline of Christ.

Israel had been blessed as a nation more than any other nation that had ever existed. God favored them; He made them His own.

But having said all of that, the logical thought that would then follow was this: if God made all of these promises to Israel, yet most of the nation of Israel has rejected God, God's Word must have failed! Paul knew that his readers would reason that the Word of God must not have "taken effect."

The rest of chapter nine really deals with that thought. Paul in the last half of this verse begins to explain why God's Word is not the problem.

For they are not all Israel, which are of Israel.

What does he mean by that? Let me illustrate. Please, ask yourself what it takes for a person to be an American.

Does it mean that a person must be a direct descendant of Amerigo Vespucci, for whom America was named? No, most of them do not live here, and most people who do live here are not descended from him.

Does it mean that a person had to have been born here? No, many people have been born here whose families have lived here for two hundred years, and they still consider themselves Italian!

Does it mean that a person must have moved here? No, many terrorists have moved here, and they are not American.

Does it mean that a person must be of European, white descent, go to college, and work a job? No, many people just like that spit on the flag, despise the Constitution, and are proud socialists and communists; they are not American.

Does it mean that a person must currently live here? No, there are many Americans whose jobs or ministries have taken them to live in foreign countries for many years.

When it gets right down to it, being American is more than just a legal matter, though the legal certainly is essential. It is also a matter of the heart, a matter of belief. It is a loyalty to the ideals upon which our nation was founded; it is a fierce devotion to freedom.

The Jews had gotten the idea that nationality was everything and that if they were descended from Abraham, Isaac, and Jacob, they were Israelites. The truth of the matter, however, was that the vast majority of people directly descended from Abraham, Isaac, and Jacob, living in the land of Israel, did not believe in the God of Israel; therefore, God did not consider them Israelites.

Being American is a matter of belief. Being Israelite was also a matter of belief, a matter of faith. The God who made the Israelites expected them to believe in Him in order to be considered Israelites by Him.

For those who believed, the true Israelites in God's sight, the Word of God had taken effect and had changed their lives.

The Word of God did not affect two million murmuring Jews in the wilderness, but it did affect Moses.

The Word of God did not affect Eli, but it did affect Samuel.

The Word of God did not affect Saul, but it did affect David.

The Word of God did not affect all of the prophets of Ahab, but it did affect Micaiah.

The Word of God did not affect Caiaphas, but it did affect John.

The Word of God, the promises of God, the laws of God, always take full effect in the hearts of those who believe.

Neither because they are the seed of Abraham, are they all children

Romans 9:7 *Neither, because they are the seed of Abraham, are they all children: but, In Isaac shall thy seed be called.*

Verse seven is an illustration of the thought begun in verse six. Just like not everyone descended physically from Israel was an Israelite in the sight of God, not everyone physically descended from Abraham was a child of Abraham in the sight of God.

Abraham had two prominent sons, Ishmael and Isaac. Ishmael came about as a result of the flesh. Abraham got impatient; Abraham did not wait on God. Sarah got impatient; Sarah did not wait on God. Sarah said, "Abraham, go sleep with my maid Hagar; we will let her be your wife too, your concubine, and that way any children that she bears can be mine."

Abraham, for his part, loved the idea. His flesh saw an opportunity to have intimate relations with another and a younger woman, and Abraham said, "Great idea, Honey, I'll get right to that." The result of that improper union, the result of that act of the flesh, was the child Ishmael. Abraham ran ahead of God, Abraham acted in the flesh, and not only did he cause himself and his family problems, but he also caused us problems. The entire modern conflict in the Middle East traces right back to that one fleshly act of Abraham.

Isaac, though, came as a result of faith. Abraham believed God. God would not have the product of the flesh as the chosen one. Isaac, the product of faith, was the chosen seed.

They which are the children of the flesh, these are not the children of God

Romans 9:8 *That is, They which are the children of the flesh, these are not the children of God: but the children of the promise are counted for the seed.*

194

Once again, this clarifies verses six through seven, and it applies to several different things.

It applies to the conflict between Arabs and Jews. Like it or not, when it comes to nations, God's chosen people are the Jews.

It also applies to the question of "what is an Israelite." Anyone who is Jewish would stand up and cheer at what I just wrote about the Arabs and the Jews and about the Jews being God's chosen people. But when it gets down to this truth, they are probably going to stop cheering. You see, while the national is important and while God loves them and real Christians do as well, the national is not nearly as essential as the spiritual. And spiritually, a person cannot be an Israelite in God's eyes without believing the way that God expects them to believe, and that means receiving His Son, the Lord Jesus Christ, as their Savior, just like Paul the Jew did.

But it also applies to the question of what a Christian is. Everywhere you go here in America, people claim to be Christians. Yet if you examine how they behave, it will tell you what they believe because belief always impacts behavior. And it is very clear on that basis that a great many people that claim to be Christians are not Christians just as a great many people who claim to be Israelites are not Israelites.

Our relationship with Christ is not a matter of where we were born or of what our parents were like or of what rituals we have kept. The word of God produces in us a relationship with Christ only when we believe, and that belief will produce in us a conformity to Christ.

If a person does not get saved, it is not God's fault, and it is not the Bible's fault. Everything you need is right there in it; it is just a matter of whether you are going to apply your belief to it or not.

Chapter Fifteen
O - Observations on Election

Romans 9:8 *That is, They which are the children of the flesh, these are not the children of God: but the children of the promise are counted for the seed.* **9** *For this is the word of promise, At this time will I come, and Sara shall have a son.* **10** *And not only this; but when Rebecca also had conceived by one, even by our father Isaac;* **11** *(For the children being not yet born, neither having done any good or evil, that the purpose of God according to election might stand, not of works, but of him that calleth;)* **12** *It was said unto her, The elder shall serve the younger.* **13** *As it is written, Jacob have I loved, but Esau have I hated.* **14** *What shall we say then? Is there unrighteousness with God? God forbid.* **15** *For he saith to Moses, I will have mercy on whom I will have mercy, and I will have compassion on whom I will have compassion.* **16** *So then it is not of him that willeth, nor of him that runneth, but of God that sheweth mercy.* **17** *For the scripture saith unto Pharaoh, Even for this same purpose have I raised thee up, that I might shew my power in thee, and that my name might be declared throughout all the earth.* **18** *Therefore hath he mercy on whom he will have mercy, and whom he will he hardeneth.* **19** *Thou wilt say then unto me, Why doth he yet find fault? For who hath resisted his will?* **20** *Nay but, O man, who art thou that repliest against God? Shall the thing formed say to him that formed it, Why hast thou made me thus?* **21** *Hath not the potter power over the clay, of the same lump to make one vessel unto honour, and another unto dishonour?* **22**

What if God, willing to shew his wrath, and to make his power known, endured with much longsuffering the vessels of wrath fitted to destruction: **23** *And that he might make known the riches of his glory on the vessels of mercy, which he had afore prepared unto glory,* **24** *Even us, whom he hath called, not of the Jews only, but also of the Gentiles?* **25** *As he saith also in Osee, I will call them my people, which were not my people; and her beloved, which was not beloved.* **26** *And it shall come to pass, that in the place where it was said unto them, Ye are not my people; there shall they be called the children of the living God.* **27** *Esaias also crieth concerning Israel, Though the number of the children of Israel be as the sand of the sea, a remnant shall be saved:* **28** *For he will finish the work, and cut it short in righteousness: because a short work will the Lord make upon the earth.* **29** *And as Esaias said before, Except the Lord of Sabaoth had left us a seed, we had been as Sodoma, and been made like unto Gomorrha.* **30** *What shall we say then? That the Gentiles, which followed not after righteousness, have attained to righteousness, even the righteousness which is of faith.* **31** *But Israel, which followed after the law of righteousness, hath not attained to the law of righteousness.* **32** *Wherefore? Because they sought it not by faith, but as it were by the works of the law. For they stumbled at that stumblingstone;* **33** *As it is written, Behold, I lay in Sion a stumblingstone and rock of offence: and whosoever believeth on him shall not be ashamed.*

The circumstances of election

Remember that in verses one through eight, God has been dealing with the nation of Israel. But he has been dealing with the fact that not all Israel *was* Israel, meaning that not everyone descended physically from Jacob believed in the God of Jacob. The result of this was that they were regarded as the children of the flesh rather than the children of God. Paul illustrated this in verses seven and eight by showing that Abraham's son Ishmael was regarded as a child of the flesh, but Abraham's son Isaac was regarded as a child of the promise. So, even though we are dealing with nations, salvation still comes into play, because all those descendants of Abraham who did not believe in the God of Abraham were doomed to hell. So, in this passage, you must see two ideas inextricably tied together: the main idea of God's election of a nation and the interwoven idea of God's election in salvation.

Let us then look at the circumstances of election.

Romans 9:9 *For this is the word of promise, At this time will I come, and Sara shall have a son.*

This verse is a quote from Genesis 18:14.

Genesis 18:14 *Is any thing too hard for the LORD? At the time appointed I will return unto thee, according to the time of life, and Sarah shall have a son.*

By the time of Genesis 18:14, Abraham already had a son, Ishmael. Ishmael came from Hagar, not from Sarah. But Ishmael was not God's promise. Ishmael was not even God's idea. God had chosen from the foundation of time that Isaac would be the promised seed. In other words, there was a "rather than" when it came to what God was going to do. God chose Isaac *rather than* Ishmael. God chose the son of Sarah *rather than* the son of Hagar.

The thought continues, but we should take note of the fact that verse eleven is a parenthetical thought. So, we will look at verses ten and twelve together first.

Romans 9:10 *And not only this; but when Rebecca also had conceived by one, even by our father Isaac;* **12** *It was said unto her, The elder shall serve the younger.*

After the time of Abraham and Sarah and Isaac and Ishmael, the Bible records the events surrounding Isaac and Rebekah. There was one father, Isaac, one mother, Rebekah, and two twins in her womb, Esau the older and Jacob the younger. God chose that the older would serve the younger. That was completely contrary to the expected custom of the day. Not only that, God chose for the bloodline of Christ to come through Jacob the younger, not Esau the older. Why? The text does not **yet** say why, but it does say why not. Do you remember that parenthesis that we skipped? Here it is:

Romans 9:11 *(For the children being not yet born, neither having done any good or evil, that the purpose of God according to election might stand, not of works, but of him that calleth;)*

When you see the word *election* in the Bible, you need to know that it simply means *choice*. For instance, during an election, you choose a person for office.

Some years ago, I lost my first election for public office. Now, the most interesting part of that was that I did not even realize that I had been running for public office! But when the election was over, there it was in the newspaper in black and white: I had received three votes for Head of the Sanitary District. I am really not certain if I should be happy that, for whatever reason, three people in Cleveland County thought enough of me to vote for me or unhappy that about thirty thousand did not vote for me! One way or the other, I was not elected; I was not chosen.

Election in the Bible indicates that God made a choice. God had a purpose, and God called according to that purpose. And though the text does not **yet** say why He chose the way He chose, it does say why not. The two important phrases to note in verse eleven are *neither having **done** good or evil* and *not of* **works**.

At this point in our study of the doctrine of election, what we see applies to the election of nations and to the election of individuals to salvation. In neither case is it by what people have done or by their works. When it comes to salvation, you should have a couple of verses going through your mind right now.

Ephesians 2:8 *For by grace are ye saved through faith; and that not of yourselves: it is the gift of God:* **9** *Not of works, lest any man should boast.*

Titus 3:5 *Not by works of righteousness which we have done, but according to his mercy he saved us, by the washing of regeneration, and renewing of the Holy Ghost;*

Election as a nation is not based on good or evil deeds; it is not of works. Election to salvation is not based on good or evil deeds; it is not of works.

200

And it is generally at this point that embracers of Calvinism do something strange with this verse. They say, "Behold! Salvation has nothing to do with anything but an arbitrary choice of God!" But that is not what this verse says. It says not of works nor of good or evil done.

Question: When has salvation ever had anything to do with the good or evil done or with our works? Never! Question number two: When has faith, belief, ever been a work? Never! Never, never, never, never!

Verse eleven proves beyond a shadow of a doubt that works have nothing at all to do with salvation, but that is **all** that it proves.

Romans 9:13 *As it is written, Jacob have I loved, but Esau have I hated.*

Verse thirteen follows up on verse twelve, but there is an important time factor to take note of. Verses ten and twelve are spoken by God before the children were born. The words of verse thirteen, though, were spoken by God a thousand years after they were both dead.

Malachi 1:2 *I have loved you, saith the LORD. Yet ye say, Wherein hast thou loved us? Was not Esau Jacob's brother? saith the LORD: yet I loved Jacob,* **3** *And I hated Esau, and laid his mountains and his heritage waste for the dragons of the wilderness.*

God does not elect to salvation based on works, but He does "hate" based on works. And even the word hate in this context can be grievously misunderstood when we forget that even though God hated Esau, He still loved him enough to die to pay for his sins. In other words, He took all of that hatred of Esau and put it on His Son on the cross of Calvary. Only God can "hate" like that!

The compassion of the election

Romans 9:14 *What shall we say then? Is there unrighteousness with God? God forbid.*

That is an interesting question that Paul asked, isn't it? It is a question designed to ask what Paul already knew people were going to be thinking. Any time we say that God has made a choice and that choice has resulted in people being saved or lost, somebody is going to accuse God of being unrighteous.

But that accusation is just exactly as fair as if a doctor had two patients with the exact same fatal disease, offered the cure to both of them, had one of them storm out of the office without receiving the cure, administered the cure to the one who sat there and willingly received it, and then got accused of malpractice by the family of the one who left without the cure.

I guarantee you that if that doctor were asked if he had been unrighteous in "choosing to save only one," he would say, "God forbid!" And that is the exact same thing that God would say if anyone accused Him of being unrighteous in regard to the election, and for the exact same reason.

Romans 9:15 *For he saith to Moses, I will have mercy on whom I will have mercy, and I will have compassion on whom I will have compassion.*

Just like most things in Romans 9, verse fifteen usually is grievously misrepresented by the well-meaning Calvinist, and their error stems from taking this completely apart from any context or history.

This verse is a quote from Exodus 33:19.

Exodus 33:19 *And he said, I will make all my goodness pass before thee, and I will proclaim the name of the LORD before thee; and will be gracious to whom I will be gracious, and will shew mercy on whom I will shew mercy.*

In Exodus 32, the children of Israel had been delivered from the bondage of Egypt. Yet while Moses was up on the mount talking with God, the people, of their own free will, chose to make and worship a false God. Judgment then fell. One chapter later, we find Moses seeking after God. We find Moses asking to see God. And it is then that God said, *I will be gracious to whom I will be gracious, and will shew mercy on whom I will shew mercy,"* which Paul quoted in Romans 9:15.

So, tell me: was God being gracious to whom He would be gracious and showing mercy on whom He would show mercy an arbitrary thing, or was there a reason for it? Was it an arbitrary thing that God showed Himself to Moses but not to others, or was there a reason for it? Clearly, there was a reason for it. God was not unjust in judging the people and blessing Moses. The people made their choice, and Moses made his. The people disbelieved; Moses believed.

God's election is compassionate and merciful, and He gets to decide to whom and on what basis He will extend this compassion, and He has decided. Look at the next verse.

Romans 9:16 *So then it is not of him that willeth, nor of him that runneth, but of God that sheweth mercy.*

Verse sixteen points back to the same idea as verse eleven. God's election is not based on works. Verse sixteen says the same thing two more ways. It is not of him that willeth [*thelo*, to resolve, will, determine], it is not of him that runneth [*treko*, to make an effort based on that resolve]. It is not based on efforts, deeds, or works but on God's mercy. But as we saw in the case of Moses and the children of Israel, that mercy was extended to the one who had already chosen to believe in God, while others were disbelieving.

Romans 9:17 *For the scripture saith unto Pharaoh, Even for this same purpose have I raised thee up, that I might shew my power in thee, and that my name might be declared throughout all the earth.*

We have thus far looked at those that God did not choose, Ishmael and Esau, and we have looked at those that he did choose, Isaac and Jacob. We have established that His choices are not based on works. Now we are given another example of one that God did not choose, Pharaoh.

Pharaoh is another character in this passage that the Calvinist loves to point to as proof of his flawed doctrine. In verse seventeen, he will commonly tell you that God created Pharaoh in order to destroy him. But the grammar of the verse that this verse quotes, Exodus 9:16, means something completely different:

Exodus 9:16 *And in very deed for this cause have I raised thee up, for to shew in thee my power; and that my name may be declared throughout all the earth.*

Matthew Henry summarizes this beautifully, saying:

"For this cause have I raised thee up to the throne at this time, and made thee to stand the shock of the plagues hitherto, to show in thee my power.

"Providence ordered it so that Moses should have a man of such a fierce and stubborn spirit as he was to deal with; and every thing was so managed in this transaction as to make it a most signal and memorable instance of the power God has to humble and bring down the proudest of his enemies. Everything concurred to signalize this, that God's name (that is, his incontestable sovereignty, his irresistible power, and his inflexible justice) might be declared throughout all the earth, not only to all places, but through all ages while the earth remains. Note, God sometimes raises up very bad men to honor and power, spares them long, and suffers them to grow insufferably insolent, that he may be so much the more glorified in their destruction at last." (Henry, 308)

Simply put, when God says that He had *raised thee up* (speaking of Pharaoh), we understand both from grammar and historical context that the phrase means that He brought him to visibility; He made him powerful.

God knew that once Pharaoh was on the throne, he would refuse to let His people go. This would be a voluntary choice on Pharaoh's part. That choice of Pharaoh would give God the opportunity to *shew my power in thee, and that my name might be declared throughout all the earth.*

Romans 9:18 *Therefore hath he mercy on whom he will have mercy, and whom he will he hardeneth.*

When we come to verse eighteen and find that reference to God hardening people, we automatically think back to the fact that God hardened Pharaoh's heart. That is exactly what Paul is referring to here. And if you did not remember the entire story, you would once again be tempted to fall into the doctrinal error of, "See! God never even gave Pharaoh a chance! Pharaoh was chosen for hell before the foundation of the world. God hardened his heart so that he could not come to know Him..."

Not so fast. Do you happen to remember when the first time is that God hardened Pharaoh's heart? That would be in chapter seven:

Exodus 7:13 *And he hardened Pharaoh's heart, that he hearkened not unto them; as the LORD had said.*

Do you also happen to remember exactly when Moses and God started dealing with Pharaoh's heart? That would be in chapter five:

Exodus 5:1 *And afterward Moses and Aaron went in, and told Pharaoh, Thus saith the LORD God of Israel, Let my people go, that they may hold a feast unto me in the wilderness.* **2** *And Pharaoh said, Who is the LORD, that I should obey his voice to let Israel go? I know not the LORD, neither will I let Israel go.*

God did not harden Pharaoh's heart until *after* Pharaoh made a conscious decision not to obey Him. When Pharaoh said, *I know not the Lord*, the word that he used for *know* [*yada*] does not mean that he did not even know who God was and that he was utterly unfamiliar with Him, it means that he did not choose to recognize Him as God; it means that he would not admit that He was God.

Pharaoh was actually quite well acquainted with the God of the Hebrews. He had more than two million people in his land at least nominally claiming allegiance to that God. The account of what Moses had done refusing the gods of Egypt and following the God of Israel was still recent enough to be very fresh on everyone's mind. Pharaoh knew who God was; he just chose not to believe in Him. Only after Pharaoh made that choice did God then harden Pharaoh's heart.

You say, "But God did, in fact, harden his heart!" Yes, He did, and He had every right to do so. God in mercy offers every person the opportunity to believe in Him and receive Him into his or her heart. But God does not have to continually offer and offer. The fact that He offers every man, woman, boy, and girl at least one opportunity is one opportunity more than any of us actually deserve. If you push Him away like Pharaoh did, you may very well find Him hardening your heart just like He did Pharaoh's.

Romans 9:19 *Thou wilt say then unto me, Why doth he yet find fault? For who hath resisted his will?*

Here is yet another verse that the Calvinist inadvertently twists. They say, "See! No one can resist God's will! He chooses some for heaven and some for hell, and no one can resist that will and do anything about it."

But wait, what is the first word of verse nineteen? "THOU." *Thou wilt say then unto me.* Paul did not say this; Paul said that they were going to say this! They, the scoffers and skeptics, were going to say that no one has ever resisted God's will. But they were completely wrong, and that was Paul's entire point.

People throughout the Bible resisted the will of God. In fact, you will be hard-pressed to find more than a handful of pages in the Bible where somebody did not resist the will of God! Satan resisted the will of God when he rebelled and fell. One-third of the angels of heaven resisted the will of God when they rebelled along with him. Eve resisted the will of God when she ate the forbidden fruit. Adam resisted the will of God when he joined her. The entire world resisted the will of God in Noah's day. David resisted the will of God when he sinned with Bathsheba. Samson resisted the will of God when he put his head in a harlot's lap. Jerusalem resisted God when Jesus offered Himself to them, and they rejected Him. When have people not resisted the will of God?

Paul's point is that when we accuse God of leaving man with no choice in the matter, we are falsely accusing Him because He does give us a choice. When we say that He does not, we are speaking against Him.

Romans 9:20 *Nay but, O man, who art thou that repliest against God? Shall the thing formed say to him that formed it, Why hast thou made me thus?*

God has His plan, which is to *elect* us on something other than our works. And though He often calls and calls and calls, He is not obligated to do so. If He chooses, He can call one time, and then, upon our refusal, harden our hearts and never give us another opportunity. And if He does so, we, the thing formed, have no right to say to Him, "Why did you make me like this?"

Romans 9:21 *Hath not the potter power over the clay, of the same lump to make one vessel unto honour, and another unto dishonour?*

There are two things to take note of in this verse. One is the fact that it is God's work that makes a vessel out of a lump, not our works. Everyone starts out as a "lump of clay," and God then forms that vessel into a vessel either of honor or of dishonor. But the second thing to take note of is the "when factor." When did God make some of the vessels unto honor, which is a euphemism for salvation, and all the vessels unto dishonor, which is a euphemism for not being saved? Did He do it before we ever came into existence for no reason whatsoever, or did He do it afterward, and did he have a reason for it?

Well, what illustration did he just finish giving? Pharaoh, who had the witness and choice of Moses as a testimony to him. So what is the obvious answer? Yes, God makes some vessels unto dishonor. But His desire was to make every vessel a vessel of honor; His desire was to save everyone.

Romans 9:22 *What if God, willing to shew his wrath, and to make his power known, endured with much longsuffering the vessels of wrath fitted to destruction:*

In verse twenty-two, Paul asks a "what if" question that he is not going to begin to answer until verse thirty. Keep that in mind.

In this verse, Paul mentions God's wrath. Before there ever was an earth or humanity or sin, God already had the full range of emotions within Himself, including wrath. It was His desire for us to know everything there is to know about Him, including His wrath, which, by the way, is always exercised justly and properly.

We then read that God endured with much longsuffering the *vessels of wrath fitted to destruction*. This is clearly speaking of the lost. But when we read that they are *fitted to destruction* (made fit to be destroyed), we need to know who exactly it was that fitted them to destruction.

Understand that this phrase can either be regarded as a passive voice verb or a middle voice verb. And in the context of everything we are reading, it is very clearly a middle voice verb. In other words, they did it to themselves! They fitted themselves to destruction. We will see this very clearly when we get down to verse thirty, where Paul begins to answer the question that he asked here in verse twenty-two.

Romans 9:23 *And that he might make known the riches of his glory on the vessels of mercy, which he had afore prepared unto glory,* **24** *Even us, whom he hath called, not of the Jews only, but also of the Gentiles?*

In these verses, we are given a description of people called *vessels of mercy*. That clearly contrasts with the *vessels of wrath* in verse twenty-two. The vessels of wrath are the lost; the vessels of mercy are the saved.

We find concerning the vessels of mercy that God *afore prepared* them *unto glory*. In verse twenty-two, we find that lost man fits himself to destruction, but the saved are prepared by God for glory, and they are prepared *afore,* they are prepared before there ever was an earth or humanity or sin. Yes, we know that God prepared them because of His foreknowledge of the fact that they would willingly receive Him. But think of what this means when you tie it together.

God never says He prepared the lost for destruction before there was an earth or sin or humanity, but it does say that He prepared the saved for glory before there ever was an earth or sin or humanity. Since He knows not only who will receive Him but also who will reject Him, why would He not prepare the lost for hell before time? Because He loves them so much that He gives them every chance to be saved, even while knowing they will reject Him and stay lost!

In verse twenty-four, we find that God did not just do this for the Jews, but also for the Gentiles.

Romans 9:25 *As he saith also in Osee, I will call them my people, which were not my people; and her beloved, which was not beloved.* **26** *And it shall come to pass, that in the place where it was said unto them, Ye are not my people; there shall they be called the children of the living God.*

These two verses are from Hosea 2:23 and 1:10.

Hosea 2:23 *And I will sow her unto me in the earth; and I will have mercy upon her that had not obtained mercy; and I will say to them which were not my people, Thou art my people; and they shall say, Thou art my God.*

Hosea 1:10 *Yet the number of the children of Israel shall be as the sand of the sea, which cannot be measured nor numbered; and it shall come to pass, that in the place where it was said unto them, Ye are not my people, there it shall be said unto them, Ye are the sons of the living God.*

Just like God called Israel to Him when they were so far astray that they were not His people, He also chose to call the Gentiles to Him when we were so far astray that we were not His people.

Romans 9:27 *Esaias also crieth concerning Israel, Though the number of the children of Israel be as the sand of the sea, a remnant shall be saved:* **28** *For he will finish the work, and cut it short in righteousness: because a short work will the Lord make upon the earth.* **29** *And as Esaias said before, Except the Lord of Sabaoth* [armies] *had left us a seed, we had been as Sodoma, and been made like unto Gomorrha.*

This is from Isaiah 10:22-23 and 28:22. Israel would become so numerous that they seemed like grains of sand by the sea, yet they would be so anti-God that it would seem like all of them were lost. But not all of them actually would be lost; there would always be a remnant who were saved. The exact same thing would be (and already is) true of the Gentiles.

When verse twenty-eight says *For he will finish the work, and cut it short in righteousness: because a short work will the Lord make upon the earth,* the he is God, and the work being referenced is Him, for a time, setting Israel aside as He brings in the Gentiles. That will be a *short work,* meaning a work that He cuts short rather than allowing it to go on forever; God will restore His people, the Jews.

Verse twenty-nine describes how God has been working on Israel in judgment. They have been devastated repeatedly. They cried, "Let His blood be on us and on our children," and it has. Yet God loves them and will not ever let them be totally consumed as Sodom and Gomorrah were. Likewise, we Gentiles have been often judged due to our disobedience and disbelief, but God will preserve a remnant of us as well. Some Jews will be saved; some Gentiles will be saved. God has compassion!

The conclusion of election

I have always enjoyed reading a good "whodunnit" book. All throughout the book, options are eliminated. But you *must* have the last chapter in order to tie everything together. Verses thirty through thirty-three are the conclusion to the chapter and also to the question that Paul asked in verse twenty-two.

For twenty-nine verses, Paul has done everything possible to prove one thing only: the election of God of a nation or of an individual to salvation has nothing to do with works. But that still leaves a question: what is His election based on? The Calvinist will say, "Nothing! There is no basis other than the sovereign choice of God." That belief is wrong, and the last four verses will prove that conclusively.

Romans 9:30 *What shall we say then? That the Gentiles, which followed not after righteousness, have attained to righteousness, even the righteousness which is of faith.*

Let me remind you of what Paul asked in verse twenty-two.

Romans 9:22 *What if God, willing to shew his wrath, and to make his power known, endured with much longsuffering the vessels of wrath fitted to destruction:*

Now, let us put those two things together.

What if God, willing to shew his wrath, and to make his power known, endured with much longsuffering the vessels of wrath fitted to destruction: What shall we say then? That the Gentiles, which followed not after righteousness, have attained to righteousness, even the righteousness which is of faith.

Now Paul begins to answer the question, and he does so by using one of the most important words ever, a word that occurs all over the New Testament especially, but which has not yet occurred a single time in chapter nine, the word *faith.*

Do you think it is an accident that that incredibly important word has not been used a single time yet until the conclusion of chapter nine? It is no accident; it is being done for effect. Paul wants to drive this home like a nail in the coffin. The Gentiles somehow attained to righteousness while many of the Jews did not, and they did it exclusively by *faith.* Hold that thought.

Romans 9:31 *But Israel, which followed after the law of righteousness, hath not attained to the law of righteousness.*

Paul said that Israel, religious Israel, for all of their efforts and all of their following of the law, did not attain to righteousness; they did not get saved. And that begs one simple question: why? Why did they not get saved?

Look at the very first word of the next verse:

Romans 9:32 *Wherefore?*

That is Paul asking the same question I just asked. Why did they not get saved?

If the Calvinist is right, then the next words MUST be "because they were not elect. Because they were not chosen. Because they were not foreordained." But if that is *not* what comes next, then the Calvinist is one hundred percent in error. And it is NOT what comes next. What comes next is this:

Romans 9:32 *...Because they sought it not by faith, but as it were by the works of the law. For they stumbled at that stumblingstone;*

The one and only reason the Jews as a whole did not get saved was because they did not seek righteousness by faith, but by works! But do you see what this means? It was not God's choice; it was theirs! And it always is. If you go to heaven, it will be your choice, and if you go to hell, it will also be your choice.

Romans 9:33 *As it is written, Behold, I lay in Sion a stumblingstone and rock of offence: and whosoever believeth on him shall not be ashamed.*

This is a quote of Isaiah 8:14 and 24:16. Sion is another spelling of Zion.

You know who that rock is; it is Jesus. His own people refused to believe in Him and remained lost. People today, Jew and Gentile, still do the same. You can either stumble at that, or you can believe it. You can receive Him, or you can reject Him. And it is on that basis and that basis alone that you will either find yourself as one of the elected or one of the rejected.

Chapter Sixteen
P - Putting Christ in His Place

Romans 10:1 *Brethren, my heart's desire and prayer to God for Israel is, that they might be saved.* **2** *For I bear them record that they have a zeal of God, but not according to knowledge.* **3** *For they being ignorant of God's righteousness, and going about to establish their own righteousness, have not submitted themselves unto the righteousness of God.* **4** *For Christ is the end of the law for righteousness to every one that believeth.*

I have a map of the Pisgah Mountains where I have hiked many times. The map is *of* the Pisgah Mountains, but it is *not* the Pisgah Mountains. The map is a symbol of where I am going, a tool to direct me to the goal. It can *direct* me to shelter, but it cannot *give* me shelter. The map is not the goal; it is a tool to direct me to the goal. I can sit in my office for hours looking at the map, but if I never go out and follow it to a destination, it is useless.

The Jews had a divinely given map—the law. Had they followed it to where it was leading them, they would have arrived at Christ. Instead, they made the law itself the goal rather than a tool to reach the goal. In so doing, they became four things that we will study in this chapter.

Here are the four things they became:

213

An unsaved people

Romans 10:1 *Brethren, my heart's desire and prayer to God for Israel is, that they might be saved.*

One chapter earlier, Paul had said that he would be willing to die and go to hell if that would result in the children of Israel being saved. Now, here he is again expressing his heart's desire for them to get saved.

In other words, they were lost. They were incredibly religious. They were incredibly moral. But they were lost.

That did not bring Paul one ounce of pleasure. He wanted them to get saved. No real man of God is ever pleased by the idea of sinners going to hell.

Do we believe that over one billion Muslims are going to hell? Yes, we do. But that thought does not gladden our hearts; it breaks our hearts.

Do we believe that atheists and Hindus and Buddhists and new agers and cultists are going to hell? Yes, we do. But that thought does not gladden our hearts; it breaks our hearts.

Do we believe that homosexuals and lesbians and adulterers and fornicators are going to hell? Yes, we do. But that thought does not gladden our hearts; it breaks our hearts.

Do we believe that even the Jewish people who still reject Christ are going to hell? Yes, we do. But that thought does not gladden our hearts; it breaks our hearts.

Jesus does not want anyone to perish like that. We do not want anyone to perish like that.

But the Bible facts cannot be changed: anyone who does not receive the Lord Jesus Christ as their Savior is lost and on their way to hell.

John 14:6 *Jesus saith unto him, I am the way, the truth, and the life: no man cometh unto the Father, but by me.*

Revelation 20:15 *And whosoever was not found written in the book of life was cast into the lake of fire.*

Acts 4:10 *Be it known unto you all, and to all the people of Israel, that by the name of Jesus Christ of Nazareth, whom ye crucified, whom God raised from the dead, even by him doth this* *man stand here before you whole.* **11** *This is the stone which was set at nought of you builders, which is become the head of the corner.* **12** *Neither is there salvation in any other: for there is none other name under heaven given among men, whereby we must be saved.*

The Jewish people had the law. They had the roadmap that should have led them to Christ. But somewhere along the way, they substituted the roadmap for that which the roadmap was pointing to. They would hold the law in reverent hands, they would put it to their lips and kiss it, they would stand out of respect for its reading, but when the very One to whom the law was leading came and stood in their midst and offered Himself to them, they rejected Him.

I have no doubt in my mind that there are people today just like that. There are people today who reverence and respect the Bible and have never yet received as their personal Savior the One to whom all of the Bible points.

There are people who are going to kiss the Bible with their lips but will never call on Christ to save them with those very same lips.

There are people who will quote verses about Christ from the Bible and will never actually know Christ as their Savior.

No matter how much a person knows and respects their Bible, if they never put Christ in His place, they are an unsaved person.

An unstudied people

Romans 10:2 *For I bear them record that they have a zeal of God, but not according to knowledge.*

There is something that Paul does in verse two that everyone of us needs to learn from. Look at how he begins:

For I bear them record that they have a zeal of God...

This was not a bad thing; it was a good thing. The Jews despised and hated both Jesus and Paul. They were the greatest enemies that Paul ever had, but Paul loved them and wanted to win them to Christ. So, the very first thing he did was acknowledge that which was good about them.

It is very easy to get into a habit of only stating the negative about people on the opposite side of the fence from us. But if you really want to win people, you need to be honest, and honesty includes noticing both the good and the bad.

I am no longer Catholic, and I vehemently disagree with much of the doctrine of the Catholic church. But honesty compels me to point out the fact that very often, they are the ones out in front of some of the battles that we need to fight. They are generally extremely pro-life. Up until this particular Pope, they also believed exclusively in the biblical model of marriage being one man and one woman.

I am against the teachings of the Masonic Lodge. But the Shriners Hospital for children is one of the finest organizations on earth.

We ought to never be a part of any organization or church that teaches and preaches things contrary to Scripture. But we also ought to be honest about the good things that people do, because you cannot ignore all of those things and still expect them to hear you when you are trying to win them to Christ.

The Jewish people did have a zeal for God, but it is in the next thing that Paul says that we find the problem.

But not according to knowledge...

At first blush, this seems so incredible as to be almost impossible. These dear folks studied the Old Testament law constantly. They would spend hours a day reading and studying it. They memorized it. They could quote entire books.

How then did they manage to have a zeal for God but not according to knowledge?

Perhaps an illustration will make it clear. If you like shooting rifles and if you are going to shoot something a long distance off, what should you really have?

A scope. Most avid hunters know a great deal about their scope. They can give you brand names, model numbers, magnification power, and adjustment methodologies.

Think of the scope as the Old Testament Scripture. The Jews loved the scope. They spent hour after hour after hour looking at the scope. They knew so much about the scope; they could have taken it apart and then put it back together blindfolded and had it in perfect condition.

But is that the purpose of a scope? No, a scope is supposed to be something that you are looking through to give you a better view of something else. That something else was Christ! But instead of looking through the Scriptures to see Him, they looked at the Scriptures and missed Him completely.

The Bible is not just a book of rules and regulations. The Bible is not just a book of "thou shalt nots." The Bible is not just a book of facts and figures. The Bible is a roadmap to point us to Christ.

When you study the Bible, you need to study it to see Christ. The Bible ought to make you want to know Christ and to be like Christ and to see Christ.

I am all in favor of every one of us conforming our behavior to what the Bible, rightly divided, says. But if that is all we do, we are no better than the Jews who rejected Christ.

I believe with all my heart that people ought to dress and look right. But I get the distinct impression that in a lot of places, preachers would be satisfied having an entire church full of lost people on their way to hell as long as all of the people looked on the outside like they were saved.

Nicodemus looked like he was saved. Judas looked like he was saved. Our zeal for God must go beyond just figuring out the externals that Scripture expects of us. By all means, obey all of those external things. But the purpose of Scripture is to bring us to Christ; the purpose of Scripture is to bring us into a real, literal, personal relationship with Christ. If you ever get people into that kind of relationship with Christ, it is much easier to get them to obey all of the external things!

The Jewish people did not put Christ in His place, and as such, Paul regarded them as an unstudied people.

An unsubmitted people

Romans 10:3 *For they being ignorant of God's righteousness, and going about to establish their own righteousness, have not submitted themselves unto the righteousness of God.*

Paul leveled the loving accusation against his countrymen in verse three that they were ignorant of God's righteousness. After all of their study of the law, they still missed the fact that righteousness could never come by the works of that law.

Not one person in the Old Testament ever fulfilled the law perfectly. That, all by itself, should have pointed them to God's righteousness. But they were ignorant of it. And that ignorance of God's righteousness made them go about to establish their own righteousness.

Now, please do some grammar work with me. When it mentions them *going about to establish their own righteousness*, is that going about and that establishing an active thing on their part or a passive thing on their part? It is active; it is works. They believed that if they could DO enough, then God would regard them as righteous.

But the last phrase in verse three says they *have not submitted themselves unto the righteousness of God.*

Is submitting an active thing or a passive thing in the context of the means of salvation? It is passive. In other words, you can either try to work your way into God's righteousness, or you can admit that you cannot work your way into God's righteousness, and you can simply and humbly receive His righteousness. This is what God expected of His people, it is what Paul expected of his Jewish countrymen, and it is what God and Paul still expect of us, the Gentiles.

Every cult on earth teaches people that they can work their way to salvation. Christianity, the Bible, teaches that there is no work that you can do to get saved; you simply must humble yourself before God and receive what Jesus Christ did for you.

Paul said that it was a matter of submission. And that word brings up the biggest problem of man's heart: pride.

In general, mankind is far too proud to admit that there is nothing he can do to save himself. But Jesus said in **Luke 18:17** *Verily I say unto you, Whosoever shall not receive the kingdom of God as a little child shall in no wise enter therein.*

A child just simply and humbly believes and receives. And if you want to be saved, that is exactly what you are going to have to do.

An unsatisfied people

Romans 10:4 *For Christ is the end of the law for righteousness to every one that believeth.*

When Paul said that *Christ is the end of the law for righteousness,* you need to make sure that you do not misunderstand what he meant and assume that the law ever brought righteousness. It did not:

Hebrews 10:4 *For it is not possible that the blood of bulls and of goats should take away sins.*

All of the blood of animals that was shed in the Old Testament never did bring righteousness and never did get rid of sin. All it ever did was hold all the wrath of God back until the real Lamb could be slain on Calvary.

Paul said that *Christ is the end of the law for righteousness to every one that believeth.* What he meant by *end* was the goal or the conclusion. It is what all of the law was pointing to. Qurollo put it this way, "End may be used in the sense of termination or cessation, or it may be used in the sense of a goal toward which a movement is directed." (Qurollo, 167). Clearly, that latter definition is the one that fits with everything Paul has been saying about the law and righteousness. The law had as its end the goal of pointing everyone to Christ.

But what that means is that the Jewish people never did get to the last chapter of the book! They never did get to the dessert at the end of the meal. They never did get to put the ridge cap on the roof. Their search for righteousness was always incomplete, and thus they were always unsatisfied.

219

I saw a picture in a news story that says it all. There was a group of ultra-Orthodox Jews protesting women coming to the Wailing Wall to worship. The Old Testament says absolutely nothing about that. The New Testament says absolutely nothing about that. But the rigid customs of the ultra-Orthodox Jew have been to forbid women from coming to that place.

The picture was of an ultra-Orthodox Jew, a law-keeping Jew with the meanest and hateful look on his face you could possibly imagine. There was not one ounce of happiness there; there was not one ounce of satisfaction.

Having a relationship with Christ fixes that kind of thing! If you cannot seem to muster a smile on your face or a song in your heart, I question whether you have ever been born again. And if you have been born again, and yet you still find yourself continually miserable, then you may want to make sure that you have not done as the Galatians did and put yourself back under some form of bondage. Yes, we are to believe and behave right. But "right" is determined by what Scripture says, not by what a man says.

If anyone can show it to you clearly from Scripture, you ought to agree with it and abide by it. But anytime you find a situation where one person is preaching another person's opinion, who is preaching another person's opinion, you are going to find some very miserable people!

A relationship with Christ will not only bring purity, it will also bring pleasure.

A relationship with Christ will not only bring holiness, it will also bring happiness.

A relationship with Christ will not only bring some form and fashion, it will also bring freedom.

Christ is the end of the law for righteousness to them who believe. He is the goal and the conclusion of it all.

———————————〜——————————

We say it so often, but it really is true—it is all about Him.

Ronald Reagan many years ago, said it this way:

"Meaning no disrespect to the religious convictions of others, I still can't help wondering how we can explain away what to me is the greatest miracle of all and which is recorded in history. No one denies there was such a man, that he lived and that he was put to death by crucifixion. Where...is the miracle I spoke of? Well consider this and let your imagination translate the story into our own time—possibly to your own hometown. A young man whose father is a carpenter grows up working in his father's shop. One day he puts down his tools and walks out of his father's shop. He starts preaching on street corners and in the nearby countryside, walking from place to place, preaching all the while, even though he is not an ordained minister. He does this for three years. Then he is arrested, tried and convicted. There is no court of appeal, so he is executed at age 33 along with two common thieves. Those in charge of his execution roll dice to see who gets his clothing— the only possessions he has. His family cannot afford a burial place for him so he is interred in a borrowed tomb. End of story? No, this uneducated, propertyless young man who...left no written word has, for 2000 years, had a greater effect on the world than all the rulers, kings, emperors; all the conquerors, generals and admirals, all the scholars, scientists and philosophers who have ever lived—all of them put together. How do we explain that? ...unless he really was who he said he was." (Hannaford)

He was, and He is. And we need to put Him in His proper place, which begins by making sure He is in our hearts.

Chapter Seventeen
Q - Questions and Answers About Salvation

Romans 10:5 *For Moses describeth the righteousness which is of the law, That the man which doeth those things shall live by them.* **6** *But the righteousness which is of faith speaketh on this wise, Say not in thine heart, Who shall ascend into heaven? (that is, to bring Christ down from above:)* **7** *Or, Who shall descend into the deep? (that is, to bring up Christ again from the dead.)* **8** *But what saith it? The word is nigh thee, even in thy mouth, and in thy heart: that is, the word of faith, which we preach;* **9** *That if thou shalt confess with thy mouth the Lord Jesus, and shalt believe in thine heart that God hath raised him from the dead, thou shalt be saved.* **10** *For with the heart man believeth unto righteousness; and with the mouth confession is made unto salvation.* **11** *For the scripture saith, Whosoever believeth on him shall not be ashamed.* **12** *For there is no difference between the Jew and the Greek: for the same Lord over all is rich unto all that call upon him.* **13** *For whosoever shall call upon the name of the Lord shall be saved.* **14** *How then shall they call on him in whom they have not believed? and how shall they believe in him of whom they have not heard? and how shall they hear without a preacher?* **15** *And how shall they preach, except they be sent? as it is written, How beautiful are the feet of them that preach the gospel of peace, and bring glad tidings of good things!* **16** *But they have not all obeyed the gospel. For Esaias saith, Lord, who hath believed our report?* **17** *So then faith cometh by hearing, and hearing by the word of*

God. **18** *But I say, Have they not heard? Yes verily, their sound went into all the earth, and their words unto the ends of the world.* **19** *But I say, Did not Israel know? First Moses saith, I will provoke you to jealousy by them that are no people, and by a foolish nation I will anger you.* **20** *But Esaias is very bold, and saith, I was found of them that sought me not; I was made manifest unto them that asked not after me.* **21** *But to Israel he saith, All day long I have stretched forth my hands unto a disobedient and gainsaying people.*

Children learn very early to ask questions. Usually, it is "Why?"

In this text, there are ten questions, each one concerning salvation:

Who shall ascend into heaven? (that is, to bring Christ down from above)

Who shall descend into the deep? (that is, to bring up Christ again from the dead)

But what saith it? The word is nigh thee, even in thy mouth, and in thy heart: that is, the word of faith, which we preach.

How then shall they call on him in whom they have not believed?

How shall they believe in him of whom they have not heard?

How shall they hear without a preacher?

How shall they preach, except they be sent?

Lord, who hath believed our report?

Have they not heard?

Did not Israel know?

That is ten question marks in just a few short verses. You will be hard-pressed to find another portion of Scripture quite like this one. Paul knew that questions would arise about salvation, so he went ahead and asked them and then answered them. These ten questions can be divided into three headings.

Questions on the means of salvation

The last thing Paul said in verse four was *For Christ is the end of the law for righteousness to every one that believeth.*

I trust that you remember that by *end* he meant the goal, the whole point, the thing the law was directing everyone to. Now, look at how he begins verse five:

Romans 10:5 *For Moses describeth the righteousness which is of the law, That the man which doeth those things shall live by them.*

By starting with the word *for,* you know that what he is going to say is going to verify or expand on what he just said in the previous verse. This verse is a quote from **Leviticus 18:5**. *Ye shall therefore keep my statutes, and my judgments: which if a man do, he shall live in them: I am the LORD.*

The Old Testament law was to be followed, no questions asked. If a person followed it, he was allowed to live, whereas if he broke certain portions of it, his very life was forfeit.

But this also meant that if a person did keep the law, there were temporal blessings that would be his. He would not just *get to live;* he would *live,* and he would have a good life. That is all the law could offer: the ability to live and to live well. But what it could not offer was a way for you to live forever. It could help you here and now, but it could not help you with eternity. That is why the next verse starts with a word of contrast:

Romans 10:6 *But the righteousness which is of faith speaketh on this wise, Say not in thine heart, Who shall ascend into heaven? (that is, to bring Christ down from above:)* **7** *Or, Who shall descend into the deep? (that is, to bring up Christ again from the dead.)* **8** *But what saith it? The word is nigh thee, even in thy mouth, and in thy heart: that is, the word of faith, which we preach;*

There is the righteousness of the law, and there is the righteousness of faith. Throughout the book, Paul will draw this contrast.

When dealing with the law, everyone could at least agree on one thing—it was really hard. But when dealing with the righteousness which is by faith, people who did not understand would come to the exact same conclusion: it is really hard!

"How are we going to get up into heaven to bring down this Christ that you say is necessary for salvation? Or, if He is still dead, how are we going to bring Him back up?"

Paul wanted to let them know that yes, salvation is by Christ alone, but no, it is not far off. It is not way up in heaven; it is not way down in the grave or paradise. Verse eight says that it is right nearby. In fact, you carry the potential of salvation with you at all times in your mouth and in your heart! How? Look at the next verse.

Romans 10:9 *That if thou shalt confess with thy mouth the Lord Jesus, and shalt believe in thine heart that God hath raised him from the dead, thou shalt be saved.* **10** *For with the heart man believeth unto righteousness; and with the mouth confession is made unto salvation.*

These two verses answer the questions about the means of salvation, and what they make very clear is that salvation is available to all.

What do these two verses teach in regard to salvation?

We must confess with our mouth not just *Jesus*, but the *Lord Jesus*. In this one statement, we find both repentance and confession. Every sinner is the Lord of his or her own life. By acknowledging Christ as the Lord of his or her life, the sinner has fully changed direction. He used to be in control of his life, but he has now ceded that control to Jesus.

By confessing Jesus with his mouth, he has shown that change of attitude in his heart. Anyone who will not openly confess Christ as Lord has never received Him, and anyone who has received Him will willingly and readily confess Him.

We are also told that we must believe in our heart that God hath raised Him from the dead. We therefore very specifically find that not all "belief" is from the heart. There is a belief that is nothing more than a mental assent to a fact.

The devil believes in the resurrection!

But he is not saved. Belief for him has never been anything more than a set of facts in the brain—real belief, heart belief, always, always, always, results in a change of behavior.

If a person is sitting on a ticking time bomb, he can, perhaps, discuss with you all of the intricate details of the bomb itself. But if he does not move, that belief has never reached his heart!

When a sinner finally gets to the place where he believes in the resurrection of Christ in his heart, it will change everything about him. It will result in that person being born again and showing it.

The belief from the heart is mentioned again in verse ten. I hear from some quarters these days that we are in error when we speak of "receiving Christ into our hearts." But based on these two verses, it is entirely appropriate to say that we must receive Christ into our hearts. Yes, we know that it is not the literal blood-pumping organ that is being spoken of. But since the Bible euphemistically uses "the heart" as the seat of true belief, belief far deeper than mere mental assent, and since John 1:12 speaks of receiving Christ, the terminology is appropriate.

But the mouth is also mentioned again in verse ten. The second reference to confessing Him with our mouths led Paul to the thought of verse eleven.

Romans 10:11 *For the scripture saith, Whosoever believeth on him shall not be ashamed.*

There are multiple references in the Bible to believers not being ashamed. In those multiple references, we find two meanings given. One, whoever truly believes on Him will not later find out that he was wrong and have to be embarrassed by having placed their faith in something that turned out not to be true.

The second meaning, though, is that whoever truly believes in Him will not be ashamed to speak up and say so. That is what is being spoken of here. We know that because Paul just got done mentioning, twice, confessing Him with our mouths.

227

If a person is ashamed to admit that he is a Christian, he really does not need to worry about it, because he is not a Christian.

Romans 10:12 *For there is no difference between the Jew and the Greek: for the same Lord over all is rich unto all that call upon him.*

In verse eleven, Paul had been dealing with confessing with the mouth. In so doing, he quoted from several Old Testament passages that, taken together, basically said, "Whosoever believeth on him shall not be ashamed." But in quoting those verses, he brought another thought into the mix— the *whosoever* thought. And that is why he said what he said in verse twelve.

By *whosoever*, people need to understand that He really meant whosoever! Salvation was not just a gift to believing Jews; it was and is a gift to believing "whosoevers!" God desires to save people of every skin color and ethnic background on earth. Whoever you are, whatever you look like, if you will call on Him, He will pour out the riches of His salvation all over you!

Just in case that was not clear enough, he said it one more time and one more way in the very next verse:

Romans 10:13 *For whosoever shall call upon the name of the Lord shall be saved.*

This verse is a paraphrase of Joel 2:32. Paul uses it to point out that the final step in salvation is not "finally getting ourselves right." The final step in salvation is asking Him to save you. There will be people who know all of the facts about Christ and salvation who die and go to hell simply because they never humbled themselves to ask.

Before we move on to the next verse, though, we should delve more fully into that *whosoever*. You see, God did a very lovely thing when He inspired that word; He got "intentionally wordy." Most of the time in the New Testament, *whosoever* is from *hos an*, or *hos ean*. On other occasions, it will be from the word *pas*, which also means *everyone*, *each one*, *and anyone*. But in Romans 10:13, when dealing with who could call on the Lord and be saved, He used both of those, and put one in an out-of-typical-order placement for emphasis. It looks like this, *Pas gar hos ean,* and those in Paul's day would have read it as *anyone for whosoever!* So when God said *whosoever* here in Romans 10:13, please understand that He really did mean *WHOSOEVER!*

Questions on the messengers of salvation

Romans 10:14 *How then shall they call on him in whom they have not believed? and how shall they believe in him of whom they have not heard? and how shall they hear without a preacher? 15 And how shall they preach, except they be sent? as it is written, How beautiful are the feet of them that preach the gospel of peace, and bring glad tidings of good things!*

There are four questions posed back to back to back to back. Each one of them can be answered with a negative.

Salvation requires faith in Jesus. So, how then can people call on someone to save them if they do not believe in Him? The answer is, they really cannot. They can say the words, but they are not really calling on Him in faith from the heart.

I had a recent conversation with a half-drunk, fornicating atheist. Angry at me (at Scripture, really), he said, "You want me to ask Him into my heart? OK, here goes." Then he blurted out a version of the sinner's prayer and said, "Are you satisfied? I'm all good now!"

No, he was not and is not. You can say all the right words, but you really cannot call on Him until you believe in Him.

The second question is, how can a person believe in someone they have not heard about? The answer to that is incredibly obvious—they cannot. Until a person hears about Jesus, they cannot believe in Jesus.

Some years ago, I ran a jewelry store nearby to a poor neighborhood. A young boy, about thirteen years old, often came over and asked for work to earn a few dollars. I would let him clean or mow if I could.

One year just before Christmas, he came in the evening and knocked on the door. I let him in, and he asked if there was any work he could do. I told him no, there was not at that time. Then it occurred to me that I had never witnessed to the young man. I asked him if he knew what Christmas is really about. He had no clue, none at all. So I told him the real Christmas story. He was stunned; he had never heard any of it.

The very next night, he came back, bringing a friend with him. He said, "Preacher man? Could you tell him what you told me? I tried to explain it, but he had never heard it either..."

These boys lived in the shadow of five steeples and had never heard of Jesus.

The third question is, how shall they hear without a preacher? The answer is they probably will not. It is possible that they could just, at random, pick up a Bible and read it, never having heard preaching, and get saved. But it is not very likely. How many of you, the readers of this book, heard from a preacher before you got saved? The answer is likely to be the vast majority of you.

The fourth question is, how can they preach unless God sends them to preach? The answer is they really cannot. In practice, many do. There are, I believe, a massive number of people in the ministry who have never been called to the ministry. Real preaching, though, requires a call from God. There are a lot of preachers sermonizing, shouting, parsing, expounding, but not preaching, because real heaven-empowered preaching requires a call from God.

I am not talking about good, godly laymen going to nursing homes and such. Even Stephen the deacon preached. I am talking about actually being in the ministry. If you are not called, do not do it. Souls are too precious to play with, and many an uncalled preacher has sent people to hell by trying to do what they are not called to do.

Look at how Paul ends this section dealing with preachers. *How beautiful are the feet of them that preach the gospel of peace, and bring glad tidings of good things!*

This is a quote from **Isaiah 52:7** *How beautiful upon the mountains are the feet of him that bringeth good tidings, that* *publisheth peace; that bringeth good tidings of good, that publisheth salvation; that saith unto Zion, Thy God reigneth!*

The picture, both in Isaiah and Romans, is that of a man wandering the mountains and valleys, searching every nook and cranny, trying to find every single person to tell them the good news.

A person like that would have physically ugly feet from all of the abuse and wear, but those feet were regarded as beautiful by those who got the good news!

Child of God, every day that you take someone the gospel is a day that you have beautiful feet.

Questions on the mishandling of salvation

Romans 10:16 *But they have not all obeyed the gospel. For Esaias saith, Lord, who hath believed our report?*

The good news had been taken into the hills and hollows by the messengers. But sadly, not everyone received it. Some people actually denied it, disbelieved it, rejected it. Paul referenced the first words of Isaiah 53 about people not believing the message that was brought. And strikingly, Isaiah 53 is the clearest Old Testament description of the crucifixion of Christ.

Romans 10:17 *So then faith cometh by hearing, and hearing by the word of God. 18 But I say, Have they not heard? Yes verily, their sound went into all the earth, and their words unto the ends of the world.*

It is important, after you read verse sixteen, to take verses seventeen and eighteen together. If you do not, it probably will not make sense at all; it may even make you think the exact opposite of what Paul was thinking.

He had just gotten done mentioning that Isaiah preached, Isaiah gave a report, and that the people did not believe and did not get saved. Then he says *So then faith cometh by hearing and hearing by the word of God.*

Do you see how that could get confusing?

But when you immediately add verse eighteen, it begins to make sense. Yes, faith comes by hearing and hearing by the Word of God. And yes, Isaiah preached, they heard, and did not

231

believe. People were thus going to ask, "Well, if hearing the Word of God brings faith, did they not hear?"

The answer is yes, they did. In fact, even in Paul's day, he said that the message had gone unto the ends of the world! So why then did everyone not get saved if faith comes by hearing and everyone had heard? Keep reading, he will get to that.

Romans 10:19 *But I say, Did not Israel know? First Moses saith, I will provoke you to jealousy by them that are no people, and by a foolish nation I will anger you.*

What is the answer to the question asked here? Yes, Israel did know. Moses made all the things of God very clear to them. And yet, for some reason, that was not good enough, and God had to provoke them to jealousy to get them to even think of Him. This was in Deuteronomy 32:16, and it was a prophecy of the calling of the Gentiles.

The Jews never seemed to think too much of salvation, until they heard the Gentiles were getting saved, then suddenly they got jealous!

Romans 10:20 *But Esaias is very bold, and saith, I was found of them that sought me not; I was made manifest unto them that asked not after me.*

This is a quote from Isaiah 65:1.

Isaiah 65:1 *I am sought of them that asked not for me; I am found of them that sought me not: I said, Behold me, behold me, unto a nation that was not called by my name.*

Just like before, this is a reference to the calling of the Gentiles.

The Gentiles heard the preaching of the Word of God; they believed it, they received it, and they got saved. That is the way it is supposed to work. But that brings us back to our question about why the Jews heard the same preaching and the same word and did not get saved. That will be answered in the last verse.

Romans 10:21 *But to Israel he saith, All day long I have stretched forth my hands unto a disobedient and gainsaying* [*antilego,* contradictory, against the word] *people.*

There is your answer. They heard the same preaching, they had access to the same Bible truth, but their heart attitude was one of disobedience and contradiction.

It is not that they could not hear; it is that they would not listen.

Chapter Eighteen
R - Remnants and Riches

Romans 11:1 *I say then, Hath God cast away his people? God forbid. For I also am an Israelite, of the seed of Abraham, of the tribe of Benjamin.* **2** *God hath not cast away his people which he foreknew. Wot ye not what the scripture saith of Elias? how he maketh intercession to God against Israel, saying,* **3** *Lord, they have killed thy prophets, and digged down thine altars; and I am left alone, and they seek my life.* **4** *But what saith the answer of God unto him? I have reserved to myself seven thousand men, who have not bowed the knee to the image of Baal.* **5** *Even so then at this present time also there is a* **remnant** *according to the election of grace.* **6** *And if by grace, then is it no more of works: otherwise grace is no more grace. But if it be of works, then is it no more grace: otherwise work is no more work.* **7** *What then? Israel hath not obtained that which he seeketh for; but the election hath obtained it, and the rest were blinded* **8** *(According as it is written, God hath given them the spirit of slumber, eyes that they should not see, and ears that they should not hear;) unto this day.* **9** *And David saith, Let their table be made a snare, and a trap, and a stumblingblock, and a recompence unto them:* **10** *Let their eyes be darkened, that they may not see, and bow down their back alway.* **11** *I say then, Have they stumbled that they should fall? God forbid: but rather through their fall salvation is come unto the Gentiles, for to provoke them to jealousy.* **12** *Now if the fall of them be the* **riches**

*of the world, and the diminishing of them the **riches** of the Gentiles; how much more their fulness?*

I am not extremely well-versed on all things sewing. But there is one thing that I have learned: Not all fabrics are alike, either in quality or price. There are "rich" fabrics like leather and silk and velvet that will cost you a lot of money. There are "bargain" fabrics like cotton and polyester and corduroy that will not cost you as much. When a person goes to buy some of these less expensive fabrics, they might not buy everything left on the roll. The sad, homeless little piece that is left over is a "remnant." Not only is it not a "rich" fabric, it is now not even a whole piece of bargain fabric anymore. Somewhere, somebody may know about and desire that little remnant, but it is not nearly as desirable as if it were a complete piece.

Israel was once a whole, beautiful, rich tapestry woven by the very hand of God. She was beautiful and ornate, desirable in every way. All of the other nations were, by comparison, cheap little scraps of torn, dirty fabric. But Israel chose to reject God. She followed hard after idols: Baal, Moloch, and Ashtoreth. Eventually, God had had enough of this and sent her into captivity. After seventy years, some of the people came home and rebuilt. Some four hundred years later, God sent not a mere prophet but His own darling Son to this rebellious people. Jesus came unto His own, but His own received Him not. They rejected Him as completely as possible, hanging Him on a cross to die in agony. Three days later, they became aware of the fact that He had risen from the dead! They knew it to be true; their own men told them what they had witnessed. Once again, rather than believing the obvious truth, they willingly rejected Christ and His apostles who were carrying His message everywhere.

Finally, Paul said this in **Acts 13:46,** *Then Paul and Barnabas waxed bold, and said, It was necessary that the word of God should first have been spoken to you: but seeing ye put it from you, and judge yourselves unworthy of everlasting life, lo, we turn to the **Gentiles**.*

The Gospel has, for the last two thousand years, been received primarily by the Gentiles. But the heart of Paul never

236

stopped beating for his people, the Jews, and the heart of God has never stopped beating for His people, the Jews.

This world is becoming, yet again, as it has been many other times in history, very anti-Semitic. A reporter named Ami Horowitz (November 2014) went to the campus of the University of California, Berkeley. He held up the flag of ISIS. You may remember them: they are the ones cutting American's heads off with hunting knives, gang-raping Christian women, and even doing the same to children. They are Muslims, and they hate everything about us and Israel.

So, how would you expect kids on an American college campus to respond? One person waved at him, another gave him a fist bump, and another wished him "good luck."

But it is the second part when Ami Horowitz waved an Israeli flag that got a lot of attention. The college students held nothing back as they accused Horowitz of murdering children. They even hailed Hamas. One student even made claims that Israel is the thief in the night and a thief in the day while another said the Israeli flag represents the psychological genocide of the planet. (Grossman)

Do you understand that? Muslims who cut people's heads off with a hunting knife and gang rape women and children: good. Jews who have the only country in the Middle East where that kind of thing does not happen: bad.

This world hates the Jewish people! But God loves them in spite of the fact that they rejected Him, and Paul loved them, and if you are right with God, you love them.

Remnants

Romans 11:1 *I say then, Hath God cast away his people? God forbid. For I also am an Israelite, of the seed of Abraham, of the tribe of Benjamin.*

By the phrasing he uses in the first half of verse one, Paul means, "In light of what I said in chapter ten, verses twenty and twenty-one, has God rejected Israel? God forbid!"

If God had *cast away His people*, if He had rejected everyone of Jewish blood just because the nation as a corporate body rejected and crucified Him, that would have put Paul in sort of a bad predicament, since he was a full-blooded Jew! Paul knew exactly what tribe he was from, Benjamin; he could literally trace his genealogy father to father to father all the way back to Abraham.

We had better be very glad God does not reject individuals based on the corporate decisions of the body of people they are in.

Romans 11:2a *God hath not cast away his people which he foreknew.*

That should be enough; that should settle it. Here it is, written in the pages of Scripture. God has not cast away His people that He foreknew as His people even before they existed to be His people. If you think God is done with the Jewish people, you do not know your Bible or the heart of God.

Romans 11:2b *Wot ye not* [Do you not know] *what the scripture saith of Elias? how he maketh intercession to God against Israel, saying, 3 Lord, they have killed thy prophets, and digged down thine altars; and I am left alone, and they seek my life. 4 But what saith the answer of God unto him? I have reserved to myself seven thousand men, who have not bowed the knee to the image of Baal.*

In these words, Paul harkened back to the days of Elijah. Elijah was completely convinced that all of his people had gone bad, and that God was done with them.

But God said, "I still have 7,000!"

Romans 11:5 *Even so then at this present time also there is a remnant according to the election of grace.*

Even so, meaning just like in the days of Elijah that were just referenced, there is still a remnant, and that remnant is *according to the election* [the choice] *of grace.* It did not have to be that way; God's grace chose to make it so. In Paul's day, it was mainly Gentiles getting saved, but thanks to the choice of grace, there were a few dear Jews as well, and there always will be. Even when it seems like that is all there will ever be, you need to understand that God has promised to redeem His people as a body. Look at what Isaiah said:

Isaiah 1:27 *Zion shall be redeemed with judgment, and her converts with righteousness.*

There is going to come a day when they recognize and receive their Messiah. Until then, He still loves them, and we still love them. His love has not ceased just because they do not believe. God made a promise to Abraham, which is what that *election of grace* is talking about, and He is going to keep it, all of it!

Romans 11:6 *And if by grace, then is it no more of works: otherwise grace is no more grace. But if it be of works, then is it no more grace: otherwise work is no more work.*

This verse has a distinct "Dr. Suess sound" to it. But it is, in reality, both simple and profound. Paul had just spoken of grace, and his desire was now to distinguish between works and grace, which, for some reason, many religious systems cannot even to this day seem to grasp.

Grace and works are mutually exclusive.

If you, Jew or Gentile, are saved by grace, it is no more works. There is nothing you can do to "earn grace." If there are works involved, such as being baptized, taking the sacraments, joining the church, going to confession, or tithing, then it is not grace anymore.

If it is by grace, then it is not by works: if it is, grace is not actually grace anymore. But if it is by works, then is it not grace anymore, and if it is by grace, then work really is not work anymore, because it will not work!

Jew or Gentile, you will get saved by grace through faith in Jesus Christ alone, or you will not get saved. If you try to add in your own efforts and morality, you will pollute grace and turn it into works, and you will stay lost.

When you get saved, you will work. The book of James is based on that very premise.

But it is salvation that produces works, not works that produce salvation.

Romans 11:7 & 8b *What then? Israel hath not obtained that which he seeketh for; but the election hath obtained it, and the rest were blinded* (parenthesis of verse 8) *unto this day.*

Let's take just a moment to compare this sentence with another, lest we end up confused and in error.

Romans 9:31 *But Israel, which followed after the law of righteousness, hath not attained to the law of righteousness.* **32** *Wherefore? Because they sought it not by faith, but as it were by the works of the law. For they stumbled at that stumblingstone;*

All of Romans 9 was about the doctrine of election. We covered it very thoroughly and ended with these two verses which show us that election was not arbitrary and not a whim. The Calvinist view of election as being "unconditional" is simply wrong. Israel did not obtain the election because she sought it by works.

Romans 11:7 tells us that they did seek for it. But the elect, the saved of both Jews and Gentiles, sought for it and found it. And once again, everything that Paul has said makes it very clear that they sought it by faith and found it through grace. The rest were blinded even unto Paul's day, but not arbitrarily.

Romans 11:8 *(According as it is written, God hath given them the spirit of slumber, eyes that they should not see, and ears that they should not hear;) unto this day.*

The parenthesis of this passage is a paraphrase from Isaiah:

Isaiah 29:10 *For the LORD hath poured out upon you the spirit of deep sleep, and hath closed your eyes: the prophets and your rulers, the seers hath he covered.*

While reading these words, you need to remember that the slumber/separation started with them, not God. God made them His covenant people, and they broke that covenant, leading God to harden them in their rebellion as a judgment against them.

Their rejection of God started a long time ago and was still going on in Paul's day. They have had a "one-sided relationship" with God almost since Egypt.

Romans 11:9 *And David saith, Let their table be made a snare, and a trap, and a stumblingblock, and a recompence unto them:* **10** *Let their eyes be darkened, that they may not see, and bow down their back alway.*

This is from **Psalm 69:22-23** *Let their table become a snare before them: and that which should have been for their welfare, let it become a trap. Let their eyes be darkened, that they see not; and make their loins continually to shake.*

Paul's use of Psalm 69 in this place is very interesting. Psalm 69 has many prophetical references to Christ within it, and was used as such frequently in the New Testament. But in the days that it was penned, it was David lamenting against his enemies. So it seems that his enemies at that time were those of his own people, the Jews, and David was calling for their blindness, which would remove their ability to attack him any further.

Paul uses this as another example of how Israel went from being a tapestry to being a remnant. They fixated on works, rejected God, and were given blindness that made them miss the One the works (the laws of the Old Testament) were supposed to be pointing them to.

Riches

Romans 11:11 *I say then, Have they stumbled that they should fall? God forbid: but rather through their fall salvation is come unto the Gentiles, for to provoke them to jealousy.*

These verses will take us to the perspective of God. From the perspective of the Jewish people, no one could argue that there was a massive fall. They went from conquering a land to establishing a world-class kingdom, to internal decay, to falling into servitude and being carried away into bondage.

But their stumbling was not *that* [*hina*, in order that] *they should fall. Fall*, in that first phrase, is from *pipto*, meaning here *to fall into complete ruin*. To that thought, Paul once again gave a horrified *God forbid!* Anyone who believes the Jews ever have or ever will be completely ruined, abandoned by God, is not even in the same zip code as Scripture on the subject.

The other two uses of the word *fall* in verses eleven and twelve are from a different word, the word *paraptoma*. That word means *to fall near to something or someone*. Do you see and understand the stark contrast God is intentionally drawing?

241

The Jews fell, yes. But not into ruin; God would never allow that. He allowed them to *fall nearby*, right where He could pick them up again at just the right time.

The purpose of their stumbling was not that they should fall and stay down. From the perspective of God, their fall had a two-fold purpose. First, our salvation, and second, their jealousy which will one day lead to their salvation, and thus their rising from their fall.

Romans 11:12 *Now if the fall of them be the **riches** of the world, and the diminishing of them the **riches** of the Gentiles; how much more their fulness?*

We are made rich because of their fall. The riches of the gospel have been granted to the Gentile world because Jesus came unto His own, and His own received him not.

But if we have been made rich by their fall, how much richer will we be made by their restoration! How much more glorious will it be when we serve Jesus *with them* rather than *instead of them!*

That day is coming.

Chapter Nineteen
S - Severity and Goodness

Romans 11:13 *For I speak to you Gentiles, inasmuch as I am the apostle of the Gentiles, I magnify mine office:* **14** *If by any means I may provoke to emulation them which are my flesh, and might save some of them.* **15** *For if the casting away of them be the reconciling of the world, what shall the receiving of them be, but life from the dead?* **16** *For if the firstfruit be holy, the lump is also holy: and if the root be holy, so are the branches.* **17** *And if some of the branches be broken off, and thou, being a wild olive tree, wert graffed in among them, and with them partakest of the root and fatness of the olive tree;* **18** *Boast not against the branches. But if thou boast, thou bearest not the root, but the root thee.* **19** *Thou wilt say then, The branches were broken off, that I might be graffed in.* **20** *Well; because of unbelief they were broken off, and thou standest by faith. Be not highminded, but fear:* **21** *For if God spared not the natural branches, take heed lest he also spare not thee.* **22** *Behold therefore the goodness and severity of God: on them which fell, severity; but toward thee, goodness, if thou continue in his goodness: otherwise thou also shalt be cut off.* **23** *And they also, if they abide not still in unbelief, shall be graffed in: for God is able to graff them in again.* **24** *For if thou wert cut out of the olive tree which is wild by nature, and wert graffed contrary to nature into a good olive tree: how much more shall these, which be the natural branches, be graffed into their own olive tree?* **25** *For I would not, brethren, that ye should be ignorant of this* *mystery, lest ye should be wise in your own conceits; that blindness in part is happened to Israel, until the fulness of the Gentiles be come in. 26 And so all Israel shall be saved: as it is written, There shall come out of Sion the Deliverer, and shall turn away ungodliness from Jacob: 27 For this is my covenant unto them, when I shall take away their sins. 28 As concerning the gospel, they are enemies for your sakes: but as touching the election, they are beloved for the fathers' sakes. 29 For the gifts and calling of God are without repentance. 30 For as ye in times past have not believed God, yet have now obtained mercy through their unbelief: 31 Even so have these also now not believed, that through your mercy they also may obtain mercy. 32 For God hath concluded them all in unbelief, that he might have mercy upon all. 33 O the depth of the riches both of the wisdom and knowledge of God! how unsearchable are his judgments, and his ways past finding out! 34 For who hath known the mind of the Lord? or who hath been his counsellor? 35 Or who hath first given to him, and it shall be recompensed unto him again? 36 For of him, and through him, and to him, are all things: to whom be glory for ever. Amen.*

Not all vegetation is treated equally. Each year, we try our hand at gardening. The plants we fertilize, water, and care for. The weeds we yank up, chop down, and poison. The allusion to plant life is one that is used often in Scripture. Paul is going to use it in this passage to drive home a few points about God's dealings with Jews and Gentiles. The key verses we will look at in considering this entire passage are verses twenty-two and twenty-three:

Romans 11:22 *Behold therefore the **goodness** and **severity** of God: on them which fell, **severity**; but toward thee, **goodness**, if thou continue in his goodness: otherwise thou also shalt be cut off. 23 And they also, if they abide not still in **unbelief**, shall be graffed in: for God is able to graff them in again.*

Notice that God's dealing with us in either severity or goodness will be based on our belief or unbelief.

244

The provoking of Israel

Romans 11:13 *For I speak to you Gentiles, inasmuch as I am the apostle of the Gentiles, I magnify mine office:*

The office God had called him to was one that was sneered at by the "religious elite." Being an "apostle to the Gentiles" was much akin to being appointed a toilet cleaner in our day, such was their disdain for the Gentiles.

But Paul did not feel cursed by his ministry; he loved it! Others may have minimized his office, but he magnified his office. We should rejoice wherever God puts us. A nursery worker or janitor or usher or Sunday school teacher for the Lord is a lofty thing in the eyes of the Lord. A pastor of a church small in number is nonetheless doing a huge thing in the eyes of God.

Romans 11:14 *If by any means I may provoke to emulation them which are my flesh, and might save some of them.*

Paul was glorifying the blessed state of the saved Gentiles (v.12) and magnifying his office to the Gentiles (v.13) to make the Jews jealous, so that some of them might be saved. He knew he would never reach all, but he was determined to reach some, and he wanted the Gentiles to know he was doing so. He did not want them to ever get the idea that God was done with the Jews and satisfied with just them.

One important thing we should note, here, is that people often use the *any means* of this verse to justify doing wicked things to draw the wicked. We know Paul did not mean that, for he never DID that, and he also wrote **1 Thessalonians 5:22** *Abstain from all appearance of evil.*

Romans 11:15 *For if the casting away of them be the reconciling of the world, what shall the receiving of them be, but life from the dead?*

Much of the Gentile world has been reconciled to God because of the Jews' fall. If something that bad has produced something that good, how good will it be when they too accept Him! It will be *life from the dead*. The Jews as God's people will be resurrected, and the unity of mankind under the one true God will be resurrected. Have you ever just wanted "everybody to get along?" That is what this verse is describing, because the entire world will get along when the entire world has and worships the same God in spirit and in truth.

Romans 11:16 *For if the firstfruit be holy, the lump is also holy: and if the root be holy, so are the branches.*

Abraham was the first fruit of the wheat harvest and the root of the tree. The Jews, his descendants, are the lump of dough produced by the wheat harvest and the branches of the tree. The Jews, though they still reject Christ, are His holy, purchased possession, and they will one day accept Him. Some have even now, partly due to this "provoking of Israel," but one day all will, according to verse twenty-six. But you need to understand that, even while many of them are lost, God still regards them as His holy possession in the sense of them being "set apart to Himself." They may not be saved, but they are still His as far as He is concerned.

Does that mean they get to go to heaven even if they are lost? No, but it does mean that He still loves them and that you better keep your hands off of them.

The pride of the Gentiles

Romans 11:17 *And if some of the branches be broken off, and thou, being a wild olive tree, wert graffed in among them, and with them partakest of the root and fatness of the olive tree;* **18** *Boast not against the branches. But if thou boast, thou bearest not the root, but the root thee.*

Normally, a tree trunk would have all of its poor branches broken off, and good branches would be placed in the gaps. Here, the exact opposite thing is seen. The spiritual line of Abraham that God started is the strong, healthy roots and tree. Israel was the original branch, which, for a time, produced much good fruit. The Gentiles were wild, unfruitful branches on the root and stem of our father, the Devil. Because of unbelief, many of the Jews were cut off, and we were grafted in. We are blessed to partake of the strength of His roots; we are privileged to enjoy the fatness of the tree; we got saved through Jesus Christ, who came from the line of Abraham and was everything that the line of Abraham pointed to.

Now, picture yourself as a tree branch. You have been yanked out of a gnarled, warped, nasty wild olive tree. You have been grafted into a pure, strong cultivated olive tree. You look down, and underneath you are the ripped-off, discarded branches of non-believing Jews. You might look down at them in pride and sneer, "I'm on the tree and you're on the ground!" Paul has a word for you—You do not bear the root; the root bears you! If not for Christ, we would be as they are!

A Christian must never forget that every good thing that we have, we got through the line of those Jews. Our Bible came from the Jews; our Jesus came from the Jews.

Romans 11:19 *Thou wilt say then, The branches were broken off, that I might be graffed in.* **20** *Well; because of unbelief they were broken off, and thou standest by faith. Be not highminded, but fear:* **21** *For if God spared not the natural branches, take heed lest he also spare not thee.* **22** *Behold therefore the goodness and severity of God: on them which fell, severity; but toward thee, goodness, if thou continue in his goodness: otherwise thou also shalt be cut off.*

Paul opens this section of verses by stating what he knows the response of certain Gentiles will be to what he has said. And indeed, that proud "they were cut off and we were grafted in" argument is ubiquitous even in our day. But Paul's rejoinder to that began with a rather sarcastic *well*. That word is from *kalos*, and it means *beautiful!* Do you see the sarcasm dripping off of that?

Beautiful! You guys are on the tree; way to go, you. But you might want to remember that the good, natural branches were cut off because of their unbelief, and you were grafted in because of your belief, your faith. In other words, if you go the way they went, God will hack you off even quicker than He did them, since you are not even native to this tree to begin with!

No wonder Paul told them to *be not highminded, but fear.*

It is a matter of goodness and severity. Just as they were cut off, we could be as well. God has been very good to the Gentile world that has by and large followed Jesus, but that is not our permanent birthright, and America especially needs to remember that the blessings God has bestowed upon us are things He can just as easily take away from us.

This is becoming a very wicked land. We sing "America, America, God shed His grace on thee," but our wickedness could very well bring us to a point where He no longer does. If He cut off His own people, what makes us think He will refrain from doing so to us?

The promise of God

Romans 11:23 *And they also, if they abide not still in unbelief, shall be graffed in: for God is able to graff them in again.* **24** *For if thou wert cut out of the olive tree which is wild by nature, and wert graffed contrary to nature into a good olive tree: how much more shall these, which be the natural branches, be graffed into their own olive tree?*

God is ever ready to accept the believing Jew. He is able and desirous that these, His original chosen people, be saved. His heart has never stopped beating for His people.

In a national sense, God is more desirous that the Jew be saved than anyone else. Before you balk at that, look what Paul said. He said, *How much MORE shall these which be natural branches be graffed in?* God so loved the world, yes, but He has a special bond and connection with the Jewish people that goes all the way back to Abraham. We Gentiles were cut out of a wild olive tree (paganism, idolatry) and were, against nature, grafted into the good tree of belief that came through the line of Abraham. If God was willing to do that for Gentiles, no Gentile needs to think for even a moment that God will not quickly and gladly graft the Jews right back onto that tree that for them was natural to begin with.

Romans 11:25 *For I would not, brethren, that ye should be ignorant of this mystery, lest ye should be wise in your own*

248

conceits; that blindness in part is happened to Israel, until the fulness of the Gentiles be come in.

Now, I know that is very hard to imagine, but Paul was concerned that we Gentile Christians might get conceited. Yes, I write that in a pen dripping with sarcasm. Conceit is to us as natural as breathing, and Paul wanted to warn us against it.

The blindness that affects most but not all of the Jews is only temporary. When the last Gentile is saved, this blindness will be removed. How thoroughly? Look at the next verse:

Romans 11:26 *And so all Israel shall be saved: as it is written, There shall come out of Sion the Deliverer, and shall turn away ungodliness from Jacob:*

In the last days, every Jew left alive will receive Him. At the end of the Tribulation Period, they will turn their eyes to Him and will one and all acknowledge Him as their Messiah.

Romans 11:27 *For this is my covenant unto them, when I shall take away their sins.*

Are the Jews a sinful people? Yes. But God has made a covenant to remove their sins, and He will do it:

Isaiah 27:9a *By this therefore shall the iniquity of Jacob be purged;*

Ezekiel 36:26 *A new heart also will I give you, and a new spirit will I put within you: and I will take away the stony heart out of your flesh, and I will give you an heart of flesh.*

There is coming a revival like you have never seen, when the entire Jewish world that has not believed in Christ turns to Him, and He gives them brand new hearts.

Romans 11:28 *As concerning the gospel, they are enemies for your sakes: but as touching the election, they are beloved for the fathers' sakes.*

Let us slow down and get this verse exactly right because anyone who misses this and goes the wrong way with it is on the most dangerous ground you can imagine. This verse calls the Jews "enemies." But please pay very close attention to the fact that it does not call them OUR enemies; it says that they are enemies *as concerning the gospel*. In other words, the Jews have chosen to be enemies of the message of the Lord Jesus Christ. They oppose the Gospel; they do not believe it.

But the enmity is one-sided. They are the enemies of the gospel, but neither the gospel nor the Jesus of the gospel nor we who have received the gospel are their enemies. The last half of the verse makes that very clear when it says, *but as touching the election, they are beloved for the fathers' sakes.* They may not love Jesus or even us, but when it comes to God's election of them, His choice that they be His covenant people, Jesus loves them because His love comes from what Abraham did, not from what they have done.

In the divine scheme of things, they are enemies of the gospel *for our sakes.* In other words, God has used the fact that they do not currently want the gospel as a good reason to send it to us. So even in their enmity, we owe them a great debt!

Romans 11:29 *For the gifts and calling of God are without repentance.*

Why has God not rejected them totally? Because *the gifts and calling of God are without repentance.* In other words, God made up His mind based on the belief of Abraham that He would save the Jews. God has not and will not change His mind on the subject. The fact that there is still a single living Jew on earth after all these millennia of persecution is proof that God has not changed His mind!

Before we move forward, please pay attention to what I did not say about that phrase: *the gifts and calling of God are without repentance.* What do you hear ninety-nine percent of the time when someone uses that phrase?

"Well, I know what the qualifications of the pastor are, and yes, I blew it, but that doesn't matter because the gifts and calling of God are without repentance, so I'm still going to preach on..."

Why did I not use that phrase that way? Because Romans 11 does not have so much as the tiniest thing to do with that. There is this thing called "context." The entire passage is about God's dealings with the Jews. Not one single bit of it has anything to do with preaching, preachers, or those who, through their sin and wickedness, have disqualified themselves from the ministry and yet refuse to do the honorable thing and step away from it. To yank the verse completely out of context and misuse it in that manner is to do horrendous violence to the Scripture.

Romans 11:30 *For as ye in times past have not believed God, yet have now obtained mercy through their unbelief:* **31** *Even so have these also now not believed, that through your mercy they also may obtain mercy.*

Note again that God's mercy is based on our belief. Gentiles did not believe; Jews did. Then they fell into unbelief, and we were drawn to belief. Present-day Jews still do not believe, so we Gentiles are to take the gospel to them in mercy that they may believe and have mercy as well. If you want to get very close to the heart of God, evangelize the Jewish people.

Romans 11:32 *For God hath concluded them all in unbelief, that he might have mercy upon all.*

God has seen clearly that all, Jews and Gentiles, are unbelievers by birth and nature, and He has determined to offer mercy to all. That is just one more clear demonstration of the goodness of God.

The praise of His majesty

Romans 11:33 *O the depth of the riches both of the wisdom and knowledge of God! how unsearchable are his judgments, and his ways past finding out!*

You can almost hear Paul shouting as he writes these words. Put simply, they mean *This fantastic plan of salvation God has offered, this marvelous reconciliation of severity and goodness, this tremendous demonstration of wisdom and knowledge, who can fully grasp it!*

Look at what Peter said of this truth:

1 Peter 1:12 *Unto whom it was revealed, that not unto themselves, but unto us they did minister the things, which are now reported unto you by them that have preached the gospel unto you with the Holy Ghost sent down from heaven;* **which things the angels desire to look into.**

Even angels want to study this and to try and wrap their minds around it!

Romans 11:34 *For who hath known the mind of the Lord? or who hath been his counsellor?*

The answer to both questions is "no one." No human counselor would devise such a plan of salvation based simply on belief. God did not ask human counselors! Do you know what human counselors come up with? Works-based salvation, every single time.

Romans 11:35 *Or who hath first given to him, and it shall be recompensed unto him again?*

The answer to this question is also "no one." God does not owe anyone any favors; salvation is of God's grace and comes only by faith, belief. Qurollo put it this way, "God did not borrow someone's brains or ideas as human beings must. He did not get His information or ideas from someone else; and He is, therefore, not now indebted to someone for it." (195)

Romans 11:36 *For of him, and through him, and to him, are all things: to whom be glory for ever. Amen.*

Years after Paul wrote these words, John the Beloved wrote words that explain them very well:

Revelation 4:11 *Thou art worthy, O Lord, to receive glory and honour and power: for thou hast created all things, and for thy pleasure they are and were created.*

It really is all about Him!

Chapter Twenty
T - Transformed

Romans 12:1 *I beseech you therefore, brethren, by the mercies of God, that ye present your bodies a living sacrifice, holy, acceptable unto God, which is your reasonable service.* **2** *And be not conformed to this world: but be ye transformed by the renewing of your mind, that ye may prove what is that good, and acceptable, and perfect, will of God.*

Jesus had walked on earth for thirty-plus years in relative obscurity. He could pass by in a crowd and nothing about His looks would cause men to stop and stare. His clothing was ordinary; His hands were calloused. Outwardly, He was painfully ordinary. But inwardly, He concealed the very Shekinah glory of God.

In Matthew 17 and Mark 9, all of that changed as Jesus Christ was transfigured before His disciples.

Matthew 17:1 *And after six days Jesus taketh Peter, James, and John his brother, and bringeth them up into an high mountain apart,* **2** *And was transfigured before them: and his face did shine as the sun, and his raiment was white as the light.*

That day on the mountain, what was inside of Him all along was revealed. For Him, the miracle was not in revealing what was inside but in concealing what was inside!

The same word that is in Matthew 17 and Mark 20, translated as *transfigured,* appears in our text here as the word *transformed.* It is the word *metamorpha-oh.* We get our word metamorphosis from it. All throughout Romans, Paul has been dealing with matters of salvation, proving that all are lost, that works cannot save, that Christ is the end of the law for righteousness' sake, and instructing men exactly how to be born again. Now he will turn his attention somewhat from the inward to the outward. Just like Christ revealed what He was on the inside, we are also to show outwardly what we are on the inside as children of God. Unlike Christ, however, it is not easy for us to reveal outwardly what we are inwardly! In our text, Paul will now tell us how to be transfigured, transformed before the eyes of all who will behold. You see, there is nothing quite like a huge change in someone to make others stand up and take notice.

A plea - I beseech you therefore, brethren...

We do not often use the word beseech anymore. That is a bit of a shame since it is a very strong word. It basically means to plead with, to implore, to beg, to urge.

To whom was Paul speaking when he began this beseeching? It only takes you three more words to figure that out. Paul was talking to brethren; he was talking to saved people.

That is very fitting because what he is about to ask is not something that a lost person has the capacity to do! What he is about to ask is something that even saved people have a hard enough time with.

You do realize, don't you, saved people, that because you are still flesh, you are going to have to wrestle and argue with your body all the way home to Glory? You do realize that you are going to be tempted every which way imaginable?

You do realize that it is possible for you to be saved and still sin; it is possible for you to be saved and still be carnal?

I hope you also realize that what Paul did here as a man of God is what men of God today are supposed to be doing. Every pastor is supposed to actually care about how his people live, and any pastor who does not is not really a pastor; he is a hireling. He is not a man of God; he is a lazy bum in search of a cushy living.

A power - ...by the mercies of God...

You likely know these two verses well enough to know what he is going to ask of them. That thing that he is going to ask, the presenting of their bodies as a living sacrifice, that not being conformed to the world, that being transformed by the renewing of their minds, that is a pretty big thing.

Anytime one person is asking another for something else, especially something big, there will be a "ground of appeal for it."

Do you have a child who could wrap dad around his or her finger with the puppy-eyed "Daaaaady, I love you?" That is their power for what they are asking; it is their ground of appeal.

A pastor will often say, "Look, I have been here forever; I have loved you and your family; I have been there when you were sick and hurting; I need you to trust me on this." The years of faithful service and love are his grounds of appeal for what he is asking.

A boss will often say, "I need you to do thus and so," and without even having to spell it out, you know that the paycheck he hands you at the end of each week is his grounds of appeal.

Paul had an excellent power, an excellent grounds of appeal, for what he was going to ask. He said, *I beseech you by the mercies of God...*

God had been merciful to them, not just once but repeatedly. Can you relate to that?

A mother once approached Napoleon seeking a pardon for her son. The emperor replied that the young man had committed a certain offense **twice,** and justice demanded death.

"But I don't ask for justice," the mother explained. "I plead for mercy."

"But your son does not deserve mercy," Napoleon replied.

"Sir," the woman cried, "it would not be mercy if he deserved it, and mercy is all I ask for."

"Well, then," the emperor said, "I will have mercy." And he spared the woman's son. (Palau)

A recent news story has gone viral. A police officer was called to a Dollar General about a shoplifter. When he arrived, he caught a grandmother trying to shoplift five eggs. For some reason, he asked her why, and she explained that she had hungry grandchildren and no way to feed them. The officer said, "We get called out there all the time and find people shoplifting iPods, headsets, cosmetics. This was way different."

The officer paid for a dozen eggs out of his own pocket for her. (Goldstein)

God has been merciful to us, oh, so merciful, especially after all that we have cost Him.

A presentation - ...that ye present your bodies a living sacrifice, holy, acceptable unto God, which is your reasonable service...

Lots of people get saved, but a lot of those "lots of people who got saved" never grow much at all beyond salvation. In fact, many of them get downright carnal, and to observe them, you really would not have much of a clue that they are actually saved! Why? Because there is a difference between being saved and being spiritual, and you will never be spiritual without doing what this one verse says.

I spoke to a great preacher recently who said, "Our churches are experiencing a drought of spirituality. Our very best people are usually about one hurt feeling away from leaving church, and we wonder why God does not seem to be moving among us."

That is profound. We desperately need to get saved people to also be spiritual people. We need, every day, to *present our bodies as a living sacrifice.*

God may one day ask us to die for Him, but right now He is asking us to LIVE for Him. Not just "in our hearts," but "with our bodies."

We are to be *holy.* It is from the word *hagios,* and it means *saintly, pure.*

We are to be *acceptable unto God.*

There is a lady we know that my family and I have been careful not to be around much, because she is (while claiming to be a Christian) very un-Christian in her behavior, and I regard her as one who would be a very bad influence on my children. Because of all this, we stay away from her. She noticed that and contacted us to ask why. I very lovingly explained why. Then she justified her behavior by saying, "Well, I know people who do worse."

I very kindly responded, "That is not the standard a Christian is to live by. The standard we are to live by is, 'Is this one hundred percent acceptable to God?' "

Living like this is not to be regarded as extraordinary; it is simply to be regarded as our *reasonable service*!

A pattern - ...And be not conformed to this world: but be ye transformed by the renewing of your mind...

Be not conformed to this world; do not be like what you see in this world.

It applies to the way you dress, and what you do with your skin, and your hair, and the way you talk, and what you post and tweet and share, and every other area of your life.

It means a Christian should not be flashing gang symbols or using the off-color speech of the world.

Saved people spend most of their time absorbing the looks and values and speech of the world and because of that they become conformed to it.

But God said we are not to be conformed; we are to be transformed! We are to look just as saved on the outside as we are on the inside.

I get so weary of people behaving one way and talking one way and then when confronted saying, "Well that's not who I really am!" Really? Then maybe you ought to stop looking like whoever it is you say you aren't!

Whatever happened to the concept of a Christian being easy to identify?

This thing Paul is asking, how does it happen? *By the renewing of your mind.*

You get saved by the regeneration of your heart.

But you get spiritual by *the renewing of your mind.* Renewing is from the word *anakainosis.* It means *a renovation, a complete change for the better.* In other words, every day in everything, you retrain your mind to think the Biblical way.

A proving - ...that ye may prove what is that good, and acceptable, and perfect will of God.

Be transformed by the renewing of your mind. Why? For what purpose? For the purpose of being able to prove what the good and acceptable and perfect will of God is.

Prove to whom? Whoever it is, to yourself or to someone else. The word it comes from is *dokimadzo,* which means *to put to the test like a precious metal.*

A person who is simply saved may very well not be able to tell what the will of God is. A person who is simply saved may even have trouble distinguishing whether or not something is sinful! But a person who has a renewed mind, a person who has not just stopped at getting saved, a person who has made themselves become spiritual, that person will be able to know and explain and demonstrate what the will of God is.

A lost person is a very poor guide, but a saved person is just about as bad if he or she has never obeyed Romans 12:1-2.

I know a man who I believe truly is saved, but he is carnal, unspiritual, and I cringe at the thought of anyone ever looking up to that person or going to him for advice! A person like that may talk a good game, but he is not even capable of knowing what the good and acceptable and perfect will of God is.

You better be very careful who you look to.

And you need to not be satisfied with just being saved. After eleven chapters teaching about salvation, Paul still thought it was necessary to say, "Yes, your soul is secure, but let's talk about your body for a while. Yes, your soul is secure, but let's talk about your mind for a while."

It is time to be transformed! It is time to be spiritual! It is time to fast and pray and read and hunger and thirst after righteousness! It is time to move way beyond the very edge of the mire that God pulled you out of! It is time to quit being a sissy and start being a soldier! It is time to quit being wishy-washy and start being a warrior! It is time to stop settling for average.

It is time to have our own transfiguration experience and start actually showing on the outside what we say we are on the inside.

Chapter Twenty-one
U - Us and We

Romans 12:3 *For I say, through the grace given unto me, to every man that is among you, not to think of himself more highly than he ought to think; but to think soberly, according as God hath dealt to every man the measure of faith.* **4** *For as we have many members in one body, and all members have not the same office:* **5** *So we, being many, are one body in Christ, and every one members one of another.* **6** *Having then gifts differing according to the grace that is given to us, whether prophecy, let us prophesy according to the proportion of faith;* **7** *Or ministry, let us wait on our ministering: or he that teacheth, on teaching;* **8** *Or he that exhorteth, on exhortation: he that giveth, let him do it with simplicity; he that ruleth, with diligence; he that sheweth mercy, with cheerfulness.* **9** *Let love be without dissimulation. Abhor that which is evil; cleave to that which is good.* **10** *Be kindly affectioned one to another with brotherly love; in honour preferring one another;* **11** *Not slothful in business; fervent in spirit; serving the Lord;* **12** *Rejoicing in hope; patient in tribulation; continuing instant in prayer;* **13** *Distributing to the necessity of saints; given to hospitality.* **14** *Bless them which persecute you: bless, and curse not.* **15** *Rejoice with them that do rejoice, and weep with them that weep.* **16** *Be of the same mind one toward another. Mind not high things, but condescend to men of low estate. Be not wise in your own conceits.* **17** *Recompense to no man evil for evil. Provide things honest in the sight of all men.*

Personal pronouns tell a lot about a person. If a person has their focus on "I" or "Me," they are usually pretty annoying to be around. "Well, I just know that I am a very intelligent person and that everyone loves me. I am going to Aspen next week, and I drive a Bentley, and everyone wants to be me. But enough of me talking about me: how do YOU feel about me?"

If a person is constantly in a negative manner mentioning "They" or "Them," the same thing is true. "Well, they just aren't nearly as good as they should be, and they ought to take a good look at how all of them can be more like me!"

But may I tell you about a really beautiful pronoun? One of the most beautiful personal pronouns is capital H "Him." There is no better place to focus! But after that beautiful pronoun, some of the most joyful personal pronouns you can master in the Christian vocabulary are "Us" and "We." The Christian life is not lived alone. We are a part of the **family** of God. We have a bunch of brothers and sisters. Yes, just like any family, we sometimes get on each other's nerves.

And truthfully, not all of the members of our family are exactly... normal. I guess another way to put it is, some in the family of God are just like our families; we have some folks who could best be described as "odd."

People often look at us and say, "Do they even like each other?" One of the greatest things Christians can learn is how to relate to each other. Every one of us should take it upon ourselves to have a good relationship with each other. If we are going to spend eternity together, maybe we ought to not make the world wonder how we even keep from killing each other now! Maybe, if we are Christians, we should not be quite as WWE:

"In this corner, Sister Bad Breath, the undefeated champion of the Sanctuary Smackdown. And in the other corner, the challenger, Brother Face Frown, and his legendary stare of death.

"And there's the bell, and OHHH! Sister Bad Breath has Brother Face Frown in a headlock. It looks like it may be curtains for yet another challenger. Oh, but wait, Brother Face

Frown is actually lifting Sister Bad Breath, all of her, off the ground! If his back can hold out, and his legs and knees don't buckle, and if he can avoid a hernia, this may be a backward slam I see coming!

"And there it is! That had to measure 7.5 on the Richter scale! I think that one may just shake the steeple off the building! And yes! We have a new champion of the Sanctuary Smackdown, Brother Face Frown!"

Maybe, just maybe, it should not be like that.

So, how do we make things as good as possible with "Us and We?" The text we are studying in this chapter deals with that; it has a great deal to say about how we relate to each other and about how we should relate to each other.

A proper view of self

Romans 12:3 *For I say, through the grace given unto me, to every man that is among you, not to think of himself more highly than he ought to think; but to think soberly, according as God hath dealt to every man the measure of faith.*

Paul is about to say something pretty unpopular, so he reminds them that he is saying this by the grace of God, meaning that God has instructed and empowered him to say this. The message is, "Do not overestimate yourself." If you do, you are in effect acting drunk! Do not underestimate yourself; do not overestimate yourself; think soberly. God has given to you a measure of faith, meaning the ability to trust Him to do things for and through you. All of this, by the way, ties back to what came before it in verses one and two. We know this because of that introductory phrase, *for I say*. So, in the context of being transformed rather than being conformed, which will be key to all that follows in the text, evaluate yourself accurately if you intend for that to happen.

A great many conflicts could be headed off before they ever start by this one thing: not thinking of ourselves more highly than we ought to. Look at what Solomon said:

Proverbs 13:10 *Only by pride cometh contention: but with the well advised is wisdom.*

263

Paul continues the thought in the next two verses.

Romans 12:4 *For as we have many members in one body, and all members have not the same office: 5 So we, being many, are one body in Christ, and every one members one of another.*

Paul has the body in mind as he begins this section of verses, and the context makes clear that while he is dealing with the saved everywhere in general, he specifically has local bodies of believers, local churches, most in mind.

In our physical bodies, we have many members. Eyes, hands, liver, kidneys, they are all important. But they all must work together.

The eye sees the Jell-O, it sends a message to the brain to tell the hand to pick it up and put it in the mouth, but then on the way up the ear demands the Jell-O, and the hand complies. That does not work out so well! We all love ears, but an ear is not equipped to swallow Jell-O; only the mouth can do that. Everybody needs to get on the same page, or we have a mess and a possible medical issue that is going to be very hard to explain to a doctor.

In the family of God, it is the same. We are not a body unto ourselves. No one person is the body of Christ; all the saved are the body of Christ. ***When we realize that we are dependent on others and they are dependent on us, it changes the way we think***!

We need each other! And by the way, the devil knows this, and that is why in every church there will be a constant attack from the devil trying to get people pitted against each other.

A proper view of service

Romans 12:6 *Having then gifts differing according to the grace that is given to us, whether prophecy, let us prophesy according to the proportion of faith;*

The next several verses will deal with spiritual gifts, which God has given us in order that we may serve others. Notice here that we have these gifts *according to the grace that is given to us,* meaning that we have them simply because God chose to give them to us as gifts. We, therefore, have no right to boast. Remember what James said:

James 1:17 *Every good gift and every perfect gift is from above, and cometh down from the Father of lights, with whom is no variableness, neither shadow of turning.*

Because God has given them to us, we also have no right to complain about what He has or has not given us, or what He has or has not given someone else.

These gifts that God gives us are *differing* meaning *different.* Just like you do not give the exact same physical gift to everybody at Christmas, God does not give the exact same spiritual gift to everyone in the body.

As Paul begins to examine the first gift, prophecy, he uses the words *whether prophecy, let us prophesy according to the proportion of faith;*

Prophecy, when it referred to the miraculous, was when God spoke directly to a person and gave that person a message to convey to others, often about the future. Whoever had that gift was to use it *according to the proportion of faith,* meaning *within the proper measure of the faith.* This was an admonition for the gift to be used fully, but not to be showy or for self-gain.

Of these things that God has given us to serve each other, some we still have, some we do not. Again, in this verse, we see prophecy. There are, in the Bible, two things referred to as prophecy. There is foretelling and forthtelling. There is the telling of what God will do in the future, and there is the telling of what God expects in the present.

The miraculous part of this, the ability to perfectly and in detail tell the future, has ceased for now. (1 Corinthians 13:8-10). The proclaiming part of it, we still have.

But please understand that no matter what your view of any of these gifts regarding whether or not they are still in effect for today, if you search the Scripture, one thing that is indisputable is that they were not given for the benefit of the one who had the gift, they were given so that the one who had the gift could be a benefit to others! God gave us our gifts as tools of service.

Romans 12:7 *Or ministry, let us wait on our ministering: or he that teacheth, on teaching;*

Ministry is mentioned next, and this particular word does not mean ministry in the sense of preaching. In fact, we get our word for deacon from it. This word refers simply to being a servant to others. If God has given you the gift to humbly and quietly help others, it is not flashy, but it is necessary. Wait on it, verse seven says. In other words, occupy yourself with it like a waiter does serving tables.

It is interesting to me that so many people want the "flashy gifts" (miracles, tongues, prophecy), but not many people seem concerned with just how necessary gifts like serving, ministering are! As a pastor of a church, I do not care whether you can miraculously speak Swahili. But if you can change the oil in a vehicle or cut down a branch or kill bugs or change a diaper, you have just vaulted to very near the top of my favorite people list.

Teaching is next in verse seven. It, too, is listed as a gift. In other words, not everyone has it. I have been in church long enough to know that many people who are quite sure they have this gift, in fact, do not. And just like with the last gift listed, this gift is to be "waited on." In other words, if God has gifted you to teach, hone that gift, refine it, use it, and do so for the benefit of others.

Romans 12:8 *Or he that exhorteth, on exhortation: he that giveth, let him do it with simplicity; he that ruleth, with diligence; he that sheweth mercy, with cheerfulness.*

Exhortation is mentioned next. It too is to be waited on, honed, refined, used. To exhort means to come alongside, call alongside, be an encourager, be a comforter.

I personally cannot think of a more needed gift.

Think about it. When you are so depressed you feel like you cannot go on, do you need someone to speak to you in tongues, or do you need someone to take you to lunch? When you are crying, do you need a Sunday school lesson to cry on or a shoulder to cry on?

If you are going to pray for a gift, by the way, pray for this one. I strongly suspect that whenever a person genuinely wants this gift, the Lord will say yes and give it to them.

Giving is mentioned next in verse eight. What a gift! All believers are commanded to give, but some people have been blessed in more than an ordinary manner to be able to give to those in need. God has given them resources to work with solely for the purpose of being able to give, and a heart willing to do so.

Others, like the churches of Macedonia that Paul wrote of in 2 Corinthians 8, give "riches of liberality" out of "deep poverty"!

We are all commanded to tithe, make no mistake about that, but God has gifted some to such a degree that their tithes and offerings and even special giving are far above average either in amount or percentage or both.

Whoever is gifted to give is commanded to do it with simplicity. Simplicity means without improper motive and without strings attached.

Now that is pretty important, I would say! As a pastor, I get to hear things that would shock you if you were the ones to hear them. Let me tell you what I have had people look me in the eye and say over the years. Things like:

"Now, Pastor, I am going to be putting in a big check this week, but I need to get an airline ticket and take a mission trip so would you rather me just not put that check in and get my ticket instead, or would you rather I put it in and the church just get me a ticket instead so I can get credit for giving?"

Yes, I actually had that said to me.

Pastors could go on at length about how people are prone to give with massive strings attached. People give with the expectation that, because they can give a lot, they need to get special privileges or be put in charge of something. That is the exact kind of foolishness Paul had in mind when he commanded people to give with simplicity.

Ruling is mentioned next in verse eight. It means to superintend, to oversee. There are people who have the God-given ability to head things up and do a good job with it. There are others that, as helpful as they are, as giving as they are, if you put them in charge of something they will absolutely panic and fall apart. It is not their gift.

Whoever is gifted to rule must do it with diligence, verse eight says. Diligence is from the word *spoude*. It means quickly and earnestly. In other words, just having the gift, the ability to lead people, is not enough. If that gift is not mixed with enough character to be on time, and to not miss, and to work through difficulties, then that gift will be useless.

Mercy is mentioned next in verse eight. Not giving people what they deserve. Now, please understand, we are all commanded to be merciful, whether we have the "gift" of mercy or not:

James 2:13 *For he shall have judgment without mercy, that hath shewed no mercy; and mercy rejoiceth against judgment.*

We are all commanded to show mercy, but some are uniquely gifted to be merciful. Have you ever known a Christian who, no matter what anybody says or does to them, seems to be able to instantly shake it off and forgive and not strike back? You are looking at a person who likely has the gift of mercy.

When we show mercy, by the way, according to verse eight, we should do so cheerfully. It does not take a rocket scientist to figure out why he would say that, because the very last thing our flesh wants to do to begin with is to be merciful.

This gift may be among the most despised yet necessary ones in the body of Christ. People are, they absolutely ARE going to hurt other people. God equips some with the gift of mercy and then directs many of those attacks to that very person who is most gifted to deal with it. Those with the gift of mercy end up sparing many a weaker Christian from ruin by taking the hits the weaker Christian could never withstand.

Verse eight ends the list of the gifts in this passage, but the subject of service, and the truth that we should have a proper view of service, will continue on.

Romans 12:9 *Let love be without dissimulation. Abhor that which is evil; cleave to that which is good.*

Everybody knows we are supposed to love each other; it is actually a part of our service, not just an emotion. But this verse teaches us that our love for each other is to be *without dissimulation*. That means "sincere." What a lack of sincerity there is among Christians! Children of God, love each other and mean it! Do not ever be guilty of "loving" a brother or sister in Christ to their face and then despising them behind their back. Do not ever be guilty of "loving" a brother or sister in Christ just so that you can get them to do something for you.

Be sincere in your love for each other. And if you sense any insincerity in your love for someone, get alone with God until you have that heart issue fixed.

At the end of verse nine, we find that our view of good and evil is to be this sincere as well. We are to literally hate evil and stick to good like glue.

Romans 12:10 *Be kindly affectioned one to another with brotherly love; in honour preferring one another;*

We are to love each other as brothers and sisters, and I mean as brothers and sisters on our "happy family" days. We are also to prefer each other over ourselves and to honor each other over ourselves.

Would there ever be a disagreement among us if we always did this? No, and that is the point.

Romans 12:11 *Not slothful in business; fervent in spirit; serving the Lord;*

These seem to go together. When serving God, which we are all supposed to be doing somehow, we are to be earnest, fervent, diligent, of good character. We are not to be lazy. If you are going to serve God, whatever "high gear" is for you, kick it into that gear!

Romans 12:12 *Rejoicing in hope; patient in tribulation; continuing instant in prayer;*

Right actions are wonderful, but the right actions can be undermined by the wrong spirit. This verse tells us what type of a spirit, what type of an attitude we are to have.

We are first told that we are to be rejoicing in hope.

May I give you a very simple, one-word definition of this? Optimistic. Not blindly optimistic, intentionally optimistic because of the hope that God has given us. Sometimes it seems as if Christians are as pessimistic as we would expect the lost world to be.

We are also to be patient in tribulation. Anyone can be patient during the good times, but as a family, we owe it to each other to be patient during the hard times as well.

We are then told that we are to be continuing instant in prayer. If we are not a praying people, we will not be a pleasant people.

Romans 12:13 *Distributing to the necessity of saints; given to hospitality.*

These terms are fairly simple. We Christians, we in the local church body, are to be in the habit of meeting each other's needs and being hospitable to each other.

Romans 12:14 *Bless them which persecute you: bless, and curse not.*

This is very hard but no harder than what Christ did for us. Scripture teaches abundantly that we are allowed to rightly defend ourselves. But it also teaches that we are not to avenge ourselves. There is a difference between defense and revenge.

This is especially important in the household of faith. The world is going to take vengeance against each other, but it ought to be different in the House of God. We are to be the ones that show the world how Christ acted, because we are to act the same way, blessing rather than cursing when we are persecuted.

Romans 12:15 *Rejoice with them that do rejoice, and weep with them that weep.*

Sympathy is not just for bad times but for good as well. We are to rejoice with those who are rejoicing and weep with those who are weeping. The really interesting part about all of that is that it means that when you are rejoicing, you still need to weep with those who are weeping, and when you are weeping, you still need to rejoice with those who are rejoicing.

Years ago, when Dana first got pregnant, we had a lady in church who already had two children but could not have any more. We had not been able to have children for five years, and suddenly God had blessed us for Dana to get pregnant. Five years of weeping had come to an end for us.

This lady got her husband to come to us and tell us, "My wife is really hurt that you all are being so happy about Dana getting pregnant. My wife can't have any more, so it hurts her for you two to be happy like this."

You talk about making me want to spit nails! For a person to be so self-centered as to already have two children and get mad when we are happy after five years of trying to finally be pregnant with our first!

Learn to be happy for others, even if you are sad. At the same time, even when you are happy, if there is someone who is hurting, I mean not just ridiculous and self-absorbed like the people I just described, but actually hurting over something, learn to be able to be happy for you while also weeping for them.

You see, in a church, in the family of God, there will never be a time when it is all good for everybody, nor will there ever be a time when it is all bad for everybody. Every single day of our lives as part of a church, it will always be a mixture. Every single day, some of us will be rejoicing and others of us will be hurting. The only possible way we can make that system work is by rejoicing with them that rejoice and weeping with them that weep.

Romans 12:16 *Be of the same mind one toward another. Mind not high things, but condescend to men of low estate. Be not wise in your own conceits.*

We are to *be of the same mind one toward another*. This means we should come to a mental agreement with each other and stay agreed. We tell our kids when they are fighting, "Work it out!" Their relationship has to be more important than whatever issue they are debating about. The same thing is true for us.

Verse sixteen then says *Mind not high things*. In other words, do not seek men's approval and advancement. Condescend to men of low estate, associate with people who are humble and may not even have much. People-worship does not bring harmony; it brings division.

Verse sixteen goes on to say *Be not wise in your own conceits*. Do not think you are indispensable. My father-in-law says, "Some people have been important for so long that they don't realize they are not very important at all."

Romans 12:17 *Recompense to no man evil for evil. Provide things honest in the sight of all men.*

Believers are not to do evil to others who have done evil to them.

Having given extensive guidance for several verses on how we, God's people, are to treat each other, Paul closes out the thought by pointing out that how we treat each other, whether we are vengeful, whether we are honest or dishonest, will be seen by all men.

The world is watching us and we. What do they see?

Chapter Twenty-two
V - Vengeance

Romans 12:18 *If it be possible, as much as lieth in you, live peaceably with all men.* **19** *Dearly beloved, avenge not yourselves, but rather give place unto wrath: for it is written, Vengeance is mine; I will repay, saith the Lord.* **20** *Therefore if thine enemy hunger, feed him; if he thirst, give him drink: for in so doing thou shalt heap coals of fire on his head.* **21** *Be not overcome of evil, but overcome evil with good.*

We now come to what are truly some of the most difficult verses in the entire Bible. Mind you, they are not difficult to understand; they are difficult to obey. But they are utterly essential, and the practice of what they teach is incomprehensibly powerful.

A possibility over vengeance

Romans 12:18 *If it be possible, as much as lieth in you, live peaceably with all men.*

Commentator Albert Barnes said, "If it be possible. If it can be done. This expression implies that it could not always be done. Still, it should be an object of desire; and we should endeavor to obtain it." (Barnes, 281)

May I simplify that? If it turns out to be impossible to be peaceable with someone in the family of God, make sure it is impossible because of them, not because of you. If it is up to you, let there be peace.

You say, "But you don't know what they did! They need to pay the price!" Perhaps. But look at the next verse.

A place for vengeance

Romans 12:19 *Dearly beloved, avenge not yourselves, but rather give place unto wrath: for it is written, Vengeance is mine; I will repay, saith the Lord.*

We are told to "give place unto wrath." The Greek word for place is *topos*. We get our word topography from it. In other words, there is a proper place for wrath and vengeance.

Notice that in this verse, wrath and vengeance are found between you and the Lord. The placement of it in this verse is a good illustration of some spiritual truths:

As long as you are intent on vengeance and wrath, there is something between you and God.

Since nothing can be allowed between you and God, vengeance and wrath must go either one way or the other. It must either become yours or God's. This verse makes it very clear, it is God's. Therefore, if we take vengeance, we are stealing! God has established governmental authorities to wield the sword for Him in vengeance (Romans 13:1-4), and He will avenge all wrong to His children (Romans 12:19).

Even the lost Jewish historian Josephus understood this. Listen to his plea to the hard-headed Jews in Jerusalem who would not surrender to Titus.

> "O miserable creatures! Are you so unmindful of those that used to assist you, that you will fight by your weapons and your hands against the Romans? When did we ever conquer any other nation by such means? And when was it that God, who is the Creator of the Jewish people, did not avenge them when they had been injured?" (Josephus, *The Wars of the Jews*, Book 5, Chapter 9, Paragraph 4)

A preference over vengeance

Having vengeance and wrath taken away from us is a difficult pill for us rebellious humans to bear! But God always gives us something better than what He takes away in the spiritual realm. Kind of like a diet plan that takes away spinach and replaces it with all the desserts we can eat and still lets us lose weight! God has removed vengeance from our hands. Vengeance leaves a bitter taste in our mouths and never satisfies. In its place, He gives us a way to settle the matter that affects us and our enemies in a major way.

Romans 12:20 *Therefore if thine enemy hunger, feed him; if he thirst, give him drink: for in so doing thou shalt heap coals of fire on his head.*

Please pay attention to this because there is something that is usually missed here. Verse nineteen said that God would take vengeance, and then the very next thing you see in verse twenty is your enemies being hungry and thirsty! In other words, by the time of verse twenty, God is already starting to hammer on them. And it is then, when God starts to hammer on them, that you will be able to come along and feed them and give them to drink.

In other words, there is a time when you will be able to demonstrate kindness. While someone is actively trying to destroy you, the best you may be able to do is not let them do so. But when God has begun to level them, then you can come alongside and show them kindness.

You say, "But why should I?" The answer is, *"For in so doing thou shalt heap coals of fire on his head."* In other words, "Feed their belly; burn their head!" Let them constantly think about the fact that they have been bad to you, but you have been good to them.

A power over vengeance

In our hands, vengeance is not very powerful. It never satisfies, and it rarely has the effects we desire. There is a far more powerful thing we have at our disposal than vengeance.

Romans 12:21 *Be not overcome of evil, but overcome evil with good.*

Evil never overcomes evil. Only good overcomes evil. Many of you reading this now are likely thinking back to times of great hurt in your life. You may be a pastor thinking back to a brutal church split. Or perhaps you have had a spouse of many years abandon you for someone else, or maybe you are still thinking back to childhood abuse.

The potential causes of anger and hurt in our lives are infinite. But no evil is ever overcome by another evil. Christ Himself set the pattern for our understanding of this truth when He hung on the cross, looked down at the howling mob, and said, "Father, forgive them, for they know not what they do."

You say, "Preacher, but it is just not natural." No, it is not. But when we stop doing what comes naturally, amazing things happen.

In WWII, captured Scottish soldiers, forced by their Japanese captors to labor on a jungle railroad in brutal conditions, had degenerated to barbarous behavior, but one afternoon, something happened. A shovel was missing. The officer in charge became enraged. He demanded that the missing shovel be produced, or else. When no one in the squadron budged, the officer got his gun and threatened to kill them all on the spot. It was obvious the officer meant what he had said. Then, finally, one man stepped forward. The officer put away his gun, picked up a shovel, and beat the man to death. When it was over, the survivors picked up the bloody corpse and carried it with them to the second tool check. This time, no shovel was missing. Indeed, there had been a miscount at the first check point. The word spread like wildfire through the whole camp. An innocent man had been willing to die to save the others! The incident had a profound effect. The men began to

276

treat each other like brothers. When the victorious Allies swept in, the survivors, human skeletons, lined up in front of their captors (and instead of attacking their captors) insisted: "No more hatred. No more killing. Now what we need is forgiveness." (Ratzlaff)

Do yourself a favor: leave vengeance to God.

Chapter Twenty-three
W - Walking the Walk

Romans 13:1 *Let every soul be subject unto the higher powers. For there is no power but of God: the powers that be are ordained of God.* **2** *Whosoever therefore resisteth the power, resisteth the ordinance of God: and they that resist shall receive to themselves damnation.* **3** *For rulers are not a terror to good works, but to the evil. Wilt thou then not be afraid of the power? do that which is good, and thou shalt have praise of the same:* **4** *For he is the minister of God to thee for good. But if thou do that which is evil, be afraid; for he beareth not the sword in vain: for he is the minister of God, a revenger to execute wrath upon him that doeth evil.* **5** *Wherefore ye must needs be subject, not only for wrath, but also for conscience sake.* **6** *For for this cause pay ye tribute also: for they are God's ministers, attending continually upon this very thing.* **7** *Render therefore to all their dues: tribute to whom tribute is due; custom to whom custom; fear to whom fear; honour to whom honour.* **8** *Owe no man any thing, but to love one another: for he that loveth another hath fulfilled the law.* **9** *For this, Thou shalt not commit adultery, Thou shalt not kill, Thou shalt not steal, Thou shalt not bear false witness, Thou shalt not covet; and if there be any other commandment, it is briefly comprehended in this saying, namely, Thou shalt love thy neighbour as thyself.* **10** *Love worketh no ill to his neighbour: therefore love is the fulfilling of the law.* **11** *And that, knowing the time, that now it is high time to awake out of sleep: for now is our salvation nearer than when*

279

we believed. **12** *The night is far spent, the day is at hand: let us therefore cast off the works of darkness, and let us put on the armour of light.* **13** *Let us walk honestly, as in the day; not in rioting and drunkenness, not in chambering and wantonness, not in strife and envying.* **14** *But put ye on the Lord Jesus Christ, and make not provision for the flesh, to fulfil the lusts thereof.*

He was rather impressive to me when I was a young boy. He had all of the best Christian books and had actually read them. He could quote volumes of Scripture with ease. He always had a Bible verse answer to any question. People had looked up to him as a Christian leader for years. The knowledge of Scripture that he had in his head was truly impressive. Oh, by the way, He also destroyed his family and showed no remorse whatsoever. All of what he had in his head did not seem to affect the way he actually lived. Knowing is good; knowing and doing is far better:

James 1:22 *But be ye doers of the word, and not hearers only, deceiving your own selves.*

James 4:17 *Therefore to him that knoweth to do good, and doeth it not, to him it is sin.*

Paul has very thoroughly covered the doctrinal aspects of salvation. But salvation is not just doctrinal but also intensely practical. In this chapter, we will see four areas in which salvation should translate into our everyday walk of life.

Law

Romans 13:1 *Let every soul be subject unto the higher powers. For there is no power but of God: the powers that be are ordained of God.*

There are a great many things that are, in my mind, "where the rubber meets the road" type of issues. It is very easy to shout for an hour on Sunday morning, praise for an hour on Sunday night, and worship for an hour on Wednesday night. But it is in the everyday issues of all of the other hours of the week that you will be far more likely to struggle as a child of God.

After all of the incredibly theological and spiritual things that Paul has expounded upon in the book of Romans, he now turns his attention to an intensely practical matter: how are we to respond to the government?

And it would do us good to remember that in this case, the government being dealt with was not one that was "of the people, by the people, and for the people." It was more like one that ran roughshod over the people. Rome was about as customer friendly as an IRS agent with permanent hemorrhoids.

But in spite of all of that, Paul told these Christians in Rome to be subject to the authorities. Why? Because he said, *There is no power but of God: the powers that be are ordained of God.* In other words, even bad government is still put in place by God and is to be obeyed! God, all throughout Scripture, put good governments in, often as a way to bless His obedient people, and bad governments in, often as a way to punish His disobedient people.

Right off the bat, though, we need to find out if there are any limits to this command to obey the government. And the clear answer is, yes:

Acts 5:29 *Then Peter and the other apostles answered and said, We ought to obey God rather than men.*

Here is the limit that Peter just specified. We obey the government until the government forces us into a place where we have to choose to obey them or obey God.

In the case of the apostles, the government told them not to preach Jesus. They had no choice but to disobey. Whenever government forces that kind of an issue, we have to disobey. But as long as it is just something that we personally do not like, we obey. Christians ought to be the best citizens in the land.

Romans 13:2 *Whosoever therefore resisteth the power, resisteth the ordinance of God: and they that resist shall receive to themselves damnation.*

When we read something like this, which basically teaches that disobeying the government is the same thing as disobeying God, it has to strike you as extremely interesting. Why would Paul feel the need to say such a thing?

What were Christ and Christians constantly being accused of?

Acts 24:5 *For we have found this man a pestilent fellow, and a mover of* **sedition** *among all the Jews throughout the world, and a ringleader of the sect of the Nazarenes:*

Sedition basically means that they were trying to overthrow the government or that they did not recognize the government's authority over them. Christ was constantly labeled that way, and His followers were constantly labeled that way as well. But do you remember what Jesus Himself said when He was confronted with a question about taxes?

Matthew 22:21 *They say unto him, Caesar's. Then saith he unto them, Render therefore unto Caesar the things which are Caesar's; and unto God the things that are God's.*

Jesus Himself instructed His followers to be good citizens, including paying their taxes. Jesus did not come at that time to overthrow the government and set up an earthly kingdom. Jesus came to seek and to save that which was lost. And He left us here to do the exact same thing. So, may I ask, exactly how are we supposed to be winning the lost if we are disobeying the government, constantly getting into trouble, constantly stirring up strife, and developing terrible reputations?

When Paul said at the end of verse two, *"And they that resist shall receive to themselves damnation,"* he was not just talking about us running afoul of the government. He was more properly saying that if we disobey the government, we have run afoul of God, and even if He uses government to do it, damnation of some sort will be coming.

Years ago, we put up a tent in the side yard of the church and had an outdoor revival. That always tends to bring out some interesting people. One man stopped me to talk after a service and told me that he did not believe in obeying the government. I looked at him and said, "So exactly how long have you been smoking pot?"

Stunned, he looked up at me and said, "How did you know?"

I said, "Just about everyone that ever tells me they don't need to obey government is either smoking pot or not paying their taxes, and you seemed more like the pot-smoking type to me."

We may not like all the rules of government, but until government commands us to do something that is contrary to Scripture or until government refuses to allow us to do something that Scripture commands us to do, we are bound by God to obey government.

Romans 13:3 *For rulers are not a terror to good works, but to the evil. Wilt thou then not be afraid of the power? do that which is good, and thou shalt have praise of the same:* **4** *For he is the minister of God to thee for good. But if thou do that which is evil, be afraid; for he beareth not the sword in vain: for he is the minister of God, a revenger to execute wrath upon him that doeth evil.*

In verses three and four, Paul wrote words that were directed as much to government as to the people under government. Paul was no dummy. He knew that the letter he was writing would end up in the hands of the authorities. He also knew that what he said about government was not true about every government official, but that it should be, and so they needed to read these words.

When a government and government officials are right, rulers are not a terror to good works, but they are a terror to evil works, and as such, we are to fear them with a proper fear. It is the government's responsibility to promote that which is good (*do that which is good, and thou shalt have praise of the same*) and punish that which is bad. It is the government's responsibility to take up the sword of vengeance and execute judgment on those who have done wrong. They are the *minister of God* in all of this, meaning that whether saved or not, they are His servants and will answer for their service in this area.

It is the government's responsibility to put lawbreakers in prison. It is also the government's responsibility to execute the death penalty when needed. Our government is rapidly moving away from that God-given responsibility to put to death those who, by their actions, have forfeited their own lives. What that means is that there will be people who were entrusted with

283

the responsibility to carry out the death penalty and yet did not do so, and those people will one day stand before God and answer for why they abdicated their responsibility.

Romans 13:5 *Wherefore ye must needs be subject, not only for wrath, but also for conscience sake.*

We have to obey the government, not just to avoid being punished, but in order to have a clear conscience. No real Christian can be an anarchist.

Romans 13:6 *For for this cause pay ye tribute also: for they are God's ministers, attending continually upon this very thing. 7 Render therefore to all their dues: tribute to whom tribute is due; custom to whom custom; fear to whom fear; honour to whom honour.*

The word tribute means taxes. The government is God's minister of judgment, and therefore is worthy of being supported by our taxes. They are also worthy of the customs that come with the position, and of the fear that comes with the position, and of the honor that comes with the position.

These verses are often used in a wider context, and justifiably so when we see that word *all*. But their primary meaning is in the context of our dealings with government.

There are a great many people in our government for whom I have had very little regard, including some presidents. But because they were in the position of being our president, in the light of what this passage teaches, I gave them the honor that was due the office. I will oppose the things that they wanted to do that were wrong, but I will try very hard not to be disrespectful in so doing.

It is easy to talk the Christian talk. But if we are going to walk the Christian walk, we must be right in regard to law.

Love

Romans 13:8 *Owe no man any thing, but to love one another: for he that loveth another hath fulfilled the law.*

No man lets us know that the context is now expanded way beyond the previous topic of our dealings with government.

This particular verse is a favorite of people who have a certain hobby horse to ride. People who believe that getting a loan or having any debt is sinful love this verse.

I remember when we got ready to build our current church building. As soon as we began to discuss getting a loan to buy the land and build the building, a man came to me really upset at my "sinfulness and lack of faith."

Naturally, that kind of thing does not sit very well with me. Especially not when I happen to know the mountain-sized hypocrisy of the one assailing me.

His position was that we needed to raise all of the money ahead of time before we began to build.

I said, "First of all, it might be a good idea under certain circumstances to raise all of the money ahead of time, but if we are talking about a lack of faith, how exactly is that demonstrating faith? 'We now have every dime to build with, so let us step out on faith and build?'

"Secondly, though, how exactly is it that our indebtedness is going to be a sin, but your indebtedness isn't a sin?"

He said, "What do you mean?"

I said, "How much do you owe on your Bible college bill?"

He said, "About $3,000, but that is different!"

Oh, how very convenient!

So, I went further. I said, "Did you ever pay for that item that you got from so and so, another member of the church?"

"No."

"When your wife went to the hospital, and you didn't have insurance, how did that bill get taken care of?"

"The hospital had to write it off."

So, in other words, apparently, only certain kinds of debt are actually sinful. I believe that what you will find is that when a person uses this verse to teach that all loans are sin, what they really mean is, all of *your* loans and all of *your* debt are sin, but all of *their* loans and all of *their* debts are just fine.

When Romans 13:8 says *owe no man anything*, the context goes back to the previous verses. We are to give people the honor that they are due, the custom that they are due, the fear that they are due, the whatever else that they are due.

In other words, if you are going to use this verse and apply it to loans and to indebtedness, you need to do so accurately. If these verses are applied to loans and indebtedness, then they mean that we are always to pay that which is due. Do not be late on your payments, and do not be short on your payments.

But the entire verse says *Owe no man any thing, but to love one another: for he that loveth another hath fulfilled the law.*

In other words, we are always to make sure that there is no debt that is left unpaid, but we are also to recognize the spiritual application. The spiritual application is that we are always to regard ourselves as owing one another love.

If you stop and think of the code of moral law in Scripture, it is huge, and it is complex. But on the human-to-human side of it, we can very easily boil it down to one thing: love one another.

You say, "How does that work?"

Easy. If you love each other, you will not steal from each other. If you love each other, you will not kill each other. If you love each other, you will not chase after someone else's spouse. Pick any command of the law, and it is probable that law deals with how we relate to each other. If you love each other, you will automatically not violate that part of the law.

And that is exactly what the next two verses mean and reconfirm:

Romans 13:9 *For this, Thou shalt not commit adultery, Thou shalt not kill, Thou shalt not steal, Thou shalt not bear false witness, Thou shalt not covet; and if there be any other commandment, it is briefly comprehended in this saying, namely, Thou shalt love thy neighbour as thyself.* **10** *Love worketh no ill to his neighbour: therefore love is the fulfilling of the law.*

So again, if we are going to walk the Christian walk, we must be right in regard to law and right in regard to love.

Light

Romans 13:11 *And that, knowing the time, that now it is high time to awake out of sleep: for now is our salvation nearer than when we believed.* **12** *The night is far spent, the day is at hand: let us therefore cast off the works of darkness, and let us put on the armour of light.*

As we begin to examine verses eleven and twelve, we need to remember that Paul is in fact writing to saved people. It is Christians he is telling to awake out of their sleep, and it is Christians he is telling to cast off the works of darkness.

He uses the words *our salvation.* He uses the pronoun *us* twice in verse twelve, thereby including himself.

What should this tell us? It should tell us that it is possible, even highly likely, that Christians would get into a condition where they are spiritually asleep and where they are living in the deeds of darkness rather than the deeds of light.

We call a condition like that being backslidden, being cold and indifferent, being carnal.

When you got saved, the only part of you that got saved was your inner man—your soul and your spirit. Your body remained just as lost as it had always been. And it is very easy to live in the assurance of our positional salvation, but God expects us to live a life of practical and purified salvation. God expects us to live on the outside the reality of what has happened on the inside.

In other words, you should tell people that you are saved, but you also should not have to tell people that you are saved. The way you live ought to make it evident that you have been saved.

According to these two verses, there is not much time left. And what is really sobering to consider is the fact that these verses were written 2,000 years ago. If Paul thought the coming of the Lord was near back then, how much nearer are we now?

God, through Paul, told us to put on the armor of light. Armor is a defensive clothing. In other words, our living right provides us with a level of defense against the attacks that the world and the devil will launch against us. If you think that you, a child of God, are going to get through this life without being attacked, you are sadly mistaken. If you know that you are going to get attacked, then it only makes sense to have a built-in defense.

A godly testimony that has been produced by a godly life is an excellent layer of defense against attack.

If we are going to walk the Christian walk, we must be right in regard to law, right in regard to love, and right in regard to light.

Lust

Romans 13:13 *Let us walk honestly, as in the day; not in rioting and drunkenness, not in chambering and wantonness, not in strife and envying.*

The last two verses of Romans 13 may well be some of the most practical verses in the Bible.

They begin with the command that we walk honestly, as in the daytime. Why would he command that? Because people tend to act differently in broad daylight than they do in the middle of the night when they think no one is watching.

The rule of life for a child of God ought to always be to live a clean and transparent life.

Verse thirteen proceeds to give us examples of some things that we ought not to be engaged in. Rioting is mentioned first. The first thing it means is exactly what you think it means, rioting in the normal English sense of the word. You cannot be a Christ-like person while rioting in the streets, looting stores, breaking glass, flipping cars, and burning buildings.

The second meaning of the word rioting is partying. Not like a birthday party, but a party-party. A drinking, carousing, ungodly excuse for fun. God's people are to never be involved in that.

Drunkenness is next. It is still a sin to get drunk. Period. No exceptions.

Chambering is next. It has to do with the word bedchamber. It means *having sex with anyone to whom you are not married.* Premarital sex is still a sin. Adultery is still a sin. Any form of fornication is still a sin. Any sexual activity that occurs between anyone other than a husband and wife who are married to each other is a sin. It is chambering, and God's people are not to do it.

Wantonness is next. It is a more general term. It means *that which is shameful or outrageous.* Can you imagine a more appropriate command for this day and age? God's people are not to do anything that is shameful or outrageous; we are always to be appropriate and respectable.

Strife comes next; it means contention or fighting. Then comes envying, which means being jealous of each other. God's people are not to be contentious, and they are not to be jealous. By contrast, verse fourteen says this:

Romans 13:14 *But put ye on the Lord Jesus Christ, and make not provision for the flesh, to fulfil the lusts thereof.*

When you got saved, you "let Jesus in," but every day of your life thereafter, you are to "put Jesus on." That sounds so odd; how are we supposed to do that? The last half of the verse will tell you how: *"and make not provision for the flesh, to fulfil the lusts thereof."*

As children of God, we have a responsibility to pre-limit our flesh. Not only are we not to do wrong, we are not even to make provision to do wrong. In other words, we are never to even put our flesh in a position to do wrong.

When you put the two halves of verse fourteen together, what you have is a situation where you daily show the world Christ by your actions and your behavior. You are "putting on Christ." And the most visible way that you will do that is by never putting yourself in a position to sin.

Do you know a great way to never commit adultery? Never be alone with anybody other than your spouse. Unless there is something very seriously wrong or twisted about your spouse, that methodology works one hundred percent of the time.

Do you know a great way to never get drunk? Never even be around alcohol. That methodology works one hundred percent of the time.

Pick a sin, any sin, this methodology always works one hundred percent of the time. Anything that you do not give yourself a chance to do, you do not do.

If we are going to walk the Christian walk, we must be right in regard to law, right in regard to love, right in regard to light, and right in regard to lust.

In his book *Integrity*, Ted Engstrom told this story: "For Coach Cleveland Stroud and the Bulldogs of Rockdale County High School, it was their championship season: twenty-one wins and five losses on the way to the Georgia boys' basketball tournament last March, then a dramatic come-from-behind victory in the state finals. They won it all, they were the champions. But now the new glass trophy case outside the high school gymnasium is bare, there is no trophy in it.

"A few weeks after they won the championship, they realized that a player who was academically ineligible had played forty-five seconds in the first of the school's five postseason games. 'We didn't know he was ineligible at the time; we didn't know it until a few weeks ago,' Mr. Stroud said. 'Some people have said we should have just kept quiet about it, that it was just forty-five seconds and the player wasn't an impact player. But you've got to do what's honest and right and what the rules say. I told my team that people forget the scores of

290

basketball games; they don't ever forget what you're made of.'" (Engstrom)

Child of God, walk the Christian walk.

Chapter Twenty-four
X - X Rays of the Heart,
Getting Below the Surface

Romans 14:1 *Him that is weak in the faith receive ye, but not to doubtful disputations. 2 For one believeth that he may eat all things: another, who is weak, eateth herbs. 3 Let not him that eateth despise him that eateth not; and let not him which eateth not judge him that eateth: for God hath received him. 4 Who art thou that judgest another man's servant? to his own master he standeth or falleth. Yea, he shall be holden up: for God is able to make him stand. 5 One man esteemeth one day above another: another esteemeth every day alike. Let every man be fully persuaded in his own mind. 6 He that regardeth the day, regardeth it unto the Lord; and he that regardeth not the day, to the Lord he doth not regard it. He that eateth, eateth to the Lord, for he giveth God thanks; and he that eateth not, to the Lord he eateth not, and giveth God thanks. 7 For none of us liveth to himself, and no man dieth to himself. 8 For whether we live, we live unto the Lord; and whether we die, we die unto the Lord: whether we live therefore, or die, we are the Lord's. 9 For to this end Christ both died, and rose, and revived, that he might be Lord both of the dead and living. 10 But why dost thou judge thy brother? or why dost thou set at nought thy brother? for we shall all stand before the judgment seat of Christ. 11 For it is written, As I live, saith the Lord, every knee shall bow to me, and every tongue shall confess to God. 12 So then every one of us shall give account of himself to God. 13 Let us not therefore* *judge one another any more: but judge this rather, that no man put a stumblingblock or an occasion to fall in his brother's way.* **14** *I know, and am persuaded by the Lord Jesus, that there is nothing unclean of itself: but to him that esteemeth any thing to be unclean, to him it is unclean.* **15** *But if thy brother be grieved with thy meat, now walkest thou not charitably. Destroy not him with thy meat, for whom Christ died.* **16** *Let not then your good be evil spoken of:* **17** *For the kingdom of God is not meat and drink; but righteousness, and peace, and joy in the Holy Ghost.* **18** *For he that in these things serveth Christ is acceptable to God, and approved of men.* **19** *Let us therefore follow after the things which make for peace, and things wherewith one may edify another.* **20** *For meat destroy not the work of God. All things indeed are pure; but it is evil for that man who eateth with offence.* **21** *It is good neither to eat flesh, nor to drink wine, nor any thing whereby thy brother stumbleth, or is offended, or is made weak.* **22** *Hast thou faith? have it to thyself before God. Happy is he that condemneth not himself in that thing which he alloweth.* **23** *And he that doubteth is damned if he eat, because he eateth not of faith: for whatsoever is not of faith is sin.*

In the "good old days" of our grandparents, there was a wonderful thing that doctors used on a very regular basis called "exploratory surgery." It went something like this: if you had a pain on the inside that could not be explained on the outside, they cut you open and poked around to see what was wrong. That technique is still used occasionally today, but not nearly as often as back then. You see, a better way was discovered to see what was going on on the inside. It is called X-rays. Instead of cutting you open to see if you have a kidney stone, they lay you on an ice-cold table in a flimsy gown that will not close in the back, tell you to stop shivering, and zap you with invisible rays. Those rays then strike a film, leaving an image of your inside that can be seen on the outside. If a doctor never gets below the surface, he will miss the most vital things. A person's skin tone, or eye color, or hairstyle are not nearly as significant as their arteries, or kidney function, or lung strength.

Likewise, there are some surface things that we often focus on as Christians that, though important, are not nearly as significant as the heart behind them.

In Romans 14, Paul is going to behave as a good spiritual doctor. He is going to look way beneath the surface and bring to our attention issues of the heart that we need to deal with.

Getting below the surface of the receiving of people

Romans 14:1 *Him that is weak in the faith receive ye, but not to doubtful disputations.*

On occasion, we will end up receiving into membership those that are weak, and weak in this context refers to those who are pharisaical, or people who are scared to do anything for fear that it is a sin. These are people that we love to argue with, to "dispute about their doubts." We are not to bring them in so we can fight with them; we are to bring them in out of love.

No, we cannot allow their foolishness to hurt our members.

There will always be a strain of people who believe their duty in life is to nitpick every choice, path, and preference of every other church member. We cannot allow them to wound and ruin people with their harsh Pharisaism.

But we are not to try to pick fights with them either. Teach them if they can be taught, but do not seek out a fight with them needlessly. It is sad when people are actually looking for a fight! That ought not to be.

Please pay attention to the fact that it is the one who is *weak* that is prone to these *doubtful disputations*. More about that in a bit, but just remember for now that Paul did not label the liberty-loving Christians at Rome as the weak ones; he labeled the ones who were pharisaical as weak. We will almost immediately start seeing illustrations of that from the pen of Paul.

Getting below the surface of the regulations of eating

Romans 14:2 *For one believeth that he may eat all things: another, who is weak, eateth herbs.* **3** *Let not him that eateth despise him that eateth not; and let not him which eateth not judge him that eateth: for God hath received him.* **4** *Who art thou that judgest another man's servant? to his own master he standeth or falleth. Yea, he shall be holden up: for God is able to make him stand.*

We are, in these verses, clearly dealing with Christians. Please note that it is the *weaker* Christian who thinks it is a sin to eat anything but vegetables. Paul dealt with this again in another place:

1 Timothy 4:1 *Now the Spirit speaketh expressly, that in the latter times some shall depart from the faith, giving heed to seducing spirits, and doctrines of devils;* **2** *Speaking lies in hypocrisy; having their conscience seared with a hot iron;* **3** *Forbidding to marry, and commanding to abstain from meats, which God hath created to be received with thanksgiving of them which believe and know the truth.* **4** *For every creature of God is good, and nothing to be refused, if it be received with thanksgiving:* **5** *For it is sanctified by the word of God and prayer.*

A person who actually believes that it is wrong to eat meat is not a strong person; he or she is a weak person.

This applies to any artificial set of standards that are not rooted in a good understanding of Scripture. The stronger Christian is the one who realizes the liberty he has; the weaker Christian still has a slavish dependence on standards for standards sake.

If you are dealing with minor issues that people have honest disagreements on, there is no reason for either side to despise the other.

Notice in verse three that it is indicated that the one not eating meat will even think that the meat eater is not saved. Again, this is elevating an artificial standard to the level of a "salvation measuring stick."

Verse four, though, gets to the real issue. This verse makes it clear that whether people are weak or strong, if they are saved, they are God's servants, and we are not to despise them:

Who art thou that judgest another man's servant? to his own master he standeth or falleth. Yea, he shall be holden up: for God is able to make him stand.

The one being directly pointed at is the one finding fault with another. In short, God is pretty big on believers minding their own business, because God will either help His own servants stand taller or lower them as needed, and your "help" in that is not appreciated.

The eating issue or the TV issue or the should ladies wear makeup issue is not the issue. The issue is, we are not to despise people either way. Love people, be gracious to people, be kind to people. That is way, way more important than those petty surface issues.

Getting below the surface of the regard of days

Romans 14:5 *One man esteemeth one day above another: another esteemeth every day alike. Let every man be fully persuaded in his own mind. 6 He that regardeth the day, regardeth it unto the Lord; and he that regardeth not the day, to the Lord he doth not regard it. He that eateth, eateth to the Lord, for he giveth God thanks; and he that eateth not, to the Lord he eateth not, and giveth God thanks.*

Some people believe certain days are higher and holier than others. Other people believe that absolutely every day is exactly alike. The great "December 25" debate and the great "is the Sabbath day still special" debate come to mind here.

Another "day" issue is the "is Sunday the Sabbath day" (which it is not) and is it, therefore, wrong to go out to eat on Sunday.

Paul's command concerning that is *Let every man be fully persuaded in his own mind.* Be fully persuaded from Scripture in your own mind and stop trying to make up everyone else's mind.

If you want to be a Grinch on December 25, do so quietly while the rest of us eat turkey and open presents.

If you want to stay in your house all day on Saturday and do nothing but pray and meditate, do not fuss at those who go out to yard sales.

I am absolutely in favor of respecting Sunday. I believe the pendulum has swung way too far to the side of not respecting it, but I also do not believe it is a sin to eat out.

When Paul in verse six said *He that regardeth the day, regardeth it unto the Lord; and he that regardeth not the day, to the Lord he doth not regard it. He that eateth, eateth to the Lord, for he giveth God thanks; and he that eateth not, to the Lord he eateth not, and giveth God thanks,* a short and simple explanation of those words is "everything those other believers are doing, they are doing between them and God, and for reasons that they believe are pleasing to God – so butt out."

The important thing, once again, is not the surface issues like that. It is the below the surface issues, which Paul dealt with in verse six, which I now ask you to look at one more time:

Romans 14:6 *He that regardeth the day, regardeth it unto the Lord; and he that regardeth not the day, to the Lord he doth not regard it. He that eateth, eateth to the Lord, for he giveth God thanks; and he that eateth not, to the Lord he eateth not, and giveth God thanks.*

Do you realize what this verse is saying about which one is right and which one is wrong? In essence, since we are not dealing with "thou shalts" and "thou shalt nots," both are right. Both are doing what they do for the Lord and giving God thanks for it. Both have a heart for God, both are doing what they do or not doing what they do not do because that is what they believe they are supposed to be doing.

When we get to heaven, and only when we get to heaven, God may let us know which was the more correct way on every little issue. But until then, we are just going to have to realize that we will not see eye to eye on every tiny issue.

The Bible makes all of the big things abundantly clear. When it specifies something as a sin, it is sin, period. But not everything is of such significance that God chose to label it a sin. Some things are merely a matter of preference.

People hold to their preferences very strongly. But do you know what we should hold onto far more strongly? Each other.

Getting below the surface of the reminder of ownership

Romans 14:7 *For none of us liveth to himself, and no man dieth to himself.* **8** *For whether we live, we live unto the Lord; and whether we die, we die unto the Lord: whether we live therefore, or die, we are the Lord's.* **9** *For to this end Christ both died, and rose, and revived, that he might be Lord both of the dead and living.*

None of us liveth to himself, and no man dieth to himself. Paraphrase? We are here together, and we need each other. When we realize that, we tend to be a lot nicer to each other.

According to verses eight and nine, whether in life or death, the Christian belongs to Christ and Christ alone. When we bash Christians based on our opinions, we are vandalizing God's property.

If a Christian needs to be taken to task by a brother in Christ as Paul did to Peter, we better be sure that we are firmly Scriptural in what we are saying and that we are acting in love.

People who are saved belong to God and need each other.

Getting below the surface of the responsibility of the judgment seat

Romans 14:10 *But why dost thou judge thy brother? or why dost thou set at nought thy brother? for we shall all stand before the judgment seat of Christ.* **11** *For it is written* [Isaiah 45:23], *As I live, saith the Lord, every knee shall bow to me, and every tongue shall confess to God.* **12** *So then every one of us shall give account of himself to God.*

Some people cannot seem to help meddling and harping in the lives of others. They are worried that if they do not

299

monitor all of their Christian brothers' and sisters' activities, that they will have no motive to live right.

I am not trying to be unkind, but a person like that needs to understand that he or she is a busybody:

1 Peter 4:15 *But let none of you suffer as a murderer, or as a thief, or as an evildoer, or as a **busybody** in other men's matters.*

"Mind your own business" is still good advice!

By the way, yes, "Iron still sharpeneth iron," and we are still called and "able to admonish" one another. But there is a world of difference between lovingly confronting someone about sin in their lives that is going to hurt them and displease Christ and constantly harping and nagging over matters of preference.

And the most interesting thing is, it is not necessary! According to verses ten through twelve, we are all going to stand before the Judgement Seat of Christ and then bow before the Christ on that judgment seat, confessing and giving account of ourselves to God. In other words, everything that needs to be dealt with, God will deal with it, which means that if we are trying to do His job now, we are both stepping out of line and wasting our time! You say, "But by the time of the Judgment Seat, it's too late!" Yes, it is, but if the thought of the Judgment Seat of Christ will not motivate people, how do you think your nagging will do any better?

Getting below the surface of the restraint of charity

Romans 14:13 *Let us not therefore judge one another any more: but judge this rather, that no man put a stumblingblock or an occasion to fall in his brother's way.*

Stop judging others; judge yourself on whether or not you do something to make others fall into sin. This is the restraint that charity, love, will bring.

If you love people, you will not be constantly badgering them on issues of preference, and if you love people, you will also not be doing or saying anything to make them likely to stumble into sin. Love ought to be our restraining factor.

Romans 14:14 *I know, and am persuaded by the Lord Jesus, that there is nothing unclean of itself: but to him that esteemeth any thing to be unclean, to him it is unclean.*

By itself, nothing God has made is wrong. It becomes wrong when the devil perverts it. For instance, alcohol is not wrong until the devil makes it a drink instead of an antiseptic, hemp is not wrong until the devil makes it a drug instead of a rope. Music is not wrong until the devil gives it a worldly beat or bad lyrics or both. Dynamite is not wrong until the devil gets people to use it for suicide bombings instead of mining or stump removal.

But here is the catch: according to the last half of this verse, even if the devil has not yet perverted something, if you *think* something is wrong (say, for instance, a seesaw), then for you, it is! But not for anyone else.

I want to stop here just for a moment and really drive home a point. People often say things that sound so right but are so wrong. I am not talking here about cultists; I am talking about Baptists. One of those things is, "If it's a sin for anybody, it's a sin for everybody!"

That sounds so good! But it is so wrong. Let me tell you what would be right to say: "If God called it a sin, it is a sin for everybody."

But please, please be intelligent students of the word rather than simply shallow hackers. According to this verse, and many others, there are some things that are sin even if God has not specified them as sin. *"But to him that esteemeth **any thing** to be unclean, to him it is unclean."* In other words, it may not actually be a sin to eat in a restaurant that serves alcohol. But if you think it is, then for you, it is! It may not actually be a sin to eat out on Sunday, but if you think it is, then for you, it is! It is not a sin for a woman not to have her hair up in a bun. But if you think it is, then for you it is!

I do not want to jump too far ahead, but look at the last phrase of verse twenty-three: *for whatsoever is not of faith is sin.*

If you do not have faith that it is right, then for you it is wrong, because you are showing a willingness to take a chance on displeasing God. Just be careful not to project that onto others.

Romans 14:15 *But if thy brother be grieved with thy meat, now walkest thou not charitably. Destroy not him with thy meat, for whom Christ died.*

Remember that restraint that charity causes? Here it is again: flaunting your liberty is not acting in love. If you actually believe that a motorcycle rider is the spawn of Satan, then I am not going to ride one around you lest I tempt you to sin. I am going to think you are a lunatic, but I will think so quietly and refrain from tempting you.

Here is an advanced concept that baby Christians and carnal Christians may not get, but I am trusting that you are advanced enough to get it: it is not weakness to limit yourselves for the legitimate benefit of others, it is strength to do so.

There are things that I know are not wrong. But I also know some very good people who think they are, yet may be tempted to do them anyway if they see me do them or hear me talk about them. When I am around those people, I am careful not to do whatever it is they think is wrong, and I am careful not to talk about those things.

I am not trying to avoid causing myself problems; I am trying to avoid tripping them and causing them to fall into sin by doing something that they cannot do in faith.

Romans 14:16 *Let not then your good be evil spoken of:*

Abuse of liberty causes liberty itself to be mocked. There are some things that are not necessarily wrong that you will have to refrain from sometimes in order to not give Christian liberty a bad name.

There are some churches that have a faulty belief on hair coverings for women. They believe that if a woman does not wear some type of hat on her head, she is acting immorally. If I ever preach at one of those churches, my wife will doubtless choose to wear a hat. We will not do anything among our dear kinsfolk in Christ to give liberty a bad name.

There are churches that believe it is wrong for a preacher to wear anything other than a white shirt. I do not own a white shirt, so if I ever preach there, I will go and buy a white shirt.

There are churches that believe facial hair on men is a sin. I have a mustache; it and I have been together since I was fourteen. I intend on keeping it, but I do not intend on arguing with anyone who will not have me preach. They are my brothers in Christ.

Romans 14:17 *For the kingdom of God is not meat and drink; but righteousness, and peace, and joy in the Holy Ghost.*

The kingdom of God is not externals [*meat and drink*] but internals [*righteousness, and peace, and joy in the Holy Ghost*]. A right internal walk will cause us to have proper external behavior, but proper external behavior is the fruit, not the root.

Now stop and consider this. At my church, we preach a lot about Calvary and salvation, and we go through books verse by verse. But in the average place, what do you hear more preaching on, meat and drink, or righteousness, peace, and joy?

My estimation is that in most places, you will hear about ninety-five percent externals and five percent internals. That kind of focus produces very hateful, pharisaical Christians!

Romans 14:18 *For he that in these things serveth Christ is acceptable to God, and approved of men.*

Whoever serves Christ in *these things*, the righteousness, peace, and joy mentioned in verse seventeen, is acceptable to Christ, and also approved by men. Righteousness covers the outward behavior, peace and joy cover the sweet attitude. Both ought to be right.

Romans 14:19 *Let us therefore follow after the things which make for peace, and things wherewith one may edify another.*

Do not chase after the divisive, but after the peaceful. In the Christian life, plenty enough fights will come to you; you have no need to go looking for them.

It is fine to preach against sin. It is fine to respond to attacks on the faith. What is not fine is living a life where you are chasing one divisive situation after another, looking for something to fight over. Verse nineteen said: *Let us therefore follow after the things which make for peace, and things wherewith one may edify another.*

Especially in church, though we absolutely have to preach against sin, we are still to be among ourselves following after peace. And nothing destroys the peace of a church so quickly as a pharisaical attitude toward those who walk in liberty or a licentious attitude toward those who are weak and steeped in pharisaism.

Romans 14:20 *For meat destroy not the work of God. All things indeed are pure; but it is evil for that man who eateth with offence.* **21** *It is good neither to eat flesh, nor to drink wine, nor any thing whereby thy brother stumbleth, or is offended, or is made weak.*

A person violating artificial standards, such as "don't eat meat," does not destroy the work of God. It is wrong, however, to eat meat if it causes your weaker brother to sin. Please notice my exact words. "It is wrong, however, to eat meat if it causes your weaker brother to sin." In other words, if you doing something is going to tempt someone to do something they think is a sin, do not do it. But this has nothing to do with people just "being offended" at something. Never give in to those that are "professionally offended," which is far different than the actual offended of verse twenty-one, from *skandalidzo,* meaning to trip up and cause to fall into sin.

Many years ago, a Pharisee told me he was "offended" by me having my top button on a three-button shirt unbuttoned. I apologized...for causing him to lust! He did not like that at all. But if he himself was not being tempted to do as I was doing or was not being tempted to lust, then he was just being professionally offended, and you never have to give an inch to people like that! Love them, but do not allow them to put you in chains.

In the simple terms that Paul used, do not do anything that legitimately causes a brother to be one who *stumbleth, or is offended, or is made weak.* But do not worry about people who simply love to stick their noses into everyone else's business.

This was a big issue in Paul's day among the Gentiles that he was ministering to and is getting bigger in our own day.

Romans 14:22 *Hast thou faith? have it to thyself before God. Happy is he that condemneth not himself in that thing which he alloweth.*

Flaunting your liberty in a way that causes your brother to sin condemns not just him, but you.

Imagine sitting down with a weak brother who thinks it is actually a sin against God to eat meat. He orders the tofu salad, and you, out of a deep sense of mischief, order the twelve-ounce filet mignon, medium, with a side of baby back ribs. The smell wafts through the air, and you can see him beginning to drool. You have already done wrong, and he is probably about to.

Getting below the surface of the requirement of faith

Romans 14:23 *And he that doubteth is damned if he eat, because he eateth not of faith: for whatsoever is not of faith is sin.*

There is a famous *whatsoever* verse that we love to quote:

1 Corinthians 10:31 *Whether therefore ye eat, or drink, or whatsoever ye do, do all to the glory of God.*

But notice that we have just read another whatsoever verse, and it should probably be just as famous, for it is just as true. Look at it again:

Romans 14:23 *And he that doubteth is damned* [Judged worthy of punishment] *if he eat, because he eateth not of faith: for whatsoever is not of faith is sin.*

This verse teaches a great truth: when in doubt, DON'T! If you have a hunch that something you are about to do is wrong, for you at least, it is! God will deem you worthy of punishment if you take a chance at sinning against Him.

That is how very careful every child of God is supposed to be.

Romans 14 is a chapter that goes below the surface to the issues of the heart. It can be summarized like this: enjoy your liberty, do not violate your conscience, do not cause others to stumble, and regard your brothers and sisters in Christ as being so very important that you will do whatever is right to be at peace with them.

Chapter Twenty-five
Y - Your Relationship with Others

Romans 15:1 *We then that are strong ought to bear the infirmities of the weak, and not to please ourselves.* **2** *Let every one of us please his neighbour for his good to edification.* **3** *For even Christ pleased not himself; but, as it is written, The reproaches of them that reproached thee fell on me.* **4** *For whatsoever things were written aforetime were written for our learning, that we through patience and comfort of the scriptures might have hope.* **5** *Now the God of patience and consolation grant you to be likeminded one toward another according to Christ Jesus:* **6** *That ye may with one mind and one mouth glorify God, even the Father of our Lord Jesus Christ.* **7** *Wherefore receive ye one another, as Christ also received us to the glory of God.* **8** *Now I say that Jesus Christ was a minister of the circumcision for the truth of God, to confirm the promises made unto the fathers:* **9** *And that the Gentiles might glorify God for his mercy; as it is written, For this cause I will confess to thee among the Gentiles, and sing unto thy name.* **10** *And again he saith, Rejoice, ye Gentiles, with his people.* **11** *And again, Praise the Lord, all ye Gentiles; and laud him, all ye people.* **12** *And again, Esaias saith, There shall be a root of Jesse, and he that shall rise to reign over the Gentiles; in him shall the Gentiles trust.* **13** *Now the God of hope fill you with all joy and peace in believing, that ye may abound in hope, through the power of the Holy Ghost.* **14** *And I myself also am persuaded of you, my brethren, that ye also are full of goodness, filled with all* *knowledge, able also to admonish one another.* **15** *Nevertheless, brethren, I have written the more boldly unto you in some sort, as putting you in mind, because of the grace that is given to me of God,* **16** *That I should be the minister of Jesus Christ to the Gentiles, ministering the gospel of God, that the offering up of the Gentiles might be acceptable, being sanctified by the Holy Ghost.* **17** *I have therefore whereof I may glory through Jesus Christ in those things which pertain to God.* **18** *For I will not dare to speak of any of those things which Christ hath not wrought by me, to make the Gentiles obedient, by word and deed,* **19** *Through mighty signs and wonders, by the power of the Spirit of God; so that from Jerusalem, and round about unto Illyricum, I have fully preached the gospel of Christ.* **20** *Yea, so have I strived to preach the gospel, not where Christ was named, lest I should build upon another man's foundation:* **21** *But as it is written, To whom he was not spoken of, they shall see: and they that have not heard shall understand.* **22** *For which cause also I have been much hindered from coming to you.* **23** *But now having no more place in these parts, and having a great desire these many years to come unto you;* **24** *Whensoever I take my journey into Spain, I will come to you: for I trust to see you in my journey, and to be brought on my way thitherward by you, if first I be somewhat filled with your company.* **25** *But now I go unto Jerusalem to minister unto the saints.* **26** *For it hath pleased them of Macedonia and Achaia to make a certain contribution for the poor saints which are at Jerusalem.* **27** *It hath pleased them verily; and their debtors they are. For if the Gentiles have been made partakers of their spiritual things, their duty is also to minister unto them in carnal things.* **28** *When therefore I have performed this, and have sealed to them this fruit, I will come by you into Spain.* **29** *And I am sure that, when I come unto you, I shall come in the fulness of the blessing of the gospel of Christ.* **30** *Now I beseech you, brethren, for the Lord Jesus Christ's sake, and for the love of the Spirit, that ye strive together with me in your prayers to God for me;* **31** *That I may be delivered from them that do not believe in Judaea; and that my service which I have for Jerusalem may be accepted of the saints;* **32**

That I may come unto you with joy by the will of God, and may with you be refreshed. **33** *Now the God of peace be with you all. Amen.*

In Romans 14, Paul deals with Christian liberty and how we deal with others whom he calls "weaker brethren." These are people who go beyond what the Bible teaches and bind themselves beyond scriptural requirements. Do not misunderstand: God commands purity and holiness and modesty and has given us a multitude of Biblical principles by which we can determine what is right and wrong in music, dress, money, and every other area of life. There are often, though, areas in which people bind themselves and others to things that are no longer necessary or to things that never have been necessary! Paul dealt with just such a situation in the church of Galatia.

Galatians 3:1 *O foolish Galatians, who hath bewitched you, that ye should not obey the truth, before whose eyes Jesus Christ hath been evidently set forth, crucified among you?* **2** *This only would I learn of you, Received ye the Spirit by the works of the law, or by the hearing of faith?* **3** *Are ye so foolish? having begun in the Spirit, are ye now made perfect by the flesh?* **4** *Have ye suffered so many things in vain? if it be yet in vain.* **5** *He therefore that ministereth to you the Spirit, and worketh miracles among you, doeth he it by the works of the law, or by the hearing of faith?* **6** *Even as Abraham believed God, and it was accounted to him for righteousness.* **7** *Know ye therefore that they which are of faith, the same are the children of Abraham.*

The Galatians had been properly taught that righteousness is by faith and that real faith will produce righteous living. The Judaizers had then come and taught them that unless they kept the works of the law, they were not righteous. Yet Christ had fulfilled the law on Calvary.

The Judaizers said, "You must be circumcised!" Jesus said, "You are circumcised if you believe in me!" People were being pulled between the truth and an error. Paul dealt harshly with those teaching error, saying they had "bewitched" people and calling them "heretics" who are to be rejected. (Titus 3:10) But with the ones who were struggling due to the error they had been taught, Paul was firm but loving. In Chapter 15 of Romans, facing much the same thing, he deals with how to handle people, some of whom are not easy to be around. Have you ever had to deal with people, especially in a religious context, who were not always easy to be around?

Pleasing others without losing your mind

Romans 15:1 *We then that are strong ought to bear the infirmities of the weak, and not to please ourselves. 2 Let every one of us please his neighbour for his good to edification. 3 For even Christ pleased not himself; but, as it is written, The reproaches of them that reproached thee fell on me.*

The strong in this verse are the same as the strong in the previous chapter. They are the ones who live holy and pure, but who understand the liberty they have in Christ. They are the ones who do not take those things that are perfectly acceptable and label them as wicked for no scriptural reason. They realize that every day belongs to God, and they understand that God gave us meat to be received with thanksgiving. They are *"dunatos,"* strong, of great power.

The weak are the same as the weak in the last chapter; they are artificially binding themselves far beyond what God commands and desires. They are *"adunatos,"* weak, of no power. The "a" negates what it touches, as "moral" is negated by the a of "amoral."

When the weak and the strong get together, the weak have "infirmities" (of the mind) that the strong have to bear with. The tendency is to just please us, but God said to please others! Pleasing someone with a weak mindset can be maddening! The reason we do it, though, makes it worthwhile. We do it for their own good, to edify or build them up.

We have as our example in this no less an example than Christ Himself. Paul quotes from Psalm 69:9 the fact that God Himself, who was strong while we were without strength, bore our reproaches on Calvary. If He was able to deal with those as weak as us, we may certainly deal well with others weaker than ourselves. Believe it or not, we can actually do this without losing our minds. Look what the very next verse says in regard to our minds:

Romans 15:4 *For whatsoever things were written aforetime were written for our learning, that we through patience and comfort of the scriptures might have hope.*

The verse about Christ in Psalm 69:9 is from the Old Testament. People will say that it is not relevant for today. It is relevant for today. It is written that we may learn (What is God like? What does He desire?) It is written that we might develop patience; it is written that we might be comforted. It is not all *binding* upon us today, but it is all relevant! When I say it is not all binding, people begin to panic. Let me illustrate what I mean.

Deuteronomy 22:11 *Thou shalt not wear a garment of divers sorts, as of woollen and linen together.*

Could everyone check their tags, please? Why do we not observe this? Why do we not sacrifice lambs? The Law was fulfilled in Christ. The "laws" He intended for us to follow, He repeated directly or in principle in the New Testament, including nine of the ten commandments, only leaving out the Sabbath. Everything that was written in the Old Testament, though, is still for our learning. In Deuteronomy 22:11, we learn the principle of separation, which we also see in the New Testament:

2 Corinthians 6:14 *Be ye not unequally yoked together with unbelievers: for what fellowship hath righteousness with unrighteousness? and what communion hath light with darkness?*

A careful study of the Scriptures will not only teach us the differences between precepts, principles, and preferences (and there is a difference!), it will also help us to be able to please others, limiting our liberties, when necessary, without losing our minds. How? By reminding us that God, who had to put up with our weaknesses, did so as well. That is the main "learning" we ought to be doing here.

It may take work, but yes, it can be done. Go out of your way to be pleasing not just to the Lord, but to others, and not for your benefit, but for their benefit.

Consider a car engine. It is made up of very hard, precise parts. Pistons, rings, crankshaft, transmission, gears, heads. Think of those things as commandments, Biblical standards, doctrinal beliefs. Now consider this: when that engine is running, what are you going to have to have in it to keep it from seizing up in just mere minutes? Oil!

Think of the oil as this concept of pleasing others rather than ourselves. In an engine, like a church, with all of the hard-moving parts (the commandments, Biblical standards, doctrinal beliefs), a lot of friction is prone to develop, that friction causes heat, and that heat, in turn, destroys the very parts that create it.

But when you put about five quarts of kindness in, about five quarts of a determination to please others rather than self, suddenly the friction goes away, and things run smoothly. When we do that, we are doing for others what Jesus did for us.

Pulling together with others while lifting up your master

Romans 15:5 *Now the God of patience and consolation grant you to be likeminded one toward another according to Christ Jesus:* **6** *That ye may with one mind and one mouth glorify God, even the Father of our Lord Jesus Christ.*

The last verse spoke of us having patience and comfort, consolation. Verse five reminds us that it is our great and generous God who gives us this. He can also give us something else that verse five says we desperately need: likemindedness one toward another just like Christ was likeminded with the Father. God desires us to have our minds united to avoid division and strife. In other words, He wants us to pull together.

One of the things that historically has disappointed me most as a pastor is seeing people, who have more in common than they remember, fighting and bickering with each other or being cold to each other. May I remind you that we all were born in sin, we all chose to sin, we all have areas of our former behavior that people can point to as improper. **People who have been "cut some slack" should extend the same grace to others!**

Pay attention to the fact that it is our like-mindedness toward others in verse five that leads to our ability to glorify the Lord in verse six.

When we do this, when we make ourselves of one mind, we can lift up the Master together. It is much more genuine to praise God together than to try and praise Him while thinking of ways to successfully dispose of the body of the annoying person a seat or two away from you:

My Jesus, I love thee, I know thou art mine! (I'll bury that guy's body, too deeply to find)... My gracious Redeemer, my Savior art thou, (I really despise you, you pig-headed sow).

Maybe, just maybe, that is not the way to go.

Putting up with others while looking to your Maker

Romans 15:7 *Wherefore receive ye one another, as Christ also received us to the glory of God.*

Receive means to take as companions, as friends. We are to do that for each other, just like Christ did for us, to the glory of God.

"Preacher, you don't know so-and-so. They are too hard to receive! That woman has such a big mouth, she makes Rosie O'Donnell look like June Cleaver!" Verse seven says that God received us, so how hard can it be? If a person falls under the qualification of being a division causer as stated in Romans 16:17, yes, they will have to be dealt with and perhaps even removed. But quite often, what we deal with is nothing more than personality conflicts that fall under the command here in verse seven to receive one another anyway. And this verse tells us that, once again, it was Christ who set the example. If we look to Him, we once again find the right pattern to follow.

Romans 15:8 *Now I say that Jesus Christ was a minister of the circumcision for the truth of God, to confirm the promises made unto the fathers: 9 And that the Gentiles might glorify God for his mercy; as it is written* [Psalm 18:49], *For this cause I will confess to thee among the Gentiles, and sing unto thy name. 10 And again he saith* [Deuteronomy 32:43], *Rejoice, ye Gentiles, with his people. 11 And again* [Psalm 117:1], *Praise the Lord,* *all ye Gentiles; and laud him, all ye people.* **12** *And again, Esaias saith* [Isaiah 11:10], *There shall be a root of Jesse, and he that shall rise to reign over the Gentiles; in him shall the Gentiles trust.*

Verse eight was a shouting verse for the Jews. The *circumcision* in verse eight meant the Jews, because they were the ones who practiced it for religious reasons, not just for health. Yes, Jesus came to minister to the Jews, His people, but He did not stop there. In the rest of these verses, Paul quoted four different passages of the Old Testament as he reminded his readers that Christ also ministered to the Gentiles and actually joined together people as different as the Jew and the Gentile. Get over the "Jew/Gentile" distinction; we are one in Christ.

Get over the black/white distinction; we are one in Christ!

That truly is wonderful. But how about we let "the rubber meet the road," as the colloquialism goes. Get over the divisions you have one with another in church; we are one in Christ!

Romans 15:13 *Now the God of hope fill you with all joy and peace in believing, that ye may abound in hope, through the power of the Holy Ghost.*

Think of everything that has been said in the first twelve verses, then look at verse thirteen. Does it almost seem like Paul has changed subjects?

But he has not. Putting it all together, the truth you find is this: if you believe in Christ firmly enough to set aside petty, non-doctrinal differences, you will have joy, peace, hope, and Holy Ghost power! The greatest strife in a church will not likely be produced by doctrine; it will likely be produced by preference. The greatest robber of the joy and peace spoken of in verse thirteen will not likely be doctrine; it will likely be preference.

When we were building our church building, there was a part of it that we needed to hire some help for. Two bids came in. One was for $30,000, the other was for $79,000. That is a really easy call to make, I think. But I had two individuals ask me to come outside, then they chewed me out for even considering the lower bid, and when I say chewed out, you have no idea how bad it was. Why? Preference: they were buddies with the $79,000 guy. You talk about a robber of peace and joy? Try having to argue with people who actually think it is a great idea to spend $49,000 more than you have to.

There is actually a church here in our beloved Bible belt that, unless they have changed it by now, has a two-colored roof. One side is brown; one side is black. They could not agree, so they split it down the middle. Preference.

I got chewed out once for choosing one place to purchase the tires for our church bus over another place. Preference.

Verse seven told us to receive each other, take each other as true friends. We ought to love each other enough to agree on all of the essential doctrines and to be as low-key and easy-going as a sloth on any preferences. If Christ was able to join Jews and Gentiles together, then we can, under Him, by His grace, join ourselves together.

Pointing others to a life of meaning

Romans 15:14 *And I myself also am persuaded of you, my brethren, that ye also are full of goodness, filled with all knowledge, able also to admonish one another.*

This had to be one of the happiest verses Paul ever wrote. I hope the Lord looks at us and feels the same way. Paul said that those folks were full of goodness and filled with knowledge.

That is a fabulous combination. In fact, one without the other usually tends to disaster. Christians ought to be the most knowledgeable people on earth, and I mean both in Scripture and other fields as well. There is no virtue in ignorance.

Right now, as I work on this book, I am reading a 1,400-year-old Chinese book, Sun Tzu, *The Art of War*. Why? Knowledge. It makes a difference. As I write this, I have been in an argument with atheists for days now over the fact that what they believe is a religious faith. One of them decided to infer that I was an idiot who had no knowledge of the subject. Then I quoted about three pages worth of quotes from atheists themselves, and I mean famous evolutionary scientists:

Dawkins, Hoyle, Lewontin, etc. Somehow, his tune changed very quickly. Why? Knowledge.

But the other side of the coin has to be there as well, compassion. And hear me: absolute truth can make people very uncompassionate. We have the absolute truth, and because of that, Christians sometimes become the meanest people around. That ought to never be the case.

For whatever reason, it is often mean preachers that gain the biggest following. I have told my church that I cannot be like that. I am going to be truthful, I am going to speak clearly against sin, but I am not going to call people unbiblical ugly names, and I am not going to take joy in leaving blood and guts all over the walls from a message that beats the sheep to death. That isn't compassionate.

Homosexuality is wicked and immoral. But I do not hate homosexuals. Adultery is also wicked and immoral, but I do not hate adulterers either. Neither homosexuals nor adulterers can be members of an actual Bible-believing church, but it would not bother me a bit to sit across a table at a restaurant with either of them and discuss the issue kindly and then pick up the tab. Truth, compassion.

Many things that church members do are wicked and immoral. I do not hate them either. We have to be full of truth and full of compassion.

Paul also said that they were able to admonish each other. That word admonish means to counsel. They were, the members of the church, able to take their Bibles, open them up, and help their fellow members see what was right and what was wrong.

Pastors do not mind counseling people; we do it all the time. But a whole lot of it would not even be necessary if every member in a church were Biblically literate enough and filled with the Spirit enough to admonish each other.

Romans 15:15 *Nevertheless, brethren,* [though you are able to admonish] *I have written the more boldly unto you in some sort, as putting you in mind, because of the grace that is given to me of God,* **16** *That I should be the minister of Jesus*

Christ to the Gentiles, ministering the gospel of God, that the offering up of the Gentiles might be acceptable, being sanctified by the Holy Ghost.

Even though they were able to admonish each other, Paul, as God's man, claimed authority to admonish them all. Some were older than him, some richer and more successful, some smarter. But as God's man, especially as God's man who was taking Jesus Christ to the Gentiles, seeing them saved, and then preparing to offer them to God at the judgment seat of Christ as an acceptable, Holy Ghost-sanctified people, he had the right and responsibility to admonish them all. Every pastor still has that right and responsibility today. Every pastor will give an account of how he shepherded the sheep. And every sheep will give account for how easy or how hard he made it for the shepherd to direct him or her.

Romans 15:17 *I have therefore whereof I may glory through Jesus Christ in those things which pertain to God.* **18** *For I will not dare to speak of any of those things which Christ hath not wrought by me, to make the Gentiles obedient, by word and deed,* **19** *Through mighty signs and wonders, by the power of the Spirit of God; so that from Jerusalem, and round about unto Illyricum, I have fully preached the gospel of Christ.*

In verse seventeen, Paul pointed out that his ministry and life had, through God's power, produced some "credentials," some things about which he could *glory through Jesus Christ in those things which pertain to God.* In verse eighteen, he used an obscure figure of speech that basically means "I will not exaggerate; I will not go beyond the truth." But then he told the truth, that God worked mightily through him to convert and train the Gentiles. Not just in one place, Paul used Jerusalem on one end and Illyricum across from Italy on the other end, two extreme ends of His travels, to show that he had encompassed the known world with the gospel.

Paul's credentials were not on a piece of paper from a seminary; they were the bodies and buildings of Christians and churches that used to not exist.

317

I am not even one one-thousandth of what Paul was, but I can relate to his sentiment. I have plenty of degrees on my wall, but they are not nearly as important a set of credentials to my ministry as the fact that in 1997 there was absolutely nothing on the hill in Mooresboro, and now there is 20,000 square feet of buildings on fourteen acres with a bunch of people showing up each week to hear preaching who used to spend Sundays on the lake or drunk or worse.

And even if it all closed down tomorrow the souls are still saved, and there are still a bunch of other preachers and missionaries out there who came out of our church!

The best credentials you can ever carry is to do something for the Lord by pointing others to a life of meaning in Christ.

Romans 15:20 *Yea, so have I strived to preach the gospel, not where Christ was named, lest I should build upon another man's foundation:* **21** *But as it is written, To whom he was not spoken of, they shall see: and they that have not heard shall understand.*

Paul's desire was to preach where no one had ever preached before. This was not a command of God to all, but it was the desire of Paul given to him by God, a desire he gained from reading Isaiah 52:15, which he references in verse twenty-one. And it is a good principle for preachers to remember. Paul did not split someone else's church to start his own. Paul did not start a church right in the middle of other churches and then go recruiting their members. Paul went where there was an actual need and then started winning people to the Lord.

It is hard to point others to a life of meaning in Christ when even the lost world looks at the behavior of some preachers and realizes that it is so unethical that even the business world would view it as dirty.

Romans 15:22 *For which cause* [the wide-ranging ministerial travels he just spoke of] *also I have been much hindered from coming to you.* **23** *But now having no more place in these parts, and having a great desire these many years to come unto you;* **24** *Whensoever I take my journey into Spain, I* *will come to you: for I trust to see you in my journey, and to be brought on my way thitherward by you, if first I be somewhat filled with your company.*

Because of his unique ministry, Paul had not yet had the privilege of seeing the saints at Rome. His desire in doing so was to enjoy the blessing of their company.

In verse twenty-three, he spoke of *having no more place in these parts.* He was then in Corinth and had evangelized all the area. Realizing that, he thought again about his long-standing desire to travel to Rome and meet the believers in that place.

His plan was to journey into Spain [modern-day Spain and Portugal] and to come to Rome and visit them. His expressed hope was that they, then, after a good visit, would help him get to wherever the gospel was next to go.

A preacher should like meeting Christian people! One of the things I enjoy the most is traveling and meeting other Christians. But this is not just for preachers; Christians should like meeting Christians. We are family, after all, so every time you meet another believer, you are filling in another branch on the family tree.

Providing others with love and ministry

Romans 15:25 *But now I go unto Jerusalem to minister unto the saints. 26 For it hath pleased them of Macedonia and Achaia to make a certain contribution for the poor saints which are at Jerusalem. 27 It hath pleased them verily; and their debtors they are. For if the Gentiles have been made partakers of their spiritual things, their duty is also to minister unto them in carnal things.*

The church started in Jerusalem, primarily with Jews who were born again. It stayed there for a while and gained mostly Jewish converts. But after a while, the gospel made it to Gentile ears. Some of the Jews in that first church got upset about that. But when Paul explained it to them and showed them how Biblical it was, they humbly accepted it. That was smart, very smart.

But it also proved to be one of the most beneficial decisions they could have made, because years later, the church at Jerusalem had a lot of very poor, needy people in their midst and were struggling to care for them. And just as with the church at Antioch in Acts 11, those very Gentile converts who at first had been shunned by the Jews turned out to be the ones who took up an offering and sent it to them to help them.

Our relationship with our brothers and sisters in Christ should go far beyond teaching and preaching; it should also include loving and ministering. It should go beyond feeding them spiritually; it should include feeding them physically when needed. It should go beyond making sure they have a mansion in heaven; it should include doing what we can to make sure they aren't living under a bridge here on earth.

That is not much of an issue for us now, but if the Lord tarries His coming, I predict that it will become more and more of an issue, and we had better be prepared for it.

Something Paul said about the relationship between the Jews and Gentiles is interesting, especially in its application for today. He said *For if the Gentiles have been made partakers of their spiritual things, their duty is also to minister unto them in carnal things.*

The Gentiles had indeed been made partakers of the Jews' Spiritual things, things like Jesus, the gospel, the Scripture, and Heaven! Because of that, Paul argued that they had a responsibility to minister to them in carnal things, by which he specifically means money and supplies. All of us who have been helped by ministers of those spiritual things have the same responsibility to minister to those ministers in those same tangible things.

Never starve those who showed you how to get to heaven and are making sure that you look good when you get there; take the good care of them that they deserve based on the eternal riches they have brought to you.

Concerning the Gentiles and their offering and its delivery, here were Paul's plans for how things were to go:

Romans 15:28 *When therefore I have performed this, and have sealed to them this fruit, I will come by you into Spain.* **29** *And I am sure that, when I come unto you, I shall come in the fulness of the blessing of the gospel of Christ.*

These words about Paul's plan are inspired, but Paul's plan was not. When he finally got to Rome, it was in chains.

Praying for others who are laboring for the Messiah

Romans 15:30 *Now I beseech you, brethren, for the Lord Jesus Christ's sake, and for the love of the Spirit, that ye strive together with me in your prayers to God for me;*

Paul asked the believers in Rome for a very important thing: pray for me and really strive together [*sunagonidzomai*; agonize in concert] with me in those prayers. He asked that *for the Lord Jesus Christ's sake,* meaning out of honor and regard for Him. If we love Jesus, we will pray for those He is using. He also asked on this basis, *and for the love of the Spirit,* meaning for the love that the Holy Spirit produces in us for each other.

Romans 15:31 *That I may be delivered from them that do not believe in Judaea; and that my service which I have for Jerusalem may be accepted of the saints;*

Paul knew, as he contemplated his return trip to Israel, that there were many there who did not believe; he used to be one of them. He also knew that they were very dangerous toward those who did believe; he used to be one of them in that, too. So he was asking the believers in Rome to pray that people who used to be like him would not be able to kill him like he used to do to believers when he was like them.

He also, though, wanted a prayer sent upward for him concerning those who did believe. He was bringing an offering from Gentiles, and he wanted the believers in Rome to pray that God would soften the Jewish believers' hearts enough to accept it.

Romans 15:32 *That I may come unto you with joy by the will of God, and may with you be refreshed.*

The final expression of why Paul wanted those particular prayers was so that he could actually do as he intended and make it to the saints in Rome.

Romans 15:33 *Now the God of peace be with you all. Amen.*

Peace was pretty hard to come by in Christian circles due to the persecution of the day. But Paul closed chapter fifteen with a blessing, in so many words asking the God who can bring peace despite any circumstances to do so for the people whom he had never yet met but already loved so dearly.

He was generally pretty good with the whole *Your Relationship With Others* thing.

Chapter Twenty-Six
Z - Zenith of the Book

Romans 16:1 *I commend unto you Phebe our sister, which is a servant of the church which is at Cenchrea: **2** That ye receive her in the Lord, as becometh saints, and that ye assist her in whatsoever business she hath need of you: for she hath been a succourer of many, and of myself also. **3** Greet Priscilla and Aquila my helpers in Christ Jesus: **4** Who have for my life laid down their own necks: unto whom not only I give thanks, but also all the churches of the Gentiles. **5** Likewise greet the church that is in their house. Salute my wellbeloved Epaenetus, who is the firstfruits of Achaia unto Christ. **6** Greet Mary, who bestowed much labour on us. **7** Salute Andronicus and Junia, my kinsmen, and my fellowprisoners, who are of note among the apostles, who also were in Christ before me. **8** Greet Amplias my beloved in the Lord. **9** Salute Urbane, our helper in Christ, and Stachys my beloved. **10** Salute Apelles approved in Christ. Salute them which are of Aristobulus' household. **11** Salute Herodion my kinsman. Greet them that be of the household of Narcissus, which are in the Lord. **12** Salute Tryphena and Tryphosa, who labour in the Lord. Salute the beloved Persis, which laboured much in the Lord. **13** Salute Rufus chosen in the Lord, and his mother and mine. **14** Salute Asyncritus, Phlegon, Hermas, Patrobas, Hermes, and the brethren which are with them. **15** Salute Philologus, and Julia, Nereus, and his sister, and Olympas, and all the saints which are with them. **16** Salute one another with an holy kiss. The churches of Christ salute you.*

17 *Now I beseech you, brethren, mark them which cause divisions and offences contrary to the doctrine which ye have learned; and avoid them.* **18** *For they that are such serve not our Lord Jesus Christ, but their own belly; and by good words and fair speeches deceive the hearts of the simple.* **19** *For your obedience is come abroad unto all men. I am glad therefore on your behalf: but yet I would have you wise unto that which is good, and simple concerning evil.* **20** *And the God of peace shall bruise Satan under your feet shortly. The grace of our Lord Jesus Christ be with you. Amen.* **21** *Timotheus my workfellow, and Lucius, and Jason, and Sosipater, my kinsmen, salute you.* **22** *I Tertius, who wrote this epistle, salute you in the Lord.* **23** *Gaius mine host, and of the whole church, saluteth you. Erastus the chamberlain of the city saluteth you, and Quartus a brother.* **24** *The grace of our Lord Jesus Christ be with you all. Amen.* **25** *Now to him that is of power to stablish you according to my gospel, and the preaching of Jesus Christ, according to the revelation of the mystery, which was kept secret since the world began,* **26** *But now is made manifest, and by the scriptures of the prophets, according to the commandment of the everlasting God, made known to all nations for the obedience of faith:* **27** *To God only wise, be glory through Jesus Christ for ever. Amen.* <Written to the Romans from Corinthus, and sent by Phebe servant of the church at Cenchrea.>

We are now at the zenith of the book. The zenith is the highest point, the point at which you survey all around you, tie up loose ends, and say final words. Paul started with the very basics, worked us up through everything we would ever need to know about salvation, then went on to give excellent instruction in how to behave after salvation.

He was almost finished. But Paul never was just an academic. He had a heart as big as his mind and love as huge as his intelligence. And so, as he normally does, he will end this book on largely personal matters.

Salutations

Romans 16:1 *I commend unto you Phebe our sister, which is a servant of the church which is at Cenchrea:* **2** *That ye receive her in the Lord, as becometh saints, and that ye assist her in whatsoever business she hath need of you: for she hath been a succourer of many, and of myself also.*

Paul issued a commendation, a word of recommendation. And interestingly, he started his commendations with a woman. Her name was Phebe. It means *radiant*. It is a good name, and it fit. You see, she was something very radiant; she was a servant.

Phebe was not from Rome; she was from a far distant location, Cenchrea, which was a seaport of Corinth. For whatever reason, she was heading to Rome (I will show you why in just a bit), and Paul wanted the church at Rome to help her with whatever she needed.

This dear woman had been a help to many, including Paul. He called her a *succourer* of many, and that is an extremely expressive word. It is from *prostatis*, and it indicates a patroness. This woman had, among other things, used her seemingly ample financial means to help a great many people.

Paul said that to help her was to behave *as becometh saints. Becometh* is from the word *axios,* and it means *suitable and worthy.* What that means for us is that, when we know of a servant of God, some person that has a heart and hands for helping, it is up to us to help them, and it is an endeavor worthy of the saints of God when we do so.

This description of Phebe also tells us that the easiest way for us to be *radiant* is not talent; it is service. A humble diaper changer is more radiant than a showy microphone eater any day, especially these days in which the church is plagued with people looking for a red carpet to walk rather than a faded carpet to quietly weep and pray on.

Romans 16:3 *Greet Priscilla and Aquila my helpers in Christ Jesus:* **4** *Who have for my life laid down their own necks:*

unto whom not only I give thanks, but also all the churches of the Gentiles. **5a** *Likewise greet the church that is in their house.*

Here, Paul mentions Priscilla and Aquilla, the tent-making companions of Paul, the humble instructors of the eloquent Apollos. We read of them earlier in the Bible from the pen of Luke:

Acts 18:24 *And a certain Jew named Apollos, born at Alexandria, an eloquent man, and mighty in the scriptures, came to Ephesus.* **25** *This man was instructed in the way of the Lord; and being fervent in the spirit, he spake and taught diligently the things of the Lord, knowing only the baptism of John.* **26** *And he began to speak boldly in the synagogue: whom when Aquila and Priscilla had heard, they took him unto them, and expounded unto him the way of God more perfectly.*

These were some amazing people. They served the Lord together, they taught together, they worked together, and Paul said that they had for his life laid down their own necks! That means that they literally risked their lives for him.

This couple was so dear that not only did Paul give thanks for them, all the churches of the Gentiles also gave thanks for them.

They also had a church in their house. These were the days when churches generally could not meet openly because of persecution. Think of the risk they were therefore taking! But risk or no, these two gladly made their home a place where the church could assemble.

Romans 16:5b *...Salute my wellbeloved Epaenetus, who is the firstfruits of Achaia unto Christ.*

Epaenetus, whose name means *praiseworthy*, was the first convert in Achaia, which was the area of southern Greece, home to towns like Athens and Corinth.

Tying a couple of passages together, we can safely surmise that Epaenetus was of the household of Stephanus:

1 Corinthians 16:15 *I beseech you, brethren, (ye know the house of Stephanas, that it is the firstfruits of Achaia, and that they have addicted themselves to the ministry of the saints,)*

Epaenetus had at some point been saved there in Achaia, had now had time to go to Rome and establish himself there, and Paul was still able to point to him as a faithful convert. Starting for God is easy; many people do that. But the real praiseworthiness comes in "staying with the stuff," as the old-timers used to say.

Romans 16:6 *Greet Mary, who bestowed much labour on us.*

This Mary is an unknown lady who bestowed labor on God's men. How blessed are those who minister to God's weary servants! Paul did not even have to mention her by last name; she was known to the church.

Romans 16:7 *Salute Andronicus and Junia, my kinsmen, and my fellowprisoners, who are of note among the apostles, who also were in Christ before me.*

We read here of Andronicus, meaning "man of victory," and Junia, meaning "youthful." They were relatives of Paul, fellow Jews, and also fellow prisoners, either right then or at other times imprisoned for Christ and well known by God's men. They were saved before Paul and were still faithful these many years later.

Romans 16:8 *Greet Amplias my beloved in the Lord.* **9** *Salute Urbane, our helper in Christ, and Stachys my beloved.*

Amplias means *large, ample*, and Stachys means *head of grain*. Those are interesting names! But more interesting is the fact that these were people who were *beloved* to Paul. There are just some people who make themselves very dear! And in the middle of the verse, Paul greets Urbane, meaning *of the city*, and says that he was *our helper in Christ*.

Being a helper does not seem, on the surface, to be a very glorious task or label. But if you are the one "helping someone in Christ," you may rest assured that you are glorious both to Christ and to the people you are helping on His behalf.

Romans 16:10 *Salute Apelles approved in Christ. Salute them which are of Aristobulus' household.*

Appeles means *called*. Paul says that this man was *approved in Christ*, meaning *proven to be genuine*. Thank God for people that are genuine!

Also mentioned are those of the household of Aristobulus, who is mentioned nowhere else in Scripture. Nothing specific is said of them, but just the fact that Paul thought enough of them to mention them, and God thought enough of them to include them in the canon of Scripture, speaks volumes.

Romans 16:11 *Salute Herodion my kinsman. Greet them that be of the household of Narcissus, which are in the Lord.*

Herodian. He was a person whose name signifies that he was of the household of Herod and thus would be expected to be antagonistic to the gospel. Yet he was both a kinsman of Paul and clearly also a saved man. How marvelous are those who choose Christ over everyone and everything!

Also mentioned here is the household of Narcissus, but not Narcissus himself. Narcissus was a favorite of Nero and was very powerful in Rome. Some of his household, who knew of the torture to which Nero put Christians, accepted Christ anyway.

Interestingly, Narcissus lived up to his name, and many people today live up to his name. Narkissos means "stupidity." We get the word "narcotic" from it.

Something we should learn from the fact that some from the household of Narcissus followed Christ is that your family does not have to determine your future.

Romans 16:12 *Salute Tryphena and Tryphosa, who labour in the Lord. Salute the beloved Persis, which laboured much in the Lord.*

Three more women who labored for the Lord are now mentioned: Tryphena, Tryphosa, and Persis. Where would we be without godly women who labor for God? And what about all this talk of the Bible being anti-woman? They certainly are receiving many positive mentions.

Romans 16:13 *Salute Rufus* [Red] *chosen in the Lord, and his mother and mine.*

Rufus was a "choice one," as the phrase *chosen in the Lord* here indicates, and a man with a godly mother. Paul seems to have taken her as an adoptive mother of sorts, as we ourselves are still prone to do with aged women that we love and respect. Albert Barnes said, "His mother in a literal sense, and mine in a figurative one." (Barnes, 329) Thank God for godly spiritual mothers and grandmothers to all of us.

Romans 16:14 *Salute Asyncritus* [incomparable], *Phlegon* [burning], *Hermas, Patrobas* [paternal], *Hermes, and the brethren which are with them. 15 Salute Philologus* [lover of the word], *and Julia* [soft-haired], *Nereus* [Lump. What a name; thanks, mom...], *and his sister, and Olympas, and all the saints which are with them.*

Notice that Paul knows these many beloved folks by name, so dear have they become to him. A few of the names are interesting. Hermas and Hermes were names of or references to a pagan god, Mercury, yet they came to know the one true God. Olympas [Usually spelled Olympus] was the pagan version of heaven, yet these folks were headed to the real heaven. And Philologus means "lover of the word," which is a perfect name for a Christian.

Romans 16:16 *Salute one another with an holy kiss. The churches of Christ salute you.*

"Salute one another with a holy kiss." In those early times the kiss, as a token of peace, friendship, and brotherly love, was frequent among all people; and the Christians used it in their public assemblies, as well as in their occasional meetings. This was at last laid aside, not because it was abused, but because, the Church becoming very numerous, the thing was impossible. In some countries, the kiss of friendship is still common; and in such countries it is scarcely ever abused, nor is it an incentive to evil, because it is customary and common. Shaking of hands is now substituted for it in almost all Christian congregations. (Clarke, 164)

And aren't you glad! But the principle still applies. There is something wrong with someone who comes in a few minutes late so as to avoid talking to people, sits stone-faced during fellowship, and races out of the parking lot at the final amen.

Separation

Romans 16:17 *Now I beseech you, brethren, mark them which cause divisions and offences contrary to the doctrine which ye have learned; and avoid them.*

This Biblical command, in a more sensible age, used to be considered absolutely essential and logical. Now it is regarded as "mean and undemocratic." But it is just as essential and logical as ever. The devil is the devil, and he has, from the very beginning, been a division causer. Think of what he did in heaven. Think of what he did in Eden.

Paul gave a vital warning to the church. God has given us pure doctrine to follow. And anyone who comes into the midst and starts contradicting it needs to be dealt with, first by marking them, then by avoiding them. To mark means to direct everyone's attention to. We would say, "publicly call them out."

But why do that? Why risk causing controversy by exercising church discipline as we are commanded? Because as we will see in the next verse, they *by good words and fair speeches deceive the hearts of the simple.* They are not trying to sway the pastor or the person who has been saved and grounded for forty years; they are after the new Christians or the ungrounded.

And we are not to allow them to do the damage they are trying to do.

Simplicity

Romans 16:18 *For they that are such serve not our Lord Jesus Christ, but their own belly; and by good words and fair speeches deceive the hearts of the simple.*

The word *for* that begins this verse ties it back to the truth of verse seventeen, the truth we must mark and avoid division causers. This word for simple is *akakos*, and in this verse, it basically means innocent and trusting. Those who are innocent and trusting are prime targets for doctrinal division causers, who *by good words and fair speeches deceive the hearts of the simple*. This, again, is why we must mark and avoid those division causers. It is not about being cruel to "people who just want the freedom to express their opinions;" it is about being protective of the innocent. People who target the simple with false doctrine may claim to serve Christ, but Paul is very clear in this place that they, in actuality, serve their own belly, a euphemism for their own sensual desires.

Romans 16:19 *For your obedience is come abroad unto all men. I am glad therefore on your behalf: but yet I would have you wise unto that which is good, and simple concerning evil.*

The Christians in Rome were obeying the Lord, everyone was hearing about it, and that was good. But they needed to know that that was not the end of the story. Paul said, *but yet...*

Verse nineteen then tells us that we are supposed to be *wise unto that which is good*, but *simple concerning evil*, and a different word is used here than the word for simple in verse eighteen. Here it is the word *akeraios*. It means *unmixed*. Unmixed how? According to the end of verse nineteen, unmixed with evil!

In context, he is talking about the evil of contrary doctrine, as he mentioned in verse eighteen. We are going to be simple, one way or the other. We will either be simple by being open to anything, even error, in which case all kinds of impurities get mixed in, or we will be simple by being closed off to error and not letting any impurity get in.

When I worked in jewelry, there were a couple of kinds of "simple." There was metal that used to be precious, like gold or silver, but had somehow been contaminated by other things. Why did we regard that as "simple?" Because you simply could not use it or sell it. It was worthless! There was no question as to what we could do with it in that state: the answer was always "nothing."

But there was a way to make it into a different kind of "simple." We could send it off to be refined. The refiners would use heat and chemicals to separate out every ounce of impurities. Then, when they sent it back to us, we could use it for anything.

Let your simplicity be the simplicity of the pure, not the simplicity of the polluted.

Strength

Romans 16:20 *And the God of peace shall bruise Satan under your feet shortly. The grace of our Lord Jesus Christ be with you. Amen.*

There is a remarkable and exciting promise in this verse, and it should sound familiar to you:

Genesis 3:15 *And I will put enmity between thee and the woman, and between thy seed and her seed; it shall bruise thy head, and thou shalt bruise his heel.*

This was the promise of Calvary, where Jesus would step on the serpent's head. But here in Romans 16:20, we have a promise that WE will get to step on his head! Just as Jesus got the victory over him, He will let us experience what that feels like as well. Make no mistake, it will be Jesus' power that does it for us, but we still get to put our foot down. Oh, what a moment that will be!

Special Mentions

Romans 16:21 *Timotheus my workfellow, and Lucius, and Jason, and Sosipater, my kinsmen, salute you.*

We know of Timothy quite well, the young protégé of Paul himself. Lucius was probably Luke, the evangelist and writer of the books of Acts and Luke. He was an eyewitness and a friend of eyewitnesses to all that happened with Jesus and the apostles. He is such a great historian that modern scoffers try to discredit him. He mentioned eighty-four specific details that no one but an eyewitness would have known, and every single one of those details has been confirmed by history and archaeology.

Jason is likely the same person who received the apostles into his house at Thessalonica and befriended them at the risk of both his property and life.

Sosipater was a Berean, a Jew by birth, and he accompanied Paul from Greece into Asia and probably into Judea.

All of these men risked everything for God and Paul.

The last three, Lucius, Jason, and Sosipater, he calls kinsmen, likely in this case meaning fellow countrymen, much like we regard other Americans as being family, of sorts.

Romans 16:22 *I Tertius, who wrote this epistle, salute you in the Lord.*

Tertius was the amanuensis for Paul, the man who wrote down what Paul told him to say.

Romans 16:23 *Gaius mine host, and of the whole church, saluteth you. Erastus the chamberlain of the city saluteth you, and Quartus a brother.*

Gaius is usually regarded to be the same one mentioned in Acts 19, who risked his life during the riot caused by Demetrius and the silversmiths. Yet here he is, still faithful. And how long did he stay faithful? Here is your answer:

3 John 1:1 *The elder unto the wellbeloved Gaius, whom I love in the truth.*

There is about a thirty-five-year gap between the writing of these two books, and Gaius was still faithful.

Erastus the chamberlain was the treasurer of the city of Corinth. We have heard of him before:

Acts 19:22 *So he sent into Macedonia two of them that ministered unto him, Timotheus and Erastus; but he himself stayed in Asia for a season.*

Never let it be said that only poor, uneducated, backwoods people believe in and worship Christ. Erastus was one of the most powerful and influential men around.

Quartus we do not know much about, but Paul regarded him as a brother in Christ, and that is enough.

Support

Romans 16:24 *The grace of our Lord Jesus Christ be with you all. Amen.*

This is what will get us through each day. This is not just a space-filler at the end of a letter; it is a reminder. The same grace that saved us will sustain us from day to day until we find ourselves in His presence, kneeling before His throne.

Splendor

Romans 16:25 *Now to him that is of power to stablish you according to my gospel, and the preaching of Jesus Christ, according to the revelation of the mystery, which was kept secret since the world began,* **26** *But now is made manifest, and by the scriptures of the prophets, according to the commandment of the everlasting God, made known to all nations for the obedience of faith:* **27** *To God only wise, be glory through Jesus Christ for ever. Amen.* <Written to the Romans from Corinthus, and sent by Phebe servant of the church at Cenchrea.>

As Paul begins to draw his extensive letter to the Romans to a close, he does so with one long sentence that encompasses all three of these verses.

In verse twenty-five, Paul uses the pronoun "him" to point his readers' attention to God, who he said had the power to stablish them, meaning to make them stable. God is not just interested in saving us; He is interested in stabilizing us as well.

Paul goes on to say that this will be done *"according to my gospel, and the preaching of Jesus Christ."* Those two words *according to* are from the Greek preposition *kata,* meaning *down from.* In other words, the stabilizing that God will do in us will come down to us from Paul's gospel and the preaching of Jesus Christ. And while those appear to be two separate things, they are, in fact, the same thing since Jesus Christ was Paul's gospel.

If God stabilizes us, it will not come from emotion or tradition; it will come from the gospel, the preaching of Jesus Christ.

Taking things a step further, Paul then said, *according to the revelation of the mystery, which was kept secret since the world began.* Once again, this word *according* is from *kata.* So, the progression then is as follows. From the very beginning of the world, God had this plan of the gospel in place. It was not an afterthought. And yet, it was a secret. The Old Testament veiled and hinted at what the New Testament fully revealed. And Paul's gospel, his preaching of Jesus Christ, came "down from" that mystery, and God stabilizing us then comes "down from" that gospel.

In verse twenty-six, Paul says of that now revealed mystery, *But now is made manifest, and by the scriptures of the prophets, according to the commandment of the everlasting God.*

Two separate lines of thought are included in those words. When Paul begins by saying, *but now is made manifest,* he was referring again to the fact that the mystery of the gospel in the Old Testament had now been unveiled and made clear in the New Testament.

But in the second phrase, when he says, *and by the scriptures of the prophets,* he is adding the final item to his gospel and the preaching of Christ that we saw in the previous verse. In other words, the gospel was found all through the Old Testament Scriptures. Yes, it finally appeared in its fullest and clearest form in the New Testament, but it most assuredly existed in the Old Testament as was found in the prophets.

Paul then writes, *according to the commandment of the everlasting God, made known to all nations for the obedience of faith.* This tells us that all of this was done intentionally, not incidentally, and that it was at the direct command of the everlasting God. Further, it was not simply sent to the Jews; God made it known to all nations for the obedience of faith. The majority Gentile audience in Rome would doubtless rejoice at these words.

Paul closes this incomparable book in verse twenty-seven by glorifying God, whom he deems *only wise.* That word *only* is from the word *monos,* and it means *alone, just one.* Is there anything else that would be appropriate but giving God alone the glory for all of this, since He alone has real wisdom, and any wisdom that we have comes from Him?

And finally, we arrived at the postscript of this book. And while it is not part of the inspired canon, it does open a pleasing window into an aspect of the inspired canon. In this postscript, we learned that Phebe was the letter carrier! What trust Paul had in this lady from verse one! We have the book of Romans not only because God chose to preserve it for us, but because when Paul needed someone that he could really trust to get this letter to Rome, Phebe was available, and he knew that she could and would get the job done.

A dear lady with a servant's heart was willing to carry the letter to the Romans from the author to the audience.

And what she carried was the greatest doctrinal treatise on salvation the world will ever know.

But before the postscript, Paul closes this incomparable book by glorifying God for the mystery of the gospel. Is there anything else that would be appropriate? After all, He is the Author of our Salvation…From A-Z.

Works Cited

Bainton, Roland. *Here I Stand*, Penguin Books, New York, 1995

Barnes, A. (1996). *Notes on the new testament: Acts and Romans*. Baker Book House.

Clarke, Adam. *Clarke's Commentary*. Volume VI, Romans to Revelation, Abingdon-Cokesbury Press, New York.

Eddy, M. B. (1971). *Science and Health with Key to the Scripture*. The First Church of Christ, Scientist.

Engstrom, Ted. "Integrity." *Sermon Illustrations*, 2020, www.sermonillustrations.com/.

Goldstein, Sasha. "Alabama Cop Hugs Grandmother after He Buys Her Eggs She Tried to Shoplift to Feed Hungry Family (Video)." *Nydailynews.com*, New York Daily News, 10 Dec. 2014, http://www.nydailynews.com/news/national/ala-buys-grandma-eggs-caught-shoplifting-article-1.2040271.

Grossman, M. M. (2014, November 20). *Watch: How do American college students react to ISIS, Israeli flags?* The Jerusalem Post | JPost.com. Retrieved December 22, 2021, from http://www.jpost.com/Diaspora/WATCH-How-do-American-college-students-react-to-ISIS-Israeli-flags-382388

Hannaford, Peter, Ronald Reagan Daily radio commentary [syndicated] December 1978 from *The Quotable Ronald Reagan*

Henry, M. (1935). *Matthew Henry's commentary on the whole Bible* (Vol. 1). Fleming H. Revell Co.

Josephus, *The Works of Josephus*, Hendrickson Publishers, Peabody, Massachusetts, 1987.

Lenski, R. C. H. *The Interpretation of St. Paul's Epistle to the Romans.* Augsburg Publishing House, Minneapolis, 1936.

Miller, Keith, and Larson, Bruce, *The Edge of Adventure,* Fleming H. Revell Company, 1991

Morris, Henry. *Scientific Creationism.* Master Books, Green Forest, AZ, 1985

Palau, Luis, *Experiencing God's Forgiveness,* Multnomah Press, 1984

Qurollo, James. *Notes on Romas Revised Edition*, 1994

Ratzlaff, Don, "The Christian Leader," (Earnest Gordon's Miracle on the River Kwai)

"Roman Empire." *International Standard Bible Encyclopedia.* Wm. B. Eerdmans Publishing Co., Grand Rapids, 1952

Sickels, D. (n.d.). *General Ahiman Rezon: Third degree: Master mason.* Sacred-Texts.com. https://sacred-texts.com/mas/gar/gar49.htm

Smith, Jospeh (1979). *The Pearl of Great Price.* The Church of Jesus Christ of Latter-day Saints.

Ten Boom, Corrie, *The Hiding Place*, Barbour Publishing, Uhrichsville, 1971

Today in the Word, June 3, 1989.

Unger, Merril F. *The New Unger's Bible Dictionary.* Moody Bible Institute, Chicago, 1988.

Other Books by Dr. Bo Wagner

Colossians: The Treasures of Deity
Daniel: Breathtaking
Ephesians: The Treasures of Family
Esther: Five Feasts and the Fingerprints of God
Galatians: The Treasures of Liberty
Hosea: Love When It Matters Most
James: The Pen and the Plumb Line
Jonah: A Study in Greatness
Nehemiah: A Labor of Love
Philippians: The Treasures of Joy
Proverbs: Bright Lights from Dark Sayings (Vol. 1)
Proverbs: Bright Lights from Dark Sayings (Vol. 2)
Romans: Salvation From A-Z
Ruth: Diamonds in the Darkness
The Revelation: Ready or Not

More Books by Dr. Bo Wagner

Beyond the Colored Coat
Don't Muzzle the Ox
From Footers to Finish Nails
I'm Saved! Now What???
Learning Not to Fear the Old Testament
Marriage Makers/Marriage Breakers
Why Christmas?

Books in the Night Heroes Series

Cry From the Coal Mine (Vol. 1)
Free Fall (Vol. 2)
Broken Brotherhood (Vol. 3)
The Blade of Black Crow (Vol. 4)
Ghost Ship (Vol. 5)
When Serpents Rise (Vol. 6)
Moth Man (Vol. 7)

Runaway (Vol. 8)
Terror by Day (Vol. 9)
Winter Wolf (Vol. 10)
Desert Heat (Vol. 11)
Deadline (Vol. 12)
The Sword and the Iron Curtain (Vol. 13)

Devotionals

DO Drops Volume 1
DO Drops Volume 2
DO Drops Volume 3
DO Drops Volume 4
DO Drops Volume 5
DO Drops Volume 6
DO Drops Volume 7
DO Drops Volume 8
DO Drops Volume 9
DO Drops Volume 10
DO Drops Volume 11
DO Drops Volume 12

Zak Blue and the Great Space Chase Series:

Falcon Wing (Vol. 1)
Enter the Maelstrom (Vol. 2)

www.ingramcontent.com/pod-product-compliance
Lightning Source LLC
Chambersburg PA
CBHW062148080426
42734CB00010B/1607